The Footballing Morgan Family of Bristol

including

The memories of Ivy Doris Irene Morgan

Compiled and researched by
Larry Bennett

Published by New Generation Publishing in 2023

Copyright © Larry Bennett 2023

First Edition

The author asserts the moral right under the Copyright, Designs and Patents Act 1988 to be identified as the author of this work.

All Rights reserved. No part of this publication may be reproduced, stored in a retrieval system or transmitted, in any form or by any means without the prior consent of the author, nor be otherwise circulated in any form of binding or cover other than that which it is published and without a similar condition being imposed on the subsequent purchaser.

ISBN: 978-1-83563-037-2

www.newgeneration-publishing.com
New Generation Publishing

This book is dedicated to my Grandmother Ivy Doris Irene Morgan, her husband George Aldridge, and their daughters Joy (my aunt) and Barbara (my mother).

So many happy memories.

God bless them all.

PREFACE

Following the passing of my mother in 2013, I found an exercise book full of her mother's memories and stories, mostly written in the early 1980s. The contents of this book are reproduced in full. In addition, further notes, diaries and photographs have been discovered in family collections, which have been added to the original manuscript.

I have, as far as possible, kept the writing style exactly as written, except to clarify some of the meaning. It is clear that my grandmother had a hard and difficult upbringing, but the happiness and love of her family comes through clearly. She was clearly a religious lady with high moral values.

Many references are made to her family, and I have taken the opportunity to research background information on the family members she mentioned in the manuscript. Such information is included in specific chapters within this publication. Every effort has been made to check and confirm accuracy, although some dates and events are difficult to establish due to conflicting source information.

It is of course possible that some of her recollections may not be totally accurate. However there are of course no means to check the accuracy of many of these, as they are personal to her. However, I have attempted to verify as many facts as possible.

The book also serves as an overall history of the Morgan family, many of whom played professional football for Bristol Rovers and Bristol City, amongst others. A great deal of local history is included, which will be of interest to those with a background in the Barton Hill, St. George, Redfield and Lawrence Hill areas of Bristol, as well as the area around St. James in the centre of the city.

Most of the photographs have come from the family archive. However there are some which have been located from other sources, and these are included to give an idea of the area in which my grandmother was brought up. Should there be copyright issues then I will be only too glad to give credit where possible in any future editions.

Many of the street names featured in the book no longer exist, and I am indebted to the Barton Hill History Group for their help in locating addresses and public houses in the area.

Many of the family (especially the families related to the Morgan family), lived in poor and cramped accommodation in the back streets and courts of Central Bristol. Thankfully nearly all of them have been demolished, but details of the addresses have been included to give an idea of the poverty they lived in.

Birth, Baptism, Marriage and Death records have been carefully checked but it is possible there will have been transcription or spelling errors in the original documentation. Some dates are missing where accurate information could not be located. In addition, dates for the same event have been recorded differently within different databases, in which cases I have selected the most reliable database; but of course transcription errors could still have been made.

There may be, of course, some errors due to conflicting family memories, although in most cases these have been rectified; should any remain I would be glad to correct them for any future editions.

To ensure privacy, details of many living relatives have not been included in this publication.

Some photographs have been scanned from newspapers (with permission) as the originals are not available, and have been included for their historical interest.

Larry Bennett, August 2023

Contents

PREFACE iv
ACKNOWLEDGEMENTS vii
CHAPTER 1. THE MORGAN FAMILY HISTORY. 1
CHAPTER 2. THE FAMILY AND DESCENDANTS OF JOHN MORGAN. 5
CHAPTER 3. THE FAMILY AND DESCENDANTS OF THOMAS HENRY MORGAN. 9
CHAPTER 4. THE FAMILY AND DESCENDANTS OF WILLIAM JOHN MORGAN. 21
CHAPTER 5. GEORGE MORGAN. 76
CHAPTER 6. THE FAMILY AND DESCENDANTS OF HARRY MORGAN. 77
CHAPTER 7. THE FAMILY AND DESCENDANTS OF JAMES MORGAN. 95
CHAPTER 8. THE FAMILY AND DESCENDANTS OF JOHN (JACK) MORGAN. ... 145
CHAPTER 9. THOMAS MORGAN. 159
CHAPTER 10. THE FAMILY AND DESCENDANTS OF THOMAS MORGAN. 160
CHAPTER 11. THE FAMILY AND DESCENDANTS OF FLORENCE BEATRICE MORGAN. 167
CHAPTER 12. THE FAMILY OF ALICE MORGAN. 169
CHAPTER 13. THE FAMILY AND DESCENDANTS OF CLARA MORGAN. 172
CHAPTER 14. IT WAS ALWAYS SUMMER. 175
CHAPTER 15. ECHOES FROM THE PAST. 198
CHAPTER 16. WORLD WAR II AND BEYOND. 204
CHAPTER 17. THE FOOTBALL CAREER OF FREDERICK 'JERRY' MORGAN. 212
CHAPTER 18. THE FOOTBALL CAREER OF WILLIAM JAMES 'JIMMY' MORGAN. 224
CHAPTER 19. THE MORGAN FAMILY FOOTBALL TEAM. 245
CHAPTER 20. RELATED FAMILIES AND LOCATIONS. 267
APPENDIX 1. FREDERICK 'JERRY' MORGAN – APPEARANCES FOR BRISTOL CITY AND BRISTOL ROVERS FOOTBALL CLUBS. 333
APPENDIX 2. WILLIAM JAMES 'JIMMY' MORGAN – APPEARANCES FOR BRISTOL ROVERS FOOTBALL CLUB. 339
APPENDIX 3. PUBLIC HOUSES OWNED BY MEMBERS OF THE MORGAN FAMILY. 344
APPENDIX 4. PERSONAL MEMORIES OF IVY MORGAN. 369

ACKNOWLEDGEMENTS

I would like to thank the following for their valued assistance with this project:
- John Moore
- George Morgan
- Steven Morgan
- Greig Lewis
- Andy White
- Paul Finegan
- Emma Leach
- Tony White
- Tony Cutting
- Susan Sprules
- Steven John Morgan
- Don Hatfield
- Allison Hatfield
- Scott Davidson
- Adam Morgan
- Helen Morgan
- Katie Welsby
- Keith Morgan
- Ed Bennett
- Howard Bennett
- Elizabeth Millsted
- Brenda Collins
- Jeff Short
- Keith Brookman and Mike Jay of the Bristol Rovers History Group
- David Woods
- Simon Howe, Bath City Football Club
- Joy Anderson
- Fi Isaacs
- Dave Cheesley
- The Barton Hill History Group
- And my long-suffering partner Wendy, who has had to put up with numerous visits to churches, graveyards and similar family-related places over the last few years.

If I have missed anyone out, please accept my sincere apologies.

CHAPTER 1.
THE MORGAN FAMILY HISTORY.

Before we investigate the life story of Ivy, it is important and indeed fascinating to understand her family history. The Morgans were a large and well-known family in the Redfield and Barton Hill areas of Bristol, and it is of great interest to research their background.

The earliest confirmed family member found at the time of writing is one William Morgan, born in Bristol c. 1785. It is unclear who he married, possibly with the Christian name Elizabeth, and investigations are ongoing. It is unclear when or where William died, but it would appear that a death recorded in 1858 in Bristol would be a distinct possibility.

They had at least one child, one of whom is a direct ancestor of the footballing Morgan family, namely:

- **William Morgan (born 1811-death unknown).**

William married Mary Ann Fink (born 1817, Bristol; died 1857, Bristol, aged 40) on 10th May 1835, in St. John's Parish, in Bedminster, a suburb of South Bristol. Inspection of the marriage register indicates both were illiterate, hence the 'mark' of both parties.

Looking at the signatures of the witnesses, there is one Mary Fink, which is likely to have been Mary Ann's mother. Further investigation has revealed that her maiden name was Woodrow, as the formation of her signature is very similar to that of her signature on her wedding registration to James Fink on 14th February 1813, at St. Philip and Jacob Church, Bristol. James was an engineer by trade.

Mary Ann had at least six siblings, all born in Bristol.

Comparison of the signatures of Mary Woodrow and Mary Fink. Formation of the word 'Mary' appears very similar.

Together William and Mary Ann had six children:

1. **James Morgan** (born 1835, Bristol; death unknown).
2. **William Morgan** (born 1837, Bristol; death unknown).
3. **John Morgan** (born 11th February 1843, Church Lane, St. Pauls, Bristol; died 13th December 1900, Bristol, aged 57).
4. **Jane Morgan** (born 18th September 1846, 3 Cheese Lane, Bristol; death unknown).
5. **George Morgan** (born 23rd February 1850, 20 Narrow Plain, Bristol; death unknown).
6. **Thomas Henry Morgan** (born 16th May 1855, at 11 Bread Street, Bristol; died 2nd February 1927, Llantarnam, Monmouthshire, aged 71).

The marriage register entry of William Morgan and Mary Ann Fink, 10th May 1835.

The 1841 Census shows the family living in John Street, St. Philips, Bristol, where it is recorded that William's employment was that of a 'Boiler Man'. James and William are also recorded on the Census, aged 6 and 3 respectively. Another child, Henry (aged 1) also appears on the Census but inspection of the birth records does not show a child of that name being born to a mother with a maiden name of 'Fink'. In addition, no baptism record for a Henry Morgan to William and Mary Ann can be traced, so the inclusion of Henry remains a mystery.

Press reports from 1842 show that a company with which William Morgan was possibly involved went bankrupt – which could explain why by 1851 the family were resident in the Stapleton Workhouse. A similar press announcement appeared on 18th March 1843.

> **Bankruptcy Meeting.**
>
> THE Commissioners in a Fiat in Bankruptcy, bearing date the 16th day of June, 1842, awarded and issued forth gainst DANIEL WADE ACRAMAN, WILLIAM EDWARD ACRAMAN, ALFRED JOHN ACRAMAN, WILLIAM MORGAN, THOMAS HOLROYD, and JAMES NORROWAY FRANKLYN, all of the City of Bristol, Ship Builders, Boiler Makers, Engineers, dealers, chapmen, and Copartners, intend to meet on the 24th day of October next, at the COMMERCIAL ROOMS, Corn-Street, in the City of Bristol, at Two o'clock in the Afternoon, in order to Audit the Accounts of the Assignees of the separate Estate and Effects of WILLIAM MORGAN, one of the said Bankrupts, under the said Fiat, pursuant to an act of Parliament, made and passed in the sixth year of the Reign of his late Majesty King George the Fourth, intituled "An Act to amend the laws relating to Bankrupts."
>
> JOHN KERLE HABERFIELD, Solicitor.

William Morgan, Boilermaker, bankruptcy announcement, 17th September 1842.

By the time of the 1851 Census, however, it was clear that the family had not recovered from William's apparent bankruptcy. Viewing of the Census shows the family as inmates in the Stapleton Workhouse. William and Mary, together with children James, John and William have been located within the Census.

Jane and George, however, do not appear on the Census, and it is possible that they were staying with other family members or friends.

A possible solution to this issue is that the 1851 Census entry for 17 Bread Street shows a 'Mary Ann' Morgan (aged 3) is living with George Morgan (aged 1) with the Tanner family. They are described as 'Nurse Children' which is a term used for a sort of unofficial adoption. It may also be that 'Jane' was renamed 'Mary Ann' after her mother. However, this is only conjecture and there is no concrete evidence yet found to support this assumption.

The address of Bread Street is of interest as it is where William and Mary gave birth to their seventh child. Thomas Henry Morgan was born at 11 Bread Street, Bristol (see link to this street earlier) on 16th May 1855.

The 1861 Census entry has not yet been located, but the 1871 Census shows Mary with youngest son Thomas living at 5 Hammonds Buildings, St. Pauls, Bristol, along with two boarders, Caroline Cooper and Emma Jane Gardener. Mary is shown as widowed, and no occupation is shown for 16-year-old Thomas.

No death information has yet been located for Mary Ann.

WILLIAM AND MARY ANN'S CHILDREN:

1. James Morgan.

James was baptised at St. Philip & Jacob Church, Bristol, on 25th December 1835. His family address was recorded as being at Bread Street, Bristol, with his father's occupation shown as being a Boiler Maker.

He disappears from records after the 1851 Census.

2. William Morgan.

William was baptised at St. Philip & Jacob Church, Bristol, on 14th January 1838. His family address was also recorded as being at Bread Street, Bristol, with his father's occupation shown as being a Boiler Maker.

He disappears from records after the 1851 Census.

3. John Morgan.

See Chapter 2.

4. Jane Morgan.

She was baptised at St. Philip & Jacob Church, Bristol, on 7th September 1845. Her family address was vaguely recorded as being at St. James, Bristol, with her father's occupation noted as being a Labourer.

No trace of Jane can be found after the 1851 Census.

5. George Morgan.

George was baptised at St. James' Church, Bristol, on 24th March 1850. His family address was recorded as being at Narrow Plain, Bristol, with his father's occupation again noted as being a Labourer.

He disappears from records after the 1851 Census.

6. Thomas Charles Morgan.

See Chapter 3.

CHAPTER 2.

THE FAMILY AND DESCENDANTS OF JOHN MORGAN.

John Morgan married Matilda Williams (born 30th May 1844, Kingswood Hill, Oldland, near Bristol; died 3rd November 1912, Bristol, aged 68) on 29th March 1864 at Bristol Registry Office. At the time of their marriage, John was living at 2 Quaker's Friars, Merchant Street, Bristol, his occupation being noted as a Labourer. Matilda was recorded as living at Ellbroad Street, Bristol, with no occupation being shown on the marriage certificate.

Details of the Williams family can be found in **Chapter 20.**

John and Matilda had ten children:

1. **William John Morgan** (born 28th April 1864, 4 Tabernacle Row, Bristol; died 19th September 1912, Bristol, aged 48).
2. **George Morgan** (born 27th October 1866, 5 Tarr's Court, Lawrence Hill, Bristol; died 22nd May 1889, Bristol, aged 22).
3. **Henry (Harry) Morgan** (born 2nd August 1869, 5 Tarr's Court, Lawrence Hill, Bristol; died 14th July 1929, Bristol, aged 59).
4. **James Morgan** (born 12th February 1872, 5 Tarr's Court, Lawrence Hill, Bristol; died 6th July 1935, Bristol, aged 63).
5. **John (Jack) Morgan** (born 10th February 1874, 5 Tarr's Court, Lawrence Hill, Bristol; died 3rd November 1944, Bristol, aged 70).
6. **Thomas Morgan** (born 18th January 1876, 5 Tarr's Court, Lawrence Hill, Bristol; died 31st May 1877, Bristol, aged 16 months).
7. **Thomas Morgan** (born 25th March 1878, 1 Barnett's Court, Lawrence Hill, Bristol; died 19th January 1944, Bristol, aged 65).
8. **Florence (Florry) Beatrice Morgan** (born 19th September 1880, 1 Barnetts's Court, Lawrence Hill, Bristol; died 8th November 1956, Bristol, aged 76).
9. **Alice Morgan** (born 8th July 1883, 29 Catherine Street, Barrow Lane, Bristol; died 16th April 1940, Bristol, aged 56).
10. **Clara Morgan** (born 26th May 1885, 29 Catherine Street, Barrow Lane, Bristol; died 24th February 1937, Bristol, aged 51).

Details of each family group may be found in their relevant chapter.

At the time of both William's and George's baptisms on 10th November 1866, the family were living at premises in Bread Street, Bristol. The 1871 Census then shows John and Matilda with children William, George and Harry living at 5 Tarr's Court, Lawrence Hill, Bristol, John's occupation recorded as a 'Stoker'.

By 1881, five more children had been born, although Thomas, born in 1876, died the following year. The subsequent child was also named Thomas, no doubt in his memory. The family were now living at 1 Barnett's Court, Lawrence Hill, Bristol, with John being described as a 'Goods Unloading Labourer', although this was crossed out on the Census return. Eldest son William was by now in employment as a 'Smith's Labourer'.

The 1891 Census shows John and the family residing at 'Rock Cottage', Riches Lane, Lawrence Hill, Bristol. John was revealed as working as a Railway Labourer, with sons James and John also working on the Railways. Son Thomas was shown as working at the local Cotton Works.

Seven members of the Morgan Family.
Back Row L-R: Harry Morgan, John (Jack) Morgan, Thomas (Tom) Morgan, James Morgan.
Front Row L-R: Clara Morgan, Florence Morgan, Alice Morgan.

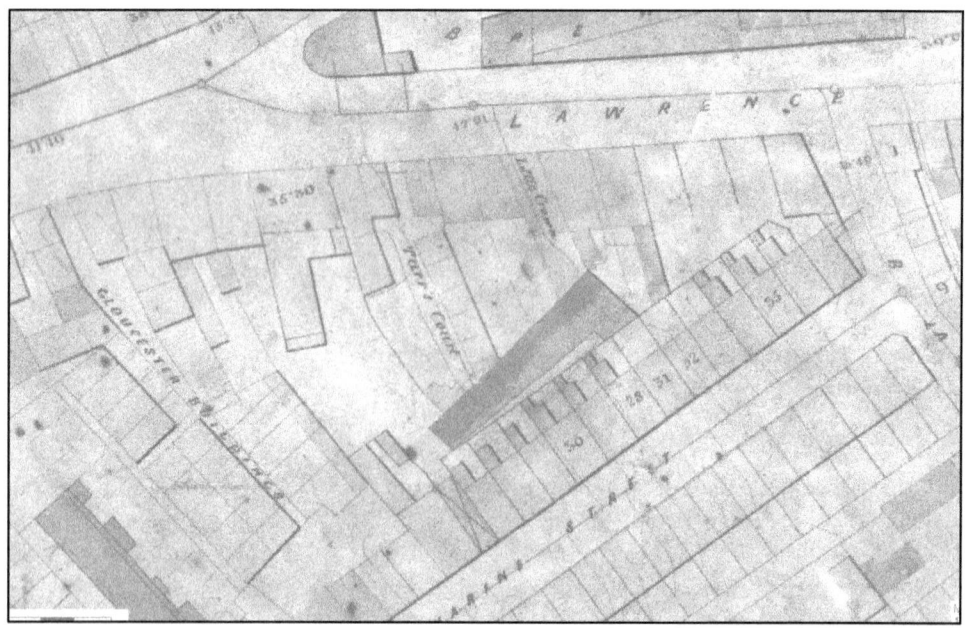

Tarr's Court (centre), showing its location close to Lawrence Hill and West Street.

John died on 13th December 1900 at home at 55 Croydon Street, Barton Hill, Bristol, leaving widow Matilda with youngest daughters Alice and Clara. The cause of death on his certificate was recorded as being by 'Abdominal Carcinoma' or Stomach Cancer. His occupation shown on the certificate was a Railway Labourer. It seems that his widow Matilda would have been illiterate as an 'x' (the mark of) is shown on the certificate as being the informant. He was buried at Avonview Cemetery, Bristol on 19th December 1900.

Matilda and her two youngest daughters continued to live at the Croydon Street address according to the 1901 Census, and her employment was recorded as being a 'Laundress' with both Alice and Clara being 'Tailoresses'.

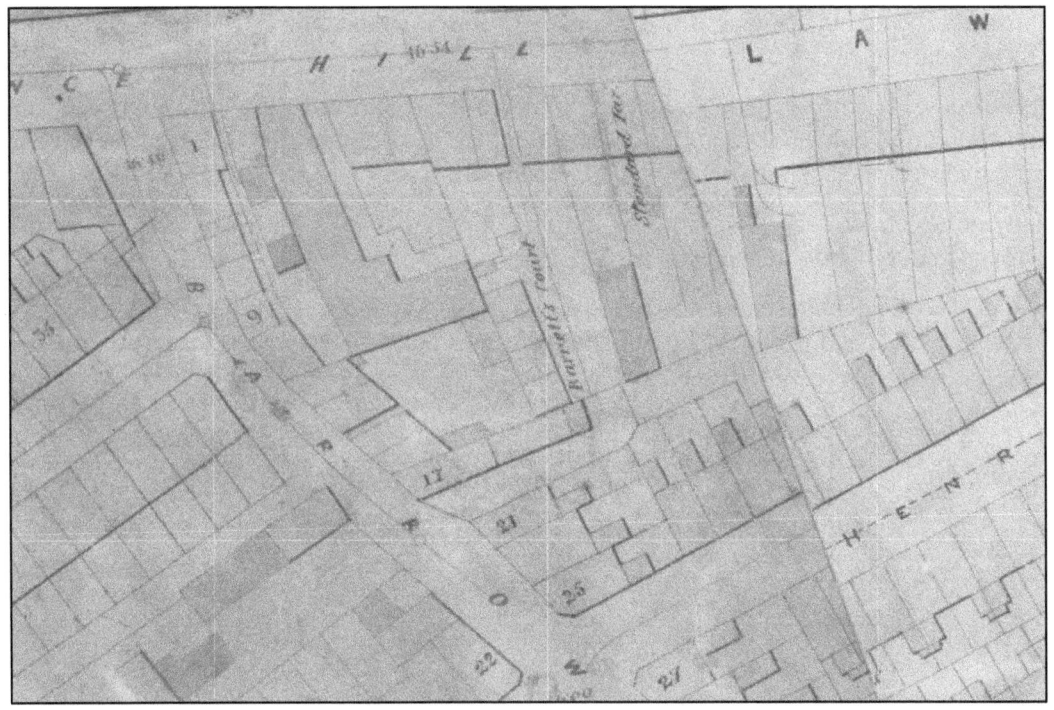

Barnett's Court can be seen in the centre of this street map, just off Lawrence Hill.

The 1911 Census showed Matilda now living alone at 13 Bright Street, Russell Town, Bristol, where she again is described as being a Laundress. However, tragedy struck on 3rd November 1912 when she was found dead in the Floating Harbour in Bristol, having committed suicide. Her death certificate simply stated that she was 'Found drowned in the Floating Harbour', although press reports the following day stated:

"Early yesterday morning the police were informed that the body of a woman was in the Floating Harbour. The River Police were apprised, and recovered the body, which was conveyed to the Mortuary. Later in the day the deceased woman was identified as Matilda Morgan, aged 69, of 22 Stafford Street, Barton Hill. Her son stated that she had been missing from her home since Saturday evening. An inquest will be held later today."

The inquest into the death of Matilda was reported on 5th November:

"The City Coroner (Mr. A. E. Barker) held an inquest at his court, Merchant Street, yesterday, relative to the death of Matilda Morgan, 69, a widow, who lived at 22 Strafford *(sic)* Street,

Barrow Road, Barton Hill, who was found drowned on Saturday in the harbour near Bristol Bridge.

A daughter of deceased said Mrs. Morgan lived with her. On Saturday, about 5.30, witness was going with her to visit her (witness's) sister, but deceased went out without saying where she was going. For about six weeks, since the death of her son, deceased had been strange, but had never threatened to take her life. Since she left nothing was heard of her mother until Sunday morning, although enquiries were made.

James Fowler, of 266 Newfoundland Road, said about nine o'clock on Sunday morning he was working at the back of Bridge Street, when he saw something in the water. He obtained a boat and rowed out. Finding it was the body of a woman, he took it to Bristol Bridge and informed the police.

Dr. Finzel said he had examined the body of deceased. There was a cut on the left eye, and the appearances pointed to death from drowning. He had attended the deceased for the last two months for melancholia. A verdict of 'Found Drowned' was returned."

Many of her children became involved in running public houses in Bristol, and details can be found under their individual sections.

Matilda was laid to rest in an unmarked grave at Avonview Cemetery, Bristol on 7th November 1912, by the wall at the Strawberry Lane side of the graveyard.

> MORGAN.—In loving memory of my dear mother, who passed away Nov. 3, 1912. Gone from sight, but to memory ever dear.—From her loving son Tom, and Lily.
>
> MORGAN.—In memory of my dear mother, Matilda Morgan, who died Nov. 3, 1912. Your end was sudden, mother dear, it made me weep and sigh; and, mother dear, it's sad to think we could not say "Good-bye." Ever remembered by your loving son Jim and daughter-in-law Lizzie, and family.
>
> MORGAN.—In memory of our dear mother, who died Nov. 3, 1912. Sadly missed by her daughters Florrie and Clara. In memory ever dear.
>
> MORGAN.—In beloved remembrance of my dear mother, who died Nov. 3, 1912. Ever remembered by her daughter and son-in-law, Alice and Albert Stephens. Not dead to those that loved her, not lost, but gone before; she lives with us in memory still, and will for evermore.

Some tributes to Matilda Morgan in the local newspaper.

CHAPTER 3.

THE FAMILY AND DESCENDANTS OF THOMAS HENRY MORGAN.

Thomas Henry Morgan married Emma Sanders (born 1853, Bristol; died 10th June 1893, Bristol, aged 40), on 18th August 1879, in St. Matthias Church, Bristol. Their address at the time was at 15 Ellbroad Street, Bristol, a street which appears regularly in the Morgan family history. Thomas's occupation was recorded as being a Plasterer, and his father appears to have been erroneously recorded as 'Henry' Morgan (rather than William), but his occupation correctly shown as being a Boiler Maker. In addition, Thomas's father should have been shown as being deceased, as his mother Mary Ann was shown as being a widow on the 1871 Census.

The marriage certificate appears to have been somewhat rushed, with a clearer but incomplete version appearing on the following page of documentation.

They had three children together:

1. **Thomas William Morgan** (born 13th December 1882, Bristol; died 1914, Newport, aged 31).

2. **Emma Sophia Morgan** (born 29th April 1885, Bristol; died 1917, Bristol, aged 31).

3. **George Sanders Morgan** (born 23rd November 1887, 20 Jubilee Street, St. Philips, Bristol; died 1961, Newport, aged 73).

The 1881 Census shows Thomas and Emma living at 22 New Bread Street, St. Philips, Bristol, where his employment was shown as being a Plasterer. The couple were living with the family of George and Emma Lavender.

By 1891 they had moved to 20 Jubilee Street, St. Philips, Bristol, along with their three children. Thomas continued in his role as a Plasterer, whilst Emma worked as a Dress Machinist.

Sadly, Thomas's wife Emma died on 10th June 1893 at home (20 Jubilee Street, St. Philips, Bristol). Her cause of death was sadly recorded as being postpartum haemorrhage during childbirth. It seems the un-named child also died at the same time.

On 12th December 1894, Thomas married Lillie Kyte (born 1st March 1872, Marshfield, Monmouthshire; died 18th June 1952, Newport), at Newport Registry Office. Both Thomas and Lillie were living at 55 Durham Road, Newport, at the time of their marriage, with Thomas's occupation being recorded as a Plasterer Journeyman.

They went on to have six further children:

1. **Frederick John Morgan** (born 26th May 1895, 55 Durham Road, Newport; died 21st October 1973, Warley, aged 78).

2. **William Henry Morgan** (born 16th April 1896, 14 Philip Street, Newport; died 6th May 1917, at sea, aged 21).

3. **John Charles Morgan** (born 18th May 1903, 2 Gordon Street, Newport; died 16th March 1972, Birmingham, aged 68).

4. **Elizabeth Gwendoline Morgan** (born 26th December 1904, 2 Gordon Street, Newport; died 22nd March 1982, Portsmouth, aged 77).

5. **Walter Morgan** (born 26th June 1906, 2 Gordon Street, Newport; died 28th May 1976, Sutton Coldfield, aged 69).

6. **Stanley Morgan** (born 4th September 1913, 5 Philip Street, Newport; died 1982, Pembroke, aged 68).

The 1901 Census interestingly does not show Thomas living with his family, his whereabouts unknown at that time. New wife Lillie is shown with her two sons and two stepsons, living at 2 Gordon Street, Newport, Monmouthshire, son Thomas being recorded as an Errand Boy.

By 1911 both Thomas and Lillie could be found, now living at 18 Llewellin Street, Newport, Monmouthshire, still engaged in his work as a Plasterer. Lillie and seven of their children/stepchildren were also shown on the Census. Son William was employed as a Potter's Labourer, and George a Builder's Labourer.

1921 saw the family living at 132 Llantarnam Road, Cwmbran. Details of the family indicated that he continued to work as a Plasterer (for Richards Builders of Panteg), whilst Lillie was engaged in home duties. Details of their children's work will be found in their relevant sections. Also shown on the Census form were two of Thomas's brothers-in-law, Stanley Kyte and Jenivus Joseph Kyte.

Lillie Kyte (1872-1952)

Thomas's occupation throughout his life was a Plasterer, and he died at 132 Llantarnam Road, Llantarnam, South Wales, on 2nd February 1927, aged 71. The cause of death was noted as being Influenza and Pneumonia.

Lillie appears on the 1939 Register, working as a housekeeper for William J. Evells (Builder) at 28 Victoria Avenue, Newport, Monmouthshire.

She died on 18th June 1952, in Newport, aged 80.

THE CHILDREN OF THOMAS AND EMMA:

1. Thomas William Morgan.

Thomas was baptised at St. Philip & Jacob Church, Bristol, on 7th March 1883. The address for his parents was recorded as being 2 Cheese Lane, Bristol, and his father's occupation noted as being a Labourer.

He never married, and can initially be found on the 1891 Census living with his family at 20 Jubilee Street, St. Philips, Bristol.

The 1901 Census shows Thomas living with his stepmother Lillie at 2 Gordon Street, Newport, Monmouthshire, along with brother George and stepbrothers Frederick and William. He was shown as being an 'Errand Boy' at the time.

He can also be found on the 1911 Census, now living with his father and stepmother, although his name was shown as William T. Morgan in this instance. His occupation was shown as being a Potter's Labourer.

Thomas died in 1914, in Newport, aged 31.

2. Emma Sophia Morgan.

Emma was baptised at St. Philip & Jacob Church, Bristol, on 7th October 1885. The address for her parents was recorded as being at 2 Cheese Lane, Bristol, and her father's occupation noted as being a Plasterer.

Emma never married, and it is assumed that she was sadly given up by the family.

Both the 1901 and 1911 Census returns show her living in the Stapleton Workhouse in Bristol, where she is curtly described as an 'Imbecile'.

Records indicate that she died in 1917, in Bristol, aged 31.

3. George Sanders Morgan.

__George Sanders Morgan (1887-1961).__

George was baptised at Emmanuel Church, St. Philips, Bristol, on 20th December 1887. The address for his parents was recorded as being at 20 Jubilee Street, Bristol, and his father's occupation noted as being a Plasterer.

George married Mercy Watkins (born 1886, Newport; died 1967, Newport, aged 81), on 5th August 1918, at St. Matthew's Church, Newport. The marriage certificate stated that George was living at 5 Manchester Street, Newport, and was employed as a Coal Tipper. Mercy's address was recorded as being at 43 Prince Street, Newport.

They had no children.

The 1921 Census shows George and Mercy still living at 5 Manchester Street, Newport, at the home of Agnes Cooper (Mercy's sister). George's occupation is noted as being a Wire Works Labourer at Guest Keen & Co., Newport.

The 1939 Register shows that George and Mercy continued to live at the same address with Agnes, although George's occupation had changed to that of a Builder's Labourer.

George died in 1961 in Newport, aged 73. Mercy died in 1967, again in Newport, aged 81.

THE CHILDREN OF THOMAS AND LILLIE:

1. **Frederick John Morgan (Kyte).**

Frederick John Morgan (Kyte) (1895-1973)

He was actually registered as 'John Thomas Frederick Morgan' according to the birth registration documents but re-arranged his Christian names and later took his mother's surname of Kyte. Frederick married Catherine Parry (born 27th July 1896, Aberdare; died 18th June 1979, Stone, Staffordshire, aged 82) in 1916, in Caernarvonshire.

They had three children:

- **Annie Lillie Kyte** (born 13th April 1917, Glasgow; died 14th June 1992, Stafford, aged 75).

Annie married Stanley Lawson Fereday (born 23rd September 1915, Kings Norton, Birmingham; died 31st December 1972, North Bierley, Yorkshire, aged 57) in 1940, in Smethwick. They had two children.

- **Lillie Kyte** (born 8th September 1918, Newport; died 17th April 2021, Alderley Edge, Cheshire, aged 102).

Lillie married Kenneth Frank Holding (born 25th June 1915, Bolton; died 14th June 1997, Chelford, Cheshire, aged 81) on 1940, in Smethwick. They had two children.

- **Catherine Elizabeth Kyte** (born 1927, Birmingham).

Catherine married Gordon James Prentice (born 25th September 1925, Orsett, Essex; died 18th December 1991, Timperley, Cheshire, aged 66) in 1948, in Smethwick. They had two children.

The 1939 Register shows the family living at 50 Cavendish Road, Birmingham, where Frederick's occupation is noted as being a Blacksmith. Daughter Annie was a Sewing Machinist by trade, and Lillie a Ledger Clerk. Daughter Catherine does not appear on this Register.

Frederick died on 21st October 1973 at 9 Frank Road, Warley, aged 78.

2. William Henry Morgan.

William never married. He joined the Royal Navy on 16th April 1914. He served on the *'Impregnable'*, *'Leviathan'* and *'Vivid I'*, and was sadly killed by torpedo action whilst serving on board the S.S. *'Alfalfa'* off the Scilly Isles on 6th May 1917, aged 21.

Reports advise that the ship was sunk on 27th April 1917, but it wasn't until 6th May that William was officially recorded as being 'presumed drowned'.

The loss of the ship was reported thus:

"The British cargo ship *'Alfalfa'*, built in 1898 by Blumer, John & Co. and owned at the time of her loss by Arthur Holland & Co., on a voyage from Newport to the Mediterranean with a cargo of coal, was torpedoed and sunk by the German submarine UB-32 (Max Viebeg), 30 miles southwest of the Scilly Isles. 31 people lost their lives."

> MORGAN, A.B. W. S.S. " Alfalfa " (London). Presumed drowned 6th May, 1917. Age 21. Son of Mr. and Mrs. Morgan, of 132, Llantarnam Rd., Cwmbran, Newport, Mon. Born at Newport, Mon.

William Henry Morgan's Commonwealth Graves Ledger Entry.

His record shows that he was 5'2" tall, with brown hair and grey eyes, and his civilian occupation was that of an outdoor porter. His home address was noted as 132 Llantarnam Road, Cwmbran.

He is remembered on the Tower Hill War Memorial in London.

3. John Charles Morgan.

John was baptised at St. Mary's Mission Church, Maindee, Newport, on 2nd June 1903. The registration shows the family living at 2 Gordon Street, Newport, where his father's occupation was recorded as being a Plasterer.

John 'Jack' Morgan, photographed in 1940.

The 1921 Census indicated that he was living at home with his parents and siblings at 132 Llantarnam Road, Cwmbran. His occupation was recorded as being a Smith's Striker and a P.A.B. Assistant Pointer. At the time of the Census he was unemployed, but his place of work was shown as being at Guest, Keen & Nettlefold, Cwmbran Forge.

Known as 'Jack', John married Florence Ethel (Floss) Taylor (born 14th December 1905, Birmingham; died 18th February 1985, Oldbury, aged 79) on 30th July 1932, in Smethwick.

They had four children:

- **Joan Morgan** (born 12th June 1932, Oldbury, died 21st December 2014, Smethwick, aged 82).
- **John Charles Morgan** (born 29th August 1935, Oldbury, died 2002, Birmingham, aged 66).
- **William J. Morgan** (born 29th August 1935, Oldbury).
- **Leslie T. Morgan** (born 1946, Oldbury).

He joined the Royal Air Force on 11th October 1921. His civilian occupation at the time was that of a Blacksmith's Striker. He served in numerous locations worldwide.

John died on 16th March 1972, in Birmingham, aged 68.

4. Elizabeth Gwendoline Morgan.

Elizabeth was baptised at St. Mary's Mission Church, Maindee, Newport, on 24th January 1905. The registration shows the family living at 2 Gordon Street, Newport, where her father's occupation was recorded as being a Plasterer.

The 1921 Census indicated that she was living at home with her parents and siblings at 132 Llantarnam Road, Cwmbran, and her name was recorded as 'Gwendoline Elizabeth'. No employment details were shown.

Elizabeth married Hector William John Milton (born 16th January 1901, 55 Alfred Street, Weston-super-Mare), on 7th April 1928 at Christ Church, Summerfield, Birmingham.

They had three children:

- **Francis John Milton** (born 4th October 1929, 35 Algernon Road, Ladywood, Birmingham, died 25th June 2014, Portsmouth, aged 84).

Francis married Valerie Ann Way (born 19th February 1931, Wendover, Buckinghamshire; died 26th May 2009, Fareham, Hampshire, aged 78) on 6th June 1953, in Portsmouth.

- **Hector Stanley Milton** (born 21st May 1931, 10 Beresford Grove, Northfield, Birmingham, died 9th November 2010, Portsmouth, aged 79).

Hector married Maureen Pamela Beazley (born 13th November 1933, Portsmouth; died 4th November 2013, Cosham, Portsmouth, aged 80), on 7th August 1954, in Portsmouth.

- **William Norman Milton** (born 24th September 1935, 12 Kelby Road, Birmingham, died 20th April 2002, Cowplain, Hampshire, aged 66).

William married Eileen P. Ellis in 1974, in Portsmouth.

The 1939 Register shows Elizabeth and her children living at 12 Kelby Road, Birmingham. Husband Hector was away at the time of the registration process, serving with the Royal Navy, with whom he had signed up since 1929. His civilian occupation was noted as being a Farm Labourer.

Elizabeth with two of her children, photograph taken in 1941.

Elizabeth died on 22nd March 1982 at Alexandra Hospital, Cosham, Portsmouth, aged 77. Hector died on 17th December 1987 at Yarborough House, Southsea, aged 86.

5. Walter Morgan.

Walter was baptised at St. Mary's Mission Church, Maindee, Newport, on 10th July 1906. The registration shows the family living at 2 Gordon Street, Newport, where his father's occupation was recorded as being a Plasterer.

The 1921 Census indicated that he was living at home with his parents and siblings at 132 Llantarnam Road, Cwmbran, and his occupation recorded as being a 'P.P.B. Assistant', Pointer of Dog Spike' – although at the time of the Census he was shown as being unemployed. His place of work shown as being at Guest, Keen & Nettlefold, Cwmbran Forge, which is where his older brother John worked.

Informally known as 'Kell', he married Edith Elizabeth Barber (born 4th August 1910, Newmarket; died 27th August 2009, Handsworth, aged 99), on 22nd December 1934, at St. James' Church. Handsworth, Staffordshire. Both Walter and Edith were recorded as living at 78 Alexandra Road, Handsworth at the time of their marriage, Walter's occupation being noted as being a Brass Worker. No occupation was shown for Edith.

Edith Elizabeth Barber (1910-2009)

They had two children:

- **David Morgan** (born 1937, Birmingham, died 26th January 2020, Chase Terrace, Staffordshire, aged 83).

David married Valerie A. Guest (born 1941, Birmingham), in 1960, in Birmingham.

- **Gillian Mary Morgan** (born 25th September 1943, Birmingham, died 20th September 2015, Birmingham, aged 71).

Gillian married John Edward George Finegan (born 7th September 1943; died 8th November 1990, Birmingham, aged 47).

The 1939 Register shows Walter and Edith residing at 76 Alexandra Road, Birmingham, where Walter is shown as being a Hydraulic Dieman at Brass Works. Edith is recorded as undertaking unpaid domestic duties.

Walter died on 28th May 1976, in Sutton Coldfield, aged 69.

Walter 'Kell' Morgan (1906-1976)

The grave of Walter and Edith Elizabeth Morgan, Birmingham.

6.   Stanley Morgan.

Stanley was baptised at St. Mary's Mission Church, Maindee, Newport, on 23rd September 1913. The registration shows the family living at 5 Philip Street, Newport, where his father's occupation was recorded as being a Plasterer.

The 1921 Census indicated that he was living at home with his parents and siblings at 132 Llantarnam Road, Cwmbran.

Stanley married Olive Mary Satchwell (born 1921, Birmingham; died 10th August 2007, Birmingham, aged 86) on 22nd June 1940, in Birmingham.

They had no children.

The 1939 Register shows that Stanley was living with the Satchwell family at the time, at 192 Frankley Beeches Road, Birmingham, where his occupation was recorded as being an Aircraft Work Assembler.

Stanley died in 1982, in Pembroke, aged 68.

CHAPTER 4.
THE FAMILY AND DESCENDANTS OF WILLIAM JOHN MORGAN.

William was born at 4 Tabernacle Row, Bristol, on 28th April 1864, and was baptised at St. Philip & Jacob Church, Bristol, on 10th November 1866. The registration shows the family living at Bread Street, Bristol, where his father's occupation was recorded as being a Plasterer.

Alice Bullock with one of her children, date unknown.

As stated earlier, he married Alice Bullock (born 25th November 1867, 1 Wellington Terrace, Bristol; died 13th August 1929, Bristol, aged 61) on 13th October 1884 at Bristol Registry Office. At the time of their marriage, William was living at 29 Catherine Street, Barton Hill, Bristol, his occupation being recorded as a Blacksmith, with Alice residing at 7 Hillingdon Place, Lawrence Hill, Bristol.

They had twelve children:

1. **William John Morgan** (born 25th July 1885, 57 Croydon Street, Bristol; died 21st October 1914, Langemarke, Belgium (WW1), aged 29).

2. **Thomas Morgan** (born 19th November 1886, 37 Gladstone Street, Bristol; died 4th July 1943, Bristol, aged 56).

3. **Alice Morgan** (born 24th May 1889, 17 Croydon Street, Bristol; died 25th May 1957, Bristol, aged 68).

4. **George Morgan** (born 24th August 1891, 17 Croydon Street, Bristol; died 9th October 1973, Bristol, aged 82).

5. **James (Jim) Morgan** (born 4th October 1893, 1 Riches Lane, Bristol; died 26th August 1920, Birmingham, aged 26).

6. **Florence Matilda Morgan** (born 6th November 1895, 22 Saffron Street, Bristol; died 19th January 1961, Bristol, aged 65).

7. **Frederick 'Jerry' Morgan** (born 5th November 1897, 22* Saffron Street, Bristol; died 9th May 1953, Bristol, aged 55).

The birth certificate states the address as 2 Saffron Street but this is likely to be an error.

8. **Harry Morgan** (born 30th May 1899, 22 Saffron Street, Bristol; died 28th April 1973, Bristol, aged 73).

9. **Clara Morgan** (born 31st March 1901, 22 Saffron Street, Bristol; died 21st August 1959, Bristol, aged 58).

10. **Violet Morgan** (born 31st May 1903, 9 Bishop Street, Bristol; died 11th June 1981, Bristol, aged 78).

11. **Elsie Morgan** (born 3rd November 1904, 9 Bishop Street, Bristol; died 9th November 1973, Bristol, aged 69).

12. **Arthur Morgan** (born 17th October 1906, 9 Bishop Street, Bristol; died 12th June 1968, Bristol, aged 61).

The Census of 1891 shows William and his family living at 21 Croydon Street, Barton Hill, Bristol, where his occupation is stated as being a Blacksmith.

By the time of the 1901 Census, the family had moved to 22 Saffron Street, Barton Hill, Bristol. William's occupation was again shown as being a Blacksmith, and sons William and Thomas were both employed as Market Garden Labourers.

The 1911 Census shows the family living at 9 Wellington Street, Easton Road, Bristol, where William's occupation was still being recorded as being a Blacksmith (although clarified as working for the Tramways), and sons Thomas (Leather Labourer), George (Wagon Works Labourer) and James (Tramways Labourer) shown as being in gainful employment.

William died on 19th September 1912, in Bristol, aged 48.

The 1921 Census shows Alice and three of her children (Frederick, Alice and Arthur) living at 30 Proctor Street, St. George, Bristol. She is described as living on her own means, but was also interestingly stated as having 'no fixed abode'.

Alice passed away on 13th August 1929, aged 61, also in Bristol. She was buried at Avonview Cemetery, Bristol, on 19th August 1929.

1. THE FAMILY AND DESCENDANTS OF WILLIAM JOHN MORGAN.

William was baptised at St. Philip & Jacob Church, Bristol, on 16th August 1885. The registration shows the family living at 51 Croydon Street, Barton Hill, Bristol, where his father's occupation was recorded as being a Blacksmith.

He married Margaret Chapman (born 4th June 1886, Southampton) at Bristol Register Office on 13th April 1908. Both William and Margaret were living at 82 Easton Road, Easton, Bristol, and William's occupation noted as being a General Labourer.

The 1911 Census shows the family living at 5 Rose Green Road, St. George, Bristol, where William worked as a Tramways Labourer. Sadly, William was killed during World War 1, on 21st Oct 1914 in Langemarke, Belgium. He had joined the 1st Battalion South Wales Borderers (Regiment Number 8039).

William John Morgan's Pension Card following his death in WW1.

A list of his effects following his death shows that his widow Margaret received the sum of £3 19/11d (just under £4) on 10th April 1915, followed by a further £5 War Gratuity on 15th July 1919.

Margaret subsequently married Walter Channell on 8th August 1923 at St. George Parish Church in Bristol, and had one child also called Walter, born on 28th Jan 1924. Margaret's address at the time of this marriage was 1 Rock Cottage, Bethel Road, Bristol, and Walter's at Hudd's Hill Road, Bristol.

Walter senior died in 1961, at 67 Shakespeare Avenue, Bristol. Margaret died on 4th February 2016 in Bristol.

Son Walter married Olive May Hazel Roberts (born 16th September 1926, Bristol; died 27th April 1995, Bristol) in 1942, in Bristol. They had one child. Walter died on 4th February 2016, in Bristol.

CHILDREN OF WILLIAM AND MARGARET:

1.   **Margaret Morgan** (born 19th February 1910, Bristol; died 1912, Bristol, aged 2).

Margaret was baptised at St. Silas Church, Bedminster, Bristol, on 23rd March 1910. The family address at the time was recorded at 48 Leadhouse Road, Easton, Bristol. Margaret sadly died in Bristol in 1912 at the age of 2. Her father's profession was recorded as a Labourer.

2.   **Catherine Gladys Morgan** (born 1st July 1913, Bristol; died 1994, Bristol, aged 80).

Catherine was baptised at All Saints Church in Fishponds, Bristol, on 23rd July 1913. At this time the family were living at 32 The Causeway (Lodge Causeway), Fishponds, Bristol, with her father's profession noted as being a Motor Driver.

She married Ronald Edwin Shackleton Street (born 4th November 1909, Keynsham, near Bristol) on 20th April 1935, at St. John the Divine's Church, Bristol. Their marriage certificate states that Catherine lived at 34 Lodge Causeway, Fishponds, Bristol, where her employment was shown as being a Brush Marker. Ronald lived at 5 Ashley Hill, Montpelier, Bristol, where his occupation was noted as being an Engineer.

By 1939 the family were living at 57 Beverley Road, Bristol. Ronald's occupation was described in detail as being a Capstan Lathe Tool Fitter, whilst Catherine undertook unpaid domestic duties.

They had two children:

1.   **Un-named male child** (died at birth).
2.   **Ronald Walter Street** (born 7th June 1938, in Bristol; died 13th June 1992, 2 George Road, Erdington, Bishop Sutton, aged 54).

The grave of Ronald Street and his son, located at Bishop Sutton,
a few miles South of Bristol.

Catherine died in Bristol in 1994, aged 80. Ronald died in Bristol on 17th December 2001 at the age of 92. The grave of Ronald Street and his son is located at Holy Trinity Church, Bishop Sutton.

2. THE FAMILY AND DESCENDANTS OF THOMAS MORGAN.

Second son Thomas (Tom) was baptised at St. Lawrence Church, Easton, Bristol, on 15th September 1891. At the time of his baptism the family were living at 17 Croydon Street, Barton Hill, Bristol, and his father's occupation being recorded as being a Blacksmith.

He married Alice Lily (Lilian) Perkins (born 8th September 1890, Trowbridge) in Bristol, on 16th September 1918, at Holy Trinity Church, Bristol.

The marriage registration shows that at the time Thomas was 'on Active Service' whilst Alice was living at 14 Beaufort Street, Bristol.

They had one child, Douglas Thomas Morgan (born 14th August 1919, Bristol).

Alice had previously been married to William Hodge (since 11th October 1909), and they had three children:

1. **William Cecil Hodge** (born 16th February 1911, Bristol; died 1912, Bristol, aged 10 months).
2. **Gordon Donald Hodge** (born 4th September 1913, Bristol; died 1993, West Coker, Somerset, aged 79).
3. **Kathleen Daisy Hodge** (born 29th November 1916, Bristol; died 2004, Portsmouth, aged 87).

William died of wounds sustained during WW1 on 29th November 1917.

William Hodge's military death index card showing his address and family information.

Thomas was a useful footballer and played on three occasions for Bristol City; His appearances are shown below.

Date	Opponents	League	Goals
12 October 1918	Royal Engineers (White City)	Bristol County Combination	0
26 December 1918	Bristol Rovers	Bristol County Combination	0
4 January 1919	Ex-Servicemen	Friendly	0

In 1921, the family's address remained at 14 Beaufort Street, Bristol, where Thomas was noted working as a labourer at the well-known local employer Brecknell, Munro & Rogers at Lawrence Hill, Bristol, whilst his wife Alice and the three surviving children remained at home.

The 1939 Register shows the Morgan family living further down the road at 4 Beaufort Street, Bristol, where Thomas is described as a Builder's Labourer. He was also noted as working for the A.R.P. (Air Raid Patrol) reserve during the war.

Stepson Gordon Hodge is also seen in the register, living with the family, having recently been widowed. His wife, Agnes Joan Bessie Horstead (born 29th May 1916, Wells, died 15th December 1937, Bristol, age 20), who he married on 11th April 1936, at Emmanuel Church, St. Philips, Bristol, was buried at Greenbank Cemetery, Bristol, on 20th December 1937.

He was recorded as working as a Traffic Clerk.

Son Douglas was shown as working at the Aircraft Works, almost certainly in the Filton area.

Thomas (Tom) Morgan with four of his brothers, photograph taken in 1926. Thomas is front row, extreme right. The back row shows William John and Frederick (Jerry), and the front row shows George and Harry (in uniform) to the left of Tom.

Thomas died on 4th July 1943, at 4 Beaufort Street, Bristol, aged 56. Cause of death was recorded as Gastric Carcinoma (Stomach Cancer). He was buried at Greenbank Cemetery, Bristol, on 9th July 1943.

Alice died in 1979, aged 88, in Bournemouth.

CHILD OF THOMAS AND ALICE MORGAN:

Douglas Thomas Morgan.

Son Douglas was baptised at Holy Trinity Church, St. Philips, Bristol, on September 3rd 1919, where his parents were recorded as living at 14 Beaufort Street, Bristol, with his father noted as being a Brass Fitter.

He married Mary Cocking (born 3rd October 1919, Bristol; died 5th December 1995, Bristol, aged 75) in Bristol in 1939, and had five children;

1. **Kaye E. Morgan** (born 1942, Bristol).
2. **Donald Anthony Morgan** (born 15th December 1943, Bristol; died 20th December 1943, Bristol, aged 5 days). He was buried at Ridgeway Park Cemetery, Bristol, on 10th January 1944.
3. **Douglas Louis Morgan** (born 15th December 1943, Bristol; died 15th December 1943, Bristol, aged only 7 hours.). Twin to Donald. Buried at Ridgeway Park Cemetery, Bristol, on 10th January 1944.
4. **Linda M. Morgan** (born 1946, Bristol).
5. **Leigh V. Morgan** (born 1952, Bristol; died 1952, Bristol, aged less than one year).

Douglas died in 1992 in Portsmouth at the age of 72. His widow Mary never re-married.

3. THE FAMILY AND DESCENDANTS OF ALICE MORGAN (1889).

Alice was baptised at St. Lawrence Church, Easton, Bristol, on 15th September 1891. At the time of her baptism the family were living at 17 Croydon Street, Barton Hill, Bristol, and her father's occupation being recorded as being a Blacksmith.

She married William Mansfield (born 1885, Bristol) on 28th January 1911 at St. Luke's Church, Barton Hill, Bristol. Alice was living at 41 Granville Street, Bristol, at the time of her marriage, and she was employed as a Cotton Spinner. William's home address was noted as being 27 Barton Street, Bristol, and his occupation shown as being a Labourer.

They had three children, two of whom sadly died young;

1. **William Mansfield** (born 28th October 1911, died 1990, Bristol, aged 78).

William was baptised on 19th November 1913 at St. Philip & Jacob Church, Bristol, where his father's occupation was recorded as being a Galvanizer, and was living at Barton Hill, Bristol.

He married Johanna (Joan) Hale (born 16th Oct 1913, Bedwellty, died 13th April 1974, Bristol, aged 60) on 11th April 1936, at St. Matthews, Moorfields, Bristol. At the time of their marriage, William was living at 30 Proctor Street, Bristol, and his occupation shown as being a Labourer. Johanna was living at 5 Hayward Road, Bristol.

The 1939 Register shows the family living at 1 Collin Road, Bristol, where William's occupation is shown as being a Bricklayer. William was an occasional player for the Morgan Family football team, appearing in local charity matches during the 1920s and 1930s.

They had two children:

- **William F. Mansfield** (born 1938, Bristol).
- **Joan P. Mansfield** (born 1945, Bristol).

2. **James Mansfield** (born 1913, Bristol; died 13th January 1915, Bristol, aged 1 year 7 months). He was buried at Avonview Cemetery, Bristol, on 17th January 1915.

3. **Albert Francis Mansfield** (born 1914, Bristol; died 29th December 1914, Bristol, aged only 7 weeks). He was buried at Avonview Cemetery, Bristol, on 3rd January 1915.

Alice's husband William was killed in action on 19th December 1915 in Flanders, Belgium, serving with the Royal Field Artillery. His pension card confirms his date of death and also his home address of 30 Proctor Street, Moorfield, Bristol.

As shown on William's pension card, Alice subsequently married Edward Henry 'Sonny' Evans (born 28th April 1884, Chase Terrace, Staffordshire) on 21st September 1916, in Bristol. It is interesting to view the note on the card which reads:

"Widow was re-married on 21.4.16 to Edward Henry Evans, civilian. The re-marriage gratuity due was £34 13/5d, which was paid to Mrs. Evans. The pension for the child is being paid to Mrs. Evans."

The 1921 Census indicates that the family lived at 21 Bishop Street, St. George, Bristol, where Edward was employed as a builder's labourer at Alban, Richards & Co., Avonmouth.

They had no children together, and she died on 25th May 1957 in Bristol General Hospital, aged 68. Edward died on 17th September 1957 in Bristol, aged 73.

William Mansfield's Pension Card from WW1.

4. THE FAMILY AND DESCENDANTS OF GEORGE MORGAN (1891).

George was baptised at St. Lawrence Church, Easton, Bristol, on 15th September 1891. At the time of his baptism the family were living at 17 Croydon Street, Barton Hill, Bristol, his father's occupation being recorded as being a Blacksmith.

He married Laura Wagland (born 17th Nov 1893, Bristol) on 12th August 1918 at St. Peter's Church in Bristol. Laura had previously been married to Robert William Hitchings (born 28th September 1891, Bristol) and they had one child, Robert William Hitchings (born 28th Sep 1913, Bristol). Robert Sr. was killed at sea on HMS Goliath on 13th May 1915 in the Dardanelles, Turkey.

> HITCHINGS, Sto. 1st Cl. Robert William, SS/110048. R.N. H.M.S. "Goliath." Killed in action with Turkish destroyer in Dardanelles 13th May, 1915. Age 23. Husband of L. Hitchings, of 3, Corbett St., Barton Hill, Bristol. Native of St. Paul's, Bristol. 6.

Commonwealth War Graves Register for Robert William Hitchings.

The 1921 Census shows the family living at 3 Corbett Street, Barton Hill, Bristol, where George was described as a General Labourer, working for McAlpines in Avonmouth. They had ten children:

1. **George Morgan** (born 15th January 1919, 3 Corbett Street, Bristol; died 23rd September 1995, Bristol, aged 76).

2. **Olive Laura Morgan** (born 27th April 1920, 3 Corbett Street, Bristol; died 10th August 2001, Bristol, aged 81).

3. **William James (Jimmy) Morgan** (born 19th June 1922, 3 Corbett Street, Bristol; died 11th October 1976, Bristol, aged 54).

4. **Doreen Morgan** (born 1924, Bristol; died 1924, Bristol, aged less than 1).

5. **Iris May Morgan** (born 13th February 1926, Bristol; died 9th April 2023, Bristol, aged 97).

6. **Doreen Jean Morgan** (born 9th December 1929, Bristol; died 15th June 2011, Bristol, aged 81).

7. **Ronald Morgan** (born 1931, Bristol; died 18th July 1956, Bristol, aged 25).

8. **Constance Ellen Morgan** (born 1933, Bristol; died 24th March 2014, Bristol, aged 81).

9. **Brenda Mary Morgan** (born 20th November 1934, Bristol; died 1st June 2017, Wokingham, aged 82).

10. **Patricia Ann Morgan** (born 10th November 1937, Bristol; died 17th May 2006, Bristol, aged 68).

Like many of his family, George was an excellent local footballer, and played for the Morgan Family football team who played many charity matches in the 1920s and 1930s. He made two appearances for Bath City during the 1925/26 season, scoring two goals in as many appearances.

He also played for the Brecknell, Munro and Rogers football team, who won the Gloucestershire Senior Amateur Cup in 1926.

The final was played at the Bristol Rovers ground at Eastville on 21st April 1926, against Bedminster Down Sports, Brecknells winning the match 3-1. According to a newspaper report on the match, George did not have the best of games: "Morgan, with practically an open goal, placed the ball outside" and "Morgan, heading outside with only the goalkeeper to beat." However, by winning this fixture they ensured they would meet a team from the north of the County to contest the overall championship.

The 1919/20 Brecknell, Munro & Rogers Football Team. George in the front row behind the trophy, and brother Harry on his right.

The 1925/26 Brecknell, Munro and Rogers football team, showing George Morgan holding the Gloucestershire Senior Amateur cup. Brother Harry is on his right.

The team defeated Broadwell (Forest of Dean) in this final 6-3, played at Broadwell on 4th September 1926. George scored twice in this match.

By 1939, the family were still living at 3 Corbett Street, Barton Hill, Bristol. William was still employed as a General Labourer, with son George being described as an Iron Moulder. All other children's details have been redacted.

The family of George and Laura, date unknown.

Front Row left to right: Laura Lewis (nee Morgan), George Morgan, Laura Morgan, Constance Pollinger (nee Morgan), Patricia Short (nee Morgan).

Middle Row: Iris Gould (nee Morgan), Brenda White (nee Morgan), Jean Morris (nee Morgan).

Back Row: Jimmy Morgan, Ronald Morgan, George Morgan, Robert (Bob) Hitchings.

George and Laura Morgan, with grandson Jeff Short, Corbett Street, Barton Hill, Bristol, 1960.

George and Laura celebrated their 50th wedding anniversary in 1968, and they were featured in a detailed article in the *'Bristol Evening Post'* on Saturday 12th April of that year:

'SOCCER FAMILY'

"Mr. and Mrs. George Morgan, of 5 Beaufort Close, St. George, Bristol, who family's footballing fortunes are well-known to enthusiasts, celebrate their golden wedding on Monday.

They were married at St. Peter's Church, Bristol, having met as teenagers when they both worked at the Great Western Cotton Factory.

Mr. Morgan is one of a family who turned their footballing talents to charity matches and raised large sums of money.

Mr. Morgan, now 76, was a well-known footballer in Bristol. Mrs. Morgan is 74.

His brother Tony* played for Bristol City before the 1914-18 war, and another, Fred 'Jerry' Morgan, turned out for Rovers after the war. Mr. Morgan's son Jimmy also turned out for the Rovers a generation later after the 1939-1945 war."

*This would be Tom Morgan, and not Tony, which is a typographical error.

Memorial card for George Morgan, 1973.

George died on 9th October 1973, in Bristol, aged 82, and was buried at Avonview Cemetery, Bristol, on 12th October 1973.

Laura passed away on 2nd January 1981, also in Bristol, aged 87, and was buried at Avonview Cemetery, Bristol, on 12th January 1981.

Memorial card for Laura Morgan, 1981.

The grave of George and Laura Morgan, Avonview Cemetery, Bristol.

GEORGE AND LAURA'S CHILDREN:

The children of George and Laura c. 1990.

Back Row (left to right): Olive (known as Laura) Lewis; Iris Gould; Doreen (known as Jean) Morris; Constance (Connie) Pollinger; Brenda White; Patricia (Pat) Short.

Front Row (left to right): Eileen Morgan (nee Rose - wife of George Morgan); George Morgan.

1. George Morgan.

George married Eileen Alice Rose (born 12th May 1923, Bristol; died 15th February 2007, Bristol, aged 83) in Bristol in 1950. They had five children.

One lovely story about George and his Bristol Rovers player brother William James (Jimmy) is recounted by his grandson Jeff Short:

"In their younger years, Jimmy and George looked very similar so much, so that on match days George would often arrive at Eastville Stadium early. He would stride towards Rovers officials with a confident smile and a tip of the hat.

Believing he was Jimmy, the officials would wave George in and he would watch the game for free. Quite what the officials did when the real Jimmy arrived no one knows.

It was just after WWII and times were tough so it was an "innovative" way of saving a few precious pennies."

George died on 23rd September 1995, in Bristol, aged 76.

Eileen was cremated at South Bristol Cemetery on 27th February 2007.

2. Olive Laura Morgan.

Olive was baptised at Moorfields St. Matthew Church, Redfield, Bristol, on 21st May 1920. The family were recorded as living at 3 Corbett Street, Barton Hill, Bristol, and her father's occupation noted as being a Labourer.

She married Frederick Alfred Lewis (born 31st December 1921, Bristol; died 18th November 1974, in Redfield, Bristol, aged 52) on 20th June 1942. They had two children.

Frederick was buried at Avonview Cemetery, Bristol, on 22nd November 1974.

Olive died on 10th August 2001, in Bristol, aged 81.

3. William James (Jimmy) Morgan.

William James (Jimmy) was baptised at Moorfields St. Matthew Church, Redfield, Bristol, on 14th July 1922. The family were recorded as living at 3 Corbett Street, Barton Hill, Bristol, and his father's occupation noted as being a Labourer.

He married Kathleen Rosina Frankcom (born 16th June 1926, Bristol). They had one child.

An interesting article about Jimmy appeared in the *'Bristol Evening World'* on 22nd February 1951:

'SOCCER'S IN HIS BLOOD'

"Twenty-six years old Jimmie (sic) Morgan, one of the 13 from whom the Rovers' cup-fighting team will be selected for the Newcastle tie*, comes from one of the most famous sporting families in Bristol.

He grew up in an atmosphere of soccer. In his teens he gloried in the prowess of his father and four uncles who wrote a page in the City's sporting history.

The five footballing brothers came from parents distinguished on the field. Jimmie's father, now 59, played for Gloucester County, like Uncle Harry, now 52. Uncle Fred, 54, played for the Rovers in 1924.

Uncle Jim and Uncle Tom, who have died, played for Wolves and Bristol City respectively.

Now Jimmie, living in rooms in Regent Terrace, Newtown, with his wife Kathleen and two-year-old son John, and cousin** Sid Morgan, the City goalkeeper, are the only ones of the new generation to share their talent.

One of his brothers is in the Army, two more are window-cleaning.

Jimmie began to distinguish himself at soccer at Avonvale School when he played at inside-left. Then he played for the University Settlement.

He landed in Normandy with the Royal Marine Commandos on D-Day, played regularly in the Forces and had his rehabilitation problems solved when the Rovers signed him up immediately he was demobilised,

Soon afterwards he married a girl he met on war-time leave. Kathleen hasn't seen him play more than twice. "I just can't get interested in the game", she says."

Sadly Jimmy was not selected for this famous F.A. Cup fixture.

**There is no evidence to suggest that Jimmy was related to Sid Morgan, despite claims in the local press.*

Jimmy is probably best remembered as a regular player for Bristol Rovers Football Club during the late 1940s and early 1950s, details of which appear in **Chapter 17.**

After retiring from full-time football in the mid-1960s, he set up a small window-cleaning business in the Lawrence Hill area of Bristol. He did, however, continue to make guest appearances for the Morgan family football team throughout the decade.

The family had moved to Leigh Street, Easton, Bristol, then finally to 111 Whitehall Road, Bristol. Jimmy apparently broke his arm working on his own window cleaning round then worked making grates for MAC (Metal Agencies Co. Ltd.) with headquarters in Queen Square, Bristol.

As recounted earlier, he served in the forces during World War 2, and one lovely story concerning him has been recounted by Jeff Short:

"Jim was conscripted to the army as part of the war effort in World War II. In 1940, Jim was dispatched to Dunkirk as part of the rescue mission. The news of this quickly spread to the wider family and his friends and to the community of Barton Hill.

Given the dire situation of British troops in Dunkirk, this would have been a very high risk deployment causing great concern to all his family and friends.

News was tightly controlled during the war so nothing was heard from Jim although it was known the Dunkirk mission had been a success. Then a letter from Jim arrived stating he was coming home on leave. This was the best news for everyone connected to Jim and it was decided a street party would be arranged for their homecoming hero.

The street party was lavish with the whole neighbourhood turning out, much to the embarrassment of Jim.

It turned out that Jim had made it to Dover, boarded a boat and was then abruptly told to disembark as the rescue mission had been completed - he never made it to Dunkirk. A story told several times amongst the family with much mirth and fond memories of Jim.

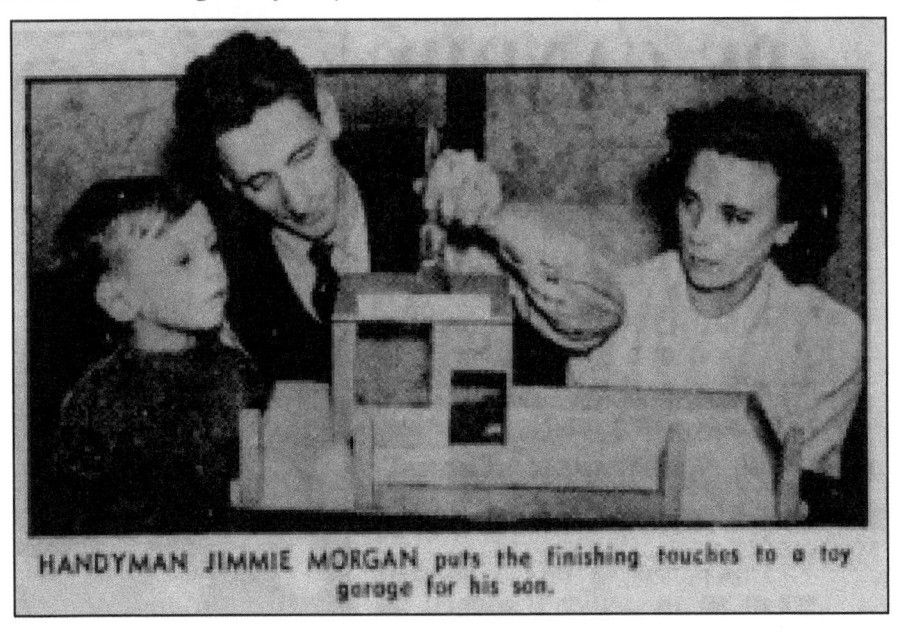

HANDYMAN JIMMIE MORGAN puts the finishing touches to a toy garage for his son.

An illustration from the 'Evening World' article; it is interesting that they referred to him as 'Jimmie'.

Steven Morgan remembers 'Uncle Jim' with affection:

I remember going to my Grandmother's prefab house in St George when Uncle Jim was there. He would look to me and say on a Sunday morning "Right - I'm off to church now - in the Lord Raglan".

Jimmy was a heavy smoker throughout his life, which no doubt contributed to his death due to lung cancer.

He died on 11th October 1976, at 111 Whitehall Road, Bristol, aged 54. He was buried at Avonview Cemetery, Bristol, on 15th October 1976.

An obituary for Jimmy appeared in the *'Bristol Evening Post'* on 12th October 1976:

'JIMMY MORGAN'

Jimmy Morgan, who played for Bristol Rovers for seven years after the war, has died after a short illness at the age of 54.

He joined the Rovers in 1945-46 after playing for the Royal Marine Commandos.

Mr. Morgan played as an inside-forward and was a member of the squad that won promotion in 1952. He progressed through the Colts and Reserve sides.

He was one of the few survivors of the Morgan family football team that helped to raise money for charity before the war.

Mr. Morgan, who lived at Whitehall Road and worked for MAC, leaves a wife and one son."

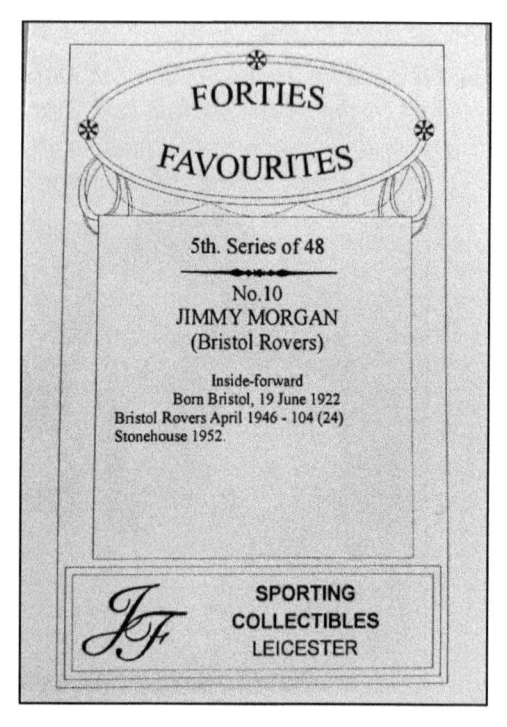

A reproduction collectors' card featuring Jimmy Morgan.

The grave of William James (Jimmy) Morgan and wife Kathleen, Avonview Cemetery, Bristol.

Kathleen died on 27th April 2006 in South Gloucestershire, aged 79. She was buried alongside her husband at Avonview Cemetery, Bristol.

4.   Doreen Morgan.

Doreen sadly died just after her birth in 1924, in Bristol.

5.   Iris May Morgan.

Iris married Royston Thomas Gould (born 17th June 1927, Bristol; died 19th July 2000, Bristol, aged 73) in 1950, in Bristol. They had three children.

Iris died on 9th April 2023, in Bristol, aged 97.

Her funeral was held on 19th May 2023 at St. Ambrose Church, Whitehall, Bristol.

6.   Doreen Jean Morgan.

Doreen married Arthur Clifford Morris (born 25th January 1926, Bristol; died 8th October 2010, Bristol, aged 84) in 1950, in Bristol. They had two children.

Their eldest child Carol was born on 11th April 1951 in Bristol. She married Robert G. Nash in 1972 in Bristol, and had two children. She sadly died on 20th April 1995, in Bristol, aged 44.

Doreen died on 15th June 2011 in Bristol, aged 81.

7. Ronald Morgan.

Ronald married Jean Short (born 31st October 1931, Bristol) in Bristol in 1950. They had one child.

In January 1934, it was reported that:

"Ronald Morgan, aged three years, of Corbett Street, Barton Hill, Bristol, was scalded about the neck when hot water from a kettle fell on him on Saturday. He was taken by the St. John Ambulance to the Bristol Royal Infirmary"

Ronald Morgan and wife Jean with their only child. Photograph dated c. 1953.

Ronald died on 18th July 1956 in Bristol, aged only 25. He was buried at Avonview Cemetery, Bristol, on 23rd July 1956.

Jean then married Ivor John Laws (born 16th June 1925, Bristol; died 3rd May 2006, Bristol, aged 80) on 9th November 1957, in Bristol. They had six children together.

The grave of Ronald Morgan, Avonview Cemetery, Bristol. Steven Evans was Ronald's son-in-law.

Jean died in Bristol on 14th June 1994, aged 62.

Ivor's funeral service took place at Westerleigh Crematorium on 11th May 2006.

8.   Constance (Connie) Ellen Morgan.

Constance married Reginald Pollinger (born 1922, Keynsham; died 26th September 2009, Bristol, aged 87) in 1951, in Bristol. They had one child.

She died on 24th March 2014, also in Bristol, aged 81. Her funeral service took place at South Bristol Crematorium on 7th April 2014.

9.   Brenda Mary Morgan.

Brenda married David John White (born 30th June 1929, Bristol; died 13th October 2009, Wokingham, aged 80) in 1954, in Bristol. They had four children.

David's funeral service took place at St. Patrick's Church, Netham Road, Redfield, Bristol, on 23rd October 2009, and he was buried at Avonview Cemetery, Bristol.

Brenda died on 1st June 2017, also in Wokingham. Her funeral service took place at Corpus Christi Church, Wokingham, on 12th July 2017, and she was buried at Avonview Cemetery, Bristol, on 13th July 2017.

The grave of Brenda and David White, Avonview Cemetery, Bristol.

10.   **Patricia Ann Morgan.**

Patricia Ann Morgan married Royston Guy Short (born 16th August 1931, Bristol; died 2nd September 2015, Bristol, aged 84.) in 1956, in Bristol. They had two children.

Patricia Ann Morgan, c. 1963

The grave of Patricia and Royston, Avonview Cemetery, Bristol.

Patricia died on 17th May 2006 in Bristol, aged 68. She was buried at Avonview Cemetery, Bristol, on 26th May 2006 following the service at St. Ambrose Church, Whitehall, Bristol.

Royston was also buried at Avonview Cemetery, Bristol.

5. THE FAMILY AND DESCENDANTS OF JAMES (JIM) MORGAN.

James married May Hart (born 24th November 1897, Bristol; died 1991, Bristol, aged 93) on 23rd August 1920, in Bristol.

They had one child, Edna May Morgan (born 4th Feb 1921, Bristol; died 10th August 2007, Bristol, aged 86). She did not appear to get married.

He played football for Bath City, and is listed as having played 31 games and scoring 4 goals in the 1919/20 season, alongside his brother Frederick (Jerry). He then signed for Wolverhampton Wanderers in June 1920, but sadly his career at the club never materialised.

Bath City F.C. 1919/20. James (Jim) Morgan pictured to the left of the goalkeeper in the back row.

James tragically died on 26th August 1920, aged 26, whilst falling from a train near Birmingham. Numerous family rumours have abounded over the years, some suggesting a suicide following war trauma. However, a press report on 4th September 1920 gives an objective view:

"Certain rumours respecting James Morgan, who played back for Bath City last season, have been in circulation in the city, and according to the *'Athletic'* of today, his death occurred last Wednesday.

"Wolverhampton Wanderers have sustained an unexpected loss," the *'Athletic News'* states. One of their latest recruits, James Morgan, of Bristol, who formerly played for Bath City, a back, was found on Wednesday evening, lying terribly injured on the railway near Birmingham, and died in hospital shortly afterwards. Morgan, who was only married on Tuesday, was unable to turn up for training at the usual time, having injured his right foot, while jumping from a wall. He left Bristol to go to Wolverhampton, and is believed that he fell from an express train."

The inquest in his death from August 1920 appeared to confirm his suicide:

"The story of the tragic death of a member of the Wolverhampton Wanderers football team was unfolded to the Birmingham coroner yesterday afternoon, when the verdict of "suicide whilst of unsound mind" was returned. Formerly a promising player of Bath City, James Morgan, aged 25, of 21, Upper Bishop Street, Moorfield, Bristol, had only recently been discharged from the Bristol Royal Infirmary, and was travelling in company with his newly-wedded wife to Wolverhampton, when he was seen to jump from the door of a corridor train.

At the time, it is estimated, the train was travelling at about 60 miles an hour. Mrs. Morgan described how she was awakened by a fellow passenger tugging at her and crying "Look." Witness was just in time to see her husband disappearing through the carriage doorway. Several witnesses spoke to finding the body near Cofton Tunnel, Northfield. Morgan was removed to the Queen's Hospital, where he died."

Another local press report published on 3rd September 1920 gave more details into the circumstances leading to his death. Under the heading of 'Bath City Player's Tragic Death', the article reports:

"Wolverhampton Wanderers have sustained an unexpected loss. One of their of their latest recruits, James Morgan, of Bristol, who formerly played for Bath City as a back, was found on Wednesday week lying terribly injured on the railway near Birmingham, and died in hospital shortly afterwards. Morgan, who was only married on the Tuesday, was unable to turn up for training at the usual time, having injured his right foot while jumping from a wall. He left Bristol on Wednesday for Wolverhampton, and it is believed that he fell from an express train.

An inquest was held at the Birmingham Coroner's Court. May Morgan, deceased's wife, said she had only been married two days when this affair happened. Morgan had been in the army and was wounded twice. He had a hasty temper, and some weeks ago quarrelled with his parents. About the same time he complained of pains in his head, and seemed dazed at times. About four weeks ago he attempted to commit suicide at his home, and had to go to the infirmary in consequence of the injuries.

On August 26th witness and her husband were travelling in a corridor train from Bristol to Wolverhampton. When near Birmingham a woman sitting on the opposite side of the compartment called, "Look."

Witness, who had been dozing, looked towards the window of the corridor side of the train, and just saw her husband's back as he disappeared from the train. The lady who had called out pulled the communication cord and the train stopped.

Nothing had occurred on the journey to suggest that such an act as the deceased's was being contemplated.

Evidence was given that the deceased seemed to jump from the train deliberately, brushing aside a little girl who was in the corridor in order to get to the door. He was picked up on the Birmingham side of the Cofton Tunnel, unconscious, and in a badly injured state.

The Coroner said deceased seems to have acted on a sudden suicidal impulse. A verdict of "Suicide while of unsound mind" was recorded.

"The Captain" writes that Jim Morgan was one of the City's best-known players last season. A native of Bristol, he played a lot of Army football, and as a right-back was one of the best the City ever possessed. He was a sportsman to the fingertips and he left the City to join the

"Wolves" with the goodwill of every Soccer adherent in Bath, who predicted for him a great career. He was one of three playing brothers, all of whom appeared with the City last season. Fred has gone to Bristol City and Tom is with a junior club in Bristol. But Jim was the best of the bunch. Built on generous lines, he could repel the stoutest stock, and when things were going badly his lion heart always rallied the failing ones. He was one of the hardest kickers in the West of England. Occasionally he was erratic, but as a rule he was the soundest of players. The City will miss hint and mourn his death. They will doubtless wear mourning at their opening match on Saturday next."

It could well be that his suicide was due to personal problems which he encountered following his return to civilian life after WW1, a condition which affected many people returning from active service. However, there is another suggestion that his suicide was due to his 'getting a chapel girl pregnant' – his wife May was carrying his daughter Edna at the time of their marriage on 23rd August 1920, and there seemed to be some degree of shame within the family at this revelation. However, this is pure family speculation and no evidence has been found to support this story.

James was buried at Avonview Cemetery, Bristol, on 3rd September 1920.

The 1921 Census shows May and Edna living with May's parents Charles and Alice Hart with their other children at 250 Newfoundland Road, Bristol, where it is sadly noted on Edna's entry that "Father Dead".

May subsequently remarried to Albert Charles Tovey (born 7th July 1890; died 16th December 1965, Manor Park Hospital, Bristol, aged 75) on 9th June 1924 at St. Agnes Church, Bristol, and they had four further children:

1. **Ronald Charles Tovey** (born 15th January 1927, Bristol; died 13th April 2003, Bristol, aged 76).

Ronald married Edna Ruby Furlong (born 15th August 1925, Bristol; died 4th March 1983, aged 57). They had four children together.

Following Edna's death, Ronald married Jean M. Hunt in 1985, in Bristol.

2. **Dennis Albert Tovey** (born 1928, Bristol; died 11th May 1932, Bristol, aged 3 years 9 months).

Dennis was buried at Greenbank Cemetery, Bristol, on 17th May 1932.

3. **June Margaret Tovey** (born 27th April 1933, Bristol; died 16th October 2011, Bristol, aged 78).

June married Gordon Arthur Pickett (born 22nd December 1933, Bristol; died 1st June 2006, Bath/N.E. Somerset, aged 72). They had two children.

4. **John Albert Tovey** (born 29th April 1940, died 1995, Bristol, aged 55).

Following her death in June 1991, May was buried at Greenbank Cemetery, Bristol, on June 13th 1991.

6. THE FAMILY OF FLORENCE MATILDA MORGAN.

Florence married George Alexander Norton (born 26th April 1896, Ivy Cottage, The Causeway, Fishponds, Bristol; died 20th January 1961, aged 64) in 1917, in Bristol. They had no children.

The 1921 Census shows Florence (also known as Matilda or Tilly) living at 21 Bishop Street, St. George, Bristol, George shown as being employed as a Piledriver at Alban, Richards & Co., Avonmouth, with Florence's younger sister Clara also living with them. Clara is shown as being a textile worker at the G.W. Cotton Works.

Neither George nor Florence can be found on the 1939 Register. However, Electoral Registers from the 1930s show the couple living at various locations in the Kensington area of London.

1932-1933: 42 Argyle Place, Hammersmith, London.

1935: 17 Heathfield Street, Kensington, London.

1936-1938: 3 Clarendon Road, Kensington, London.

1939: 1 Crescent Mansions, Elgin Crescent, Kensington, London.

Florence passed away in Manor Park Hospital, Bristol, on 19th January 1961 at the age of 66.

Their last known address was 4 Eagle Street, Easton, Bristol.

7. THE FAMILY AND DESCENDANTS OF FREDERICK 'JERRY' MORGAN.

An early photograph of Frederick.

Frederick (known as 'Jerry' for reasons unknown) married his cousin Matilda Frances (Tilly) Bullock (born 30th July 1902; died 26th January 1979, aged 76) in 1923, in Bristol. They had nine children:

1. **Winifred Joyce Morgan** (born 4th September 1923, Bristol; died 10th February 1995, Bristol, aged 71).

2. **Frederick William Morgan** (born 3rd November 1925, Bristol; died 7th February 1996, Bristol, aged 70).

3. **Ivy Doreen Morgan** (born 1927, died 28th January 1927, Bristol, aged less than 2 months).

4. **Matilda Eileen Morgan** (born 1928, died 1928, aged less than 1 month).

5. **John James (Jack) Morgan** (born 7th June 1929; died 22nd August 2006, Bristol, aged 77).

6. **George Ronald Morgan** (born 4th December 1934; died 3rd January 1999, Bristol, aged 64).

7. **William L. Morgan** (born 1942).

8. **Patricia Doreen Morgan** (born 1945; died 24th February 2017, Bristol, aged 72).

9. **Robert Morgan** (born 1947).

Frederick served in the Royal Navy during World War 1, enlisting on 14th September 1916, where his description indicated his height of 5'3" and a dark complexion. He served as a stoker on HMS *'Vivid II'* and HMS *'Marlborough'*.

He is, however, better known as a professional footballer, details of which can be found in **Chapter 16.**

The 1921 Census shows him living at home with his mother Alice and sister Elsie and brother Arthur at 30 Proctor Street, St. George, Bristol. His occupation is proudly listed as being a Professional Footballer at Bristol Rovers F.C., Eastville.

The 1939 Register shows the family living at 33 St. Bernard Road, Bristol, where his employment is noted as being a Furnace Worker at a Zinc Smelting Plant, no doubt the National Smelting Company at Avonmouth.

An early photograph of Matilda (Tilly) Bullock, date unknown.

He died of throat cancer at home in Bristol on 9th May 1953, and his wife Matilda died on 26th January 1979, in Bristol. The *'Bristol Evening Post'* carried an obituary on 14th May 1953:

"The death at the age of 55 has occurred at his home at 33 St Bernard's Road, Shirehampton, of Mr. Frederick (Jerry) Morgan who as an inside-forward played for Bristol Rovers for four seasons after the First World War. He was formerly with Horfield United and Bath City and for the latter club netted 17 goals in 10 matches. He then joined the Rovers.

A schemer and ballplayer who could make good openings, scored nine goals for the Rovers in season 1924-25 and by completing a double, helped the Eastville team beat Yeovil (4-2) in the FA Cup at Yeovil, where he gave one of his best displays for the Rovers.

Mr. Morgan put in 25 years' service with the National Smelting Co at Avonmouth. He leaves a widow, five sons and two daughters."

He maintained an interest in football after retiring from the game and turned out for the Morgan Family team on occasions, as well as managing/coaching the National Smelting Co. team at Avonmouth, where his brother Harry worked and played football for, and where his son George worked for a time.

Jerry (centre) receiving a darts trophy, date unknown.

The grave of Frederick 'Jerry' Morgan and his wife Matilda, Shirehampton Cemetery, Bristol. Their son-in-law Dennis Geater also buried in this well-maintained grave.

FREDERICK AND MATILDA'S CHILDREN:

1.   **Winifred Joyce Morgan.**

Winifred married Dennis John Raymond Geater (born 29th August 1924, Bristol; died 22nd June 1953, Bristol, aged 28), in 1944, in Bristol.

They had three children, all girls.

Following Dennis's death, Winifred married Michael James (born 3rd January 1929, Waterford, Ireland; died 30th March 2013, Bristol aged 84) in 1954. They had one further child, born in 1964.

Winifred died on 10th February 1995, aged 71, in Bristol. Her last known address was 678 Portway, Avonmouth, Bristol.

2.   **Frederick William Morgan.**

Frederick married Florence Kate Herbert (born 25th March 1930, died 25th September 2017, Bristol, aged 87), in 1952, in Bristol. They had two children.

Frederick served in the Royal Navy towards the end of World War II, but sadly made the local press on 15th August 1946:

'SUDDEN IMPULSE AT SEVERN BEACH'
Shirehampton Men Take Motor Car.

"Describing their action as a 'sudden impulse', two young men, Stanley Jeffery, of 31 Meadow Grove, Shirehampton, and Frederick William Morgan of HMS *'Ulysses'*, whose home is at 33 St. Bernard's Road, Shirehampton, were each fined £1 and 12s 6d costs at Thornbury after pleading guilty to taking and driving away a motor car worth £200, the property of Ernest Charles Fletcher, from the Severn Beach Hotel on June 22nd without the owner's consent.

Jeffery was disqualified from holding a licence for 12 months and fined £1 10s for driving without being covered by insurance, and 10s for driving without a licence."

Frederick and one of his granddaughters.

The grave of Frederick William Morgan and wife Florence Kate, St. Mary's Churchyard, Shirehampton, Bristol.

Frederick died on 7th February 1996 in Bristol, aged 70, and was buried at St. Mary's Church, Shirehampton, Bristol, with his wife Florence later in 2017.

3. **Ivy Doreen Morgan**.

Ivy sadly died on 28th January 1927, aged only two months. She was buried on 1st February 1927 at Avonview Cemetery, Bristol.

4. **Matilda Eileen Morgan**.

Similarly, Matilda died a few days after her birth in 1928.

5. **John James Morgan**.

John James (known as Jack) married Iris Evelyn Weston (born 18th April 1933, Bristol, died 18th January 2004, Bristol, aged 70), in 1952. They had six children.

Jack died on 22nd August 2006, also in Bristol, aged 77.

6. **George Ronald Morgan**.

George married Audrey Handley (born 6th June 1931, Liverpool, died 15th April 2006, Bristol, aged 74) in 1957, in Bristol, and they had two children.

George worked at the National Smelting Company in Avonmouth but injured himself in an accident in July 1957. The *'Bristol Evening Post'* reported the incident:

"An Avonmouth shunter who was caught between a moving truck and a loading platform at the National Smelting Co., St Andrew's Road, Avonmouth, was dragged clear by a colleague but sustained an injury to his thigh. An Avonmouth Docks Ambulance took the man, George Morgan (21) of 33 St Bernard's Road, Shirehampton, to the BRI for treatment."

Although the injury was not long-lasting, it no doubt contributed to his decision to leave the National Smelting Company, and he later found employment at Bristol Docks, working in Health & Safety.

The marriage of George Morgan and Audrey Handley, 1957.

He fell foul of the law in August 1963 when it was reported that:

"George Ronald Morgan (28) of 39 High Street, Shirehampton, was fined £10 when he admitted stealing one tin of corned beef worth 2s 6d."

He became one of the leading lights at Avonmouth Docks during the 1970s, when he became a Trade Union official and chairman of the Transport Union's Docks District Committee. He helped to organise the Docks Strikes at Avonmouth in 1984 and 1989, and was involved in numerous negotiations with port officials to obtain resolutions to the workers' disputes.

George died on 3rd January 1999, in Bristol, aged 64, with the funeral service held at St. Andrew's Church, Avonmouth, Bristol, on 12th January 1999.

7.   William L. Morgan.

23rd August saw the official announcement of the engagement of William and Patricia Thrush (born 1948, Bristol):

MORGAN-THRUSH.

Mr. and Mrs. A. W. Thrush, 201 Coronation Road, Southville, have pleasure in announcing the engagement of their daughter Patricia to William, son of Mrs. M. F. Morgan and the late Mr. F. Morgan, 33 St. Bernard's Road, Shirehampton.

They married on 29th March 1969 at East Street Baptist Church, Bedminster, Bristol. They had two children.

8.   Patricia Doreen Morgan.

Patricia married Leslie Foster (born 1945, Bristol; died 26th October 2016, aged 71) in 1966 in Bristol. They had no children. Patricia died on 24th February 2017, aged 72, and she was cremated at Canford Cemetery, Bristol, on 15th March 2017.

9.   Robert Morgan.

Robert married Susan Scragg (born 1949, Bristol) in 1976, in Bristol. They had one child. Robert was another talented footballer, who played for Welton Rovers in the early 1970s, along with other local clubs in Bristol.

8. THE FAMILY AND DESCENDANTS OF HARRY MORGAN.

Harry married Florence May Hobbs (born 16th July 1902, Bristol; died 15th November 1960, aged 58) in 1920, in Bristol. They had five children, all born in Bristol:

1. **Florence May Morgan** (born 4th March 1921, Bristol; died 27th July 2005, aged 84).
2. **Harry Kenneth Morgan** (born 1924, Bristol; died 1925, aged 1).
3. **Gilbert George Morgan** (born 1st November 1926, Bristol; died 13th September 1991, aged 65).
4. **Harry Morgan** (born 9th March 1932, 388 Southmead Road (Southmead Hospital), Bristol; died 20th March 2022, aged 90).
5. **Rosina Margaret Morgan** (born 9th March 1935, Bristol; died 2nd April 2012, aged 80).

The 1921 Census shows the family living at 14 Beaufort Street, St. George, Bristol, with Harry employed as a builder's labourer at McAlpines in Avonmouth. This address was also the same for his brother Thomas, so it is possible they shared the same house despite having two different Census entries.

Harry was a noted local footballer and played for his brother's National Smelting Company team as well as for the Morgan Family team. He also turned out alongside his brother George for Brecknell, Munro and Rogers, who won the Gloucester Senior Amateur Cup in 1926.

He also played one match for Bath City during the 1925/26 season.

At the time of son Harry's birth in 1932, the family were living at 30 Proctor Street, Moorfields, Bristol.

The 1939 Register shows the family living at 86 Sandholme Road, Bristol, where Harry's occupation is noted as being an Engineer's Labourer. Daughter Florence is noted as being employed as a Brewery Assistant.

A Morgan family group. Harry and wife Florence in the front, with son Gilbert, daughter Florence, daughter Rosina and son Harry behind them.

Harry died on 28th April 1973, aged 73, in Bristol.

Florence was buried at Brislington Cemetery on 18th November 1960, and Harry on 4th May 1973.

The headstone of Harry, wife Florence, and son-in-law Thomas, Brislington Cemetery, Bristol.

HARRY AND FLORENCE'S CHILDREN:

1. Florence May Morgan.

Florence May Morgan married Thomas Thornbury (born 27th May 1920, Bristol; died 27th November 1991, Bristol, aged 71), in 1943, in Bristol. They had two children.

Florence was the subject of a car accident in April 1939, and her father Harry successfully obtained compensation from the Bristol Corporation, as reported in a press report of the time:

"Judge Wethered, in Bristol County Court today, approved a settlement which had been agreed between the parties. The case was a sequel to an accident on Bristol Bridge in July, and a claim had been made for £75 damages. The plaintiff was Florence Morgan (18), who sued through her father, Mr. Harry Morgan, of 86, Sandholme Road, Brislington, and the defendants were the Lord Mayor and Corporation of Bristol, who were represented by Mr. C. Parker (Messrs. Wansbroughs, Robinson, and Co.).

Mr. E. H. Atchley, who appeared on behalf of the plaintiff, stated that the plaintiff had ridden her bicycle across Bristol Bridge, and intended going up High Street, when the traffic was held up by the police. When she stopped, a motor-van driven by an employee of the Corporation ran into the rear of her machine, and she received injuries to her thigh, bruising, and shock. An agreement had been come to between the parties of settlement for £33 and costs."

The grave of Thomas and Florence Thornbury, Brislington Cemetery, Bristol.

Thomas was buried at Brislington Cemetery, Bristol, on 3rd December 1991, along with his wife's parents.

Florence died on 27th July 2005, also in Bristol, aged 84, and was also interred in the family grave at Brislington Cemetery, Bristol.

2. **Harry Kenneth Morgan.**

Harry sadly died in 1925, aged 1.

3. **Gilbert George Morgan.**

Gilbert George Morgan.

Gilbert George Morgan married Edith Dyson (born 1st June 1925, Manchester; died 23rd June 1993, Bristol, aged 68), in Bristol, in 1947. They had three children.

Wedding of Gilbert to Edith Dyson, 1947.

L-R: Gilbert and Edith; Harry Morgan Sr. and wife Florence; Harry Morgan Jr. and twin sister Rosina; Edith's sister and husband; Tom and Florence Thornbury.

Known as 'Bert' within the family, Gilbert died on 13th September 1991, in Woolsthorpe-by-Belvoir, Grantham, Lincolnshire, aged 64.

Edith's last known address was 143A Hanham Road, Kingswood, Bristol

4.   Harry Morgan.

Harry Morgan (1932-1922)

In common with many of his family, Harry was a talented footballer and captained the Bristol Boys team when he was young.

He married Martha Devey (born 11th December 1931, Bristol; died 23rd November 2022, Bristol, aged 90) on 15th December 1951, in Bristol. They had three children.

During the 1960s and early 1970s, Harry performed in local clubs as a singer under the name of 'Don Morgan', being billed as a 'vocalist supreme'.

Along with his brother Gilbert (Bert) he operated Morgans Transport (Bristol) Ltd., based in Brislington, Bristol, although this venture was wound up in 1968.

Harry died on 20th March 2022 in Bristol, aged 90,

Bristol Boys' captain Harry Morgan (holding the ball) with his uncle Arthur Morgan behind him in the white collar.

The wedding of Harry Morgan and Martha Devey, 15th December 1951.

The wedding group at Harry's and Martha's wedding, St. Anne's Church, Bristol.

Harry, Martha and children, c. 1960

'Don' Morgan in action.

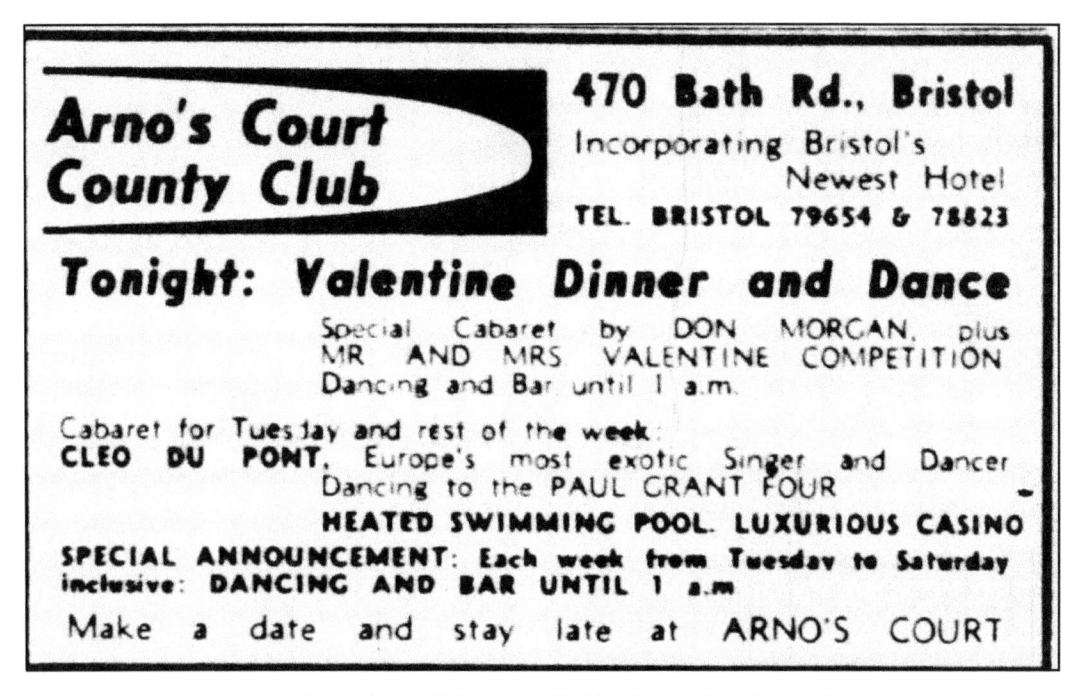

> **Arno's Court County Club**
> 470 Bath Rd., Bristol
> Incorporating Bristol's Newest Hotel
> TEL. BRISTOL 79654 & 78823
>
> **Tonight: Valentine Dinner and Dance**
> Special Cabaret by DON MORGAN, plus MR AND MRS VALENTINE COMPETITION
> Dancing and Bar until 1 a.m.
>
> Cabaret for Tuesday and rest of the week:
> CLEO DU PONT, Europe's most exotic Singer and Dancer
> Dancing to the PAUL GRANT FOUR
>
> **HEATED SWIMMING POOL. LUXURIOUS CASINO**
> SPECIAL ANNOUNCEMENT: Each week from Tuesday to Saturday inclusive: DANCING AND BAR UNTIL 1 a.m
>
> Make a date and stay late at ARNO'S COURT

A press advert from February 1966 advertising Don Morgan.

5. Rosina Margaret Morgan.

Rosina Margaret Morgan married Stanley Robin Dunsford (born 1st January 1926, Honiton, Devon; died 31st December 2017, Bristol, aged 91) in Bristol, in March 1954.

The wedding of Rosina and Stanley, 1954.

They had three children.

Rosina died on 2nd April 2012, in Bristol, aged 80.

9. THE FAMILY AND DESCENDANTS OF CLARA MORGAN.

Clara married William Frank Lewis (born 22nd Jun 1902, 20 Corbett Street, Barton Hill, Bristol) on 15th December 1923 in Bristol. They had three children:

1. **Joan Lewis** (born 9th May 1925, Bristol; died 17th July 2005, Bristol, aged 80).
2. **Royston William Lewis** (born 17th June 1929, Bristol; died 2nd June 1969, Bristol, aged 39).
3. **Dennis Lewis** (born 8th September 1933, Bristol; died 11th December 2011, Bristol, aged 78).

Clara was living with her sister Florence Matilda Morgan and her husband George Norton at 21 Bishop Street, St. George, Bristol, according to the 1921 Census. She was employed as a textile worker at the G.W. Cotton Works, Bristol, at the time.

The 1939 Register shows Clara with Joan and Dennis living at 20 Factory Street, Bristol. Royston could be found living with his paternal grandparents at 14 Granville Street, Bristol, which is the address where he was born in 1929.

Clara Morgan (1901-1959) *William Frank Lewis (1902-1981)*

Clara died on 21st August 1959, in Bristol, aged 58.

CLARA AND WILLIAM'S CHILDREN:

1. Joan Lewis.

Joan married John Evans in 1943, in Bristol.

She subsequently married George Hewitt (born 18th May 1923, Bristol; died 1st October 2016, Bristol, aged 93), in 1962.

She was cremated at South Bristol Crematorium on 25th July 2005.

Joan Lewis (1925-2005).  *George Hewitt (1923-2016).*

2. **Royston William Lewis.**

Eldest son Royston married Maureen Barbara Horler (born 17th July 1933, Bristol; died 26th October 2013, Bristol, aged 80) on 12th March 1955, in Bristol.

They had two children.

Royston William Lewis (1929-1969).  *Maureen Barbara Horler (1933-2013).*

Royston and Maureen's wedding, 12th March 1955, St. Ambrose Church, Whitehall, Bristol.

3. **Dennis Lewis.**

Youngest son Dennis married June Angela Rosemary Briffett (born 10th June 1934, Bristol; died 2nd June 1910, Bristol, aged 75) in 1959, in Bristol. They had seven children.

Wedding photograph of Dennis Lewis and June Angela Rosemary Briffett, Bristol, 1959.

He was cremated at South Bristol Crematorium on 19th December 2011.

10. THE FAMILY AND DESCENDANTS OF VIOLET MORGAN.

According to the 1921 Census, Violet was living with her sister Alice and family at 21 Bishop Street, St. George, Bristol, working as a 'General Worker' at the Globe Refinery Co., Newfoundland Road, in Bristol.

Violet married Thomas Henry Godsell (born 8th September 1902, Bristol; died 3rd May 1961, Bristol, aged 58) at Moorfields St. Matthew, Bristol on 19th April 1924. Violet was living at 21 Bishop Street, Bristol at the time of marriage. Thomas, whose occupation was interestingly listed as being a 'Clicker' was living at 30 Proctor Street, Bristol.

They had three children:

1. **Thomas William Godsell** (born 2nd March 1925, Bristol; died 2003, Thornbury, aged 77).

The 1939 Register shows that Thomas was employed at a local engineering works. He married Phyllis Mabel Bees (born 7th November 1921, Bristol; died 2003, Thornbury, aged 77), in Thornbury, near Bristol, in 1942. They had four children.

Thomas (known as 'Tom') was a useful footballer and played for Bristol St. George.

2. **Joyce Edna Godsell** (born 1927, Bristol).

Joyce married Ralph Jack Payne (born 21st May 1925, Bristol, died 1991, Bristol, aged 65), in 1947, in Bristol. They had two children.

Ralph was buried on 26th July 1991 according to the burial registers of Holy Trinity Church, Kingswood, Bristol, with his address recorded as 17 Cunningham Gardens, Oldbury Court, Bristol.

3. **Ernest Henry Godsell** (born 15th May 1930; died 10th January 2003, Bristol, aged 72).

Ernest did not appear to get married.

The 1939 Register shows Violet and Thomas, along with their children, living with the Stark family at 145 Whiteway Road, St. George, Bristol. Violet's brother Arthur is also noted as living at the same address.

Ernest played football for the Morgan family team on occasions, and even had a trial for Liverpool in his younger days. He played local football for Douglas F.C. and Cadbury Heath in the late 1950s and early 1960s.

Violet died on 11th June 1981, in Bristol, aged 78.

10. THE FAMILY AND DESCENDANTS OF ELSIE MORGAN (1904).

The 1921 Census shows Elsie living at home at 30 Proctor Street, St. George, Bristol, where it was noted that she worked as a 'Bra Maker' at Thomas Bros, Broad Plain, Bristol.

Elsie married Walter William Jordan (born 27th Sep 1902 in Bristol; died 14th November 1988, Bristol, aged 86), on 15th September 1923, at Moorfields St. Matthew, Bristol.

They had six children:

1. **Walter Kenneth Jordan** (born 21st July 1924, Bristol; died 1991, Bristol, aged 66).
2. **Ivy Doreen Jordan** (born 21st October 1925, Bristol; died 25th July 1979, Bristol, aged 53).
3. **Elsie Florence Jordan** (born 17th May 1927, Bristol; died 12th July 2019, Bristol, aged 92).
4. **Douglas William Jordan** (born 28th July 1929, Bristol; died 21st December 1977, aged 48).
5. **Raymond F. Jordan** (born 18th September 1935, Bristol).
6. **David Robert Jordan** (born 1945, Bristol).

The 1939 Register shows the family living at 13 Cossham Walk, Bristol. Walter was recorded as being a Public Works Labourer, Heavy Worker.

Elsie died on 9th November 1973, aged 69.

The grave of Elsie and Walter William Jordan.

ELSIE AND WALTER'S CHILDREN:

1.   Walter Kenneth Jordan.

Walter married Barbara Joan Dyer (born 14th March 1929, Bristol; died 10th June 1995, Bristol, aged 66) in 1949, in Bristol. They had two children.

Walter died in 1991 in Bristol, aged 66.

2.   Ivy Doreen Jordan.

Ivy married John Herbert Arthur Holder (born 7th August 1920, Thornbury; died 26th May 1986, Bristol, aged 65) in Bristol, in 1949. They had one child.

Ivy died on 25th July 1979, in Bristol, aged 53.

3.   Elsie Florence Jordan.

Elsie married Desmond Stanley Jefferies (born 10th June 1926, Bristol; died 2000, South Gloucestershire, aged 73) in 1947, in Bristol. They had three children.

Elsie died on 12th July 2019 in Bristol, aged 92.

4.   Douglas William Jordan.

Douglas married Priscilla J. Watts (born 1934, Keynsham), in 1951, in Kingswood, Bristol. They had one child.

The headstone of Douglas William Jordan.

Douglas died on 21st December 1977, in Bristol, aged 48. He was buried at Avonview Cemetery, Bristol, on 30th December 1977.

5.   **Raymond F. Jordan.**

Raymond married Hilary Fox (born 1944, Bristol). They had no children.

6.   **David Robert Jordan.**

David married Jean Margaret Wilmot (born 28th June 1948, Bristol; died 16th May 2017, Southmead Hospital, Bristol, aged 69) in 1975, in Bristol. They had one child.

The grave of Jean Jordan, Avonview Cemetery, Bristol.

Jean was buried at Avonview Cemetery, Bristol, on 16th June 2017.

11. THE FAMILY OF ARTHUR MORGAN.

Arthur Morgan (1906-1968).

In 1921, Arthur was living at home at 30 Proctor Street, St. George, Bristol, where he was noted as being in full-time education.

The 1939 Register shows he was living with the Stark family (along with his sister Violet and family) at 145 Whiteway Road, St. George, Bristol, where he was employed as a Builder's Labourer.

Arthur married Elsie Alice Lewis (born 27th April 1903, in Bristol; died 1987, Bristol, aged 83) in 1952, also in Bristol.

Elsie had been married before, having married hairdresser Herbert Leslie Dorman Marshall (born 4th October 1902, Bristol; died 18th October 1951, Bristol) at St. Agnes Church, St. George, Bristol, on 6th October 1926.

Alice and Herbert had no children, and when Alice married Arthur, no further children resulted.

Arthur died on 12th June 1968, at his home at 44 Gadshill Road, Eastville, Bristol, aged 61.

CHAPTER 5.
GEORGE MORGAN.

George was born at 5 Tarr's Court, Lawrence Hill, Bristol, on 27th October 1866, with his father's occupation recorded as a Fireman at Coal Works.

He was baptised at St. Philip & Jacob Church, Bristol, on 10th November 1866. The registration shows the family living at Bread Street, Bristol, where his father's occupation was recorded as being a Plasterer.

As a 4 year-old in the 1871 Census, he was shown living with his family at 5 Tarr's Court, Lawrence Hill, Bristol.

The 1881 Census shows George living at home at 1 Barnett's Court, Bristol, where being 14 years of age, he was shown as having no occupation.

George never married.

He sadly died on 22nd May 1889 at home at 29 Catherine Street, Barrow Lane, Bristol, aged 22. His death certificate stated that he was:

"Found dead and that his death was probably caused due to an epileptiform convulsion caused by pressure on the brain".

His employment at the time was a labourer on the Midland Railway.

He was buried at Avonview Cemetery, Bristol, on 26th May 1889.

CHAPTER 6.
THE FAMILY AND DESCENDANTS OF HARRY MORGAN.

Harry was born at 5 Tarr's Court, Lawrence Hill, Bristol, on 2nd August 1869, with his father's occupation recorded as a Stoker at Coal Works. Although seemingly baptised as 'Henry' Morgan on 16th February 1870 at Holy Trinity Church, St. Philips, Bristol, this is likely to have been an error in the baptism register.

He married Jane Williams (born 5th May 1873, Bristol) at St. Luke's Church, Barton Hill, Bristol, on 26th May 1889. At the time of marriage he was living at 33 Factory Street, Bristol, with Jane residing at 19 Great Western Street, Bristol. Jane's age on the marriage register was recorded as 18, but in fact with her birth date as shown above, her actual age was only 16.

Harry and Jane had four children:

1. **Harry Morgan** (born 26th November 1890, Bristol; died 22nd April 1968, Hanham, Bristol, aged 77).

2. **Louisa Morgan** (born 12th February 1892, Bristol; died 3rd September 1970, Sodbury, Bristol, aged 78).

3. **Jane Morgan** (born 23rd August 1894, 8 Wellington Terrace, Bristol; died 26th February 1918, Bristol, aged 23).

4. **Frederick Morgan** (born 18th January 1897, Bristol; died 26th July 1946, Weymouth, aged 49).

By the time of the 1891 Census, he was living with Jane and eldest son Harry at 12 Charlton Street, Bristol, where he was employed as a General Labourer.

At the time of daughter Jane's birth, Harry was employed as a Pork Butcher's Labourer, with the family living at 8 Wellington Terrace, Bristol.

The 1901 Census shows the family now living at 3 Berkeley Cottages, Leadhouse Road, Bristol, where his employment was recorded as a General Carter.

In 1903, Harry became landlord of 'The Talbot Inn' at 123 Easton Road, Bristol. However, a press report from February of that year showed that there were a few issues with the premises:

"Harry Morgan, Talbot, Easton Road, had his licence opposed, Mr. Vachell saying that the main objection was the back entrance to Seal Street. Mr. Wansbrough, on behalf of the tenant and the lessees, said there was not a licensed house in Seal Street, and many of the customers resided in that thoroughfare, to whom it would be extremely inconvenient to have to walk round to the front. The police had full powers of supervision, and he submitted the justices had no power to close up the back entrances of large hotels.

The chairman said they were of opinion that the passage to Seal Street should be walled off. Mr. Wansbrough remarked that the licensee objected, and the property was leased by the

United Breweries Company, and the freeholder objected to the alteration. He had to give notice of appeal. The chairman said the bench accepted the risk. The passage question would be walled off at the point they had on the plan. Mr. Wansbrough observed that if they got the permission of the freeholder to stopping up the way there might be no appeal."

By the time of the 1911 Census, Harry was still landlord of 'The Talbot Inn' at 123 Easton Road, Bristol. Son Harry had found employment as a Butcher's Assistant, Louisa had 'Domestic Duties', Jane employed as a Tailoress, and Frederick an Errand Boy.

Jane died on 19th March 1914 at the Talbot Inn, Easton, aged just 40.

Harry then took over as Landlord of the Golden Lion in Fishponds on December 7th 1914, and ran the pub until February 4th 1918,

A 1950's photograph of The Talbot, 123 Easton Road, Bristol. The pub was demolished in the late 1960s.

An early postcard of Regent Place, Fishponds with the Golden Lion on the right.

Family picture from 1917, taken outside of the Golden Lion Public House, Fishponds.
Back Row L-R: Charlotte Morgan (nee Ham), Frederick Morgan, Louisa Morgan, Unknown.
Middle Row: Robert McTavish, Unknown, Harry Morgan.
Front: William McTavish.

By the time of the 1921 Census, Harry was boarding with the Johnston family at 171 Pennywell Road, Bristol, where it was noted that he had retired, aged 51.

Harry died on 14th July 1929 at Islington Road, Southville, Bristol, aged 59.

> **MORGAN** Harry of 33 Islington-road Southville **Bristol** died 14 July 1929 Probate **Bristol** 13 August to Thomas Morgan licensed victualler and Louisa McTavish (wife of Robert McTavish). Effects £2007 19s. 7d.

Harry Morgan's Probate entry. Thomas Morgan was his brother and Louisa McTavish his sister.

The grave of Harry and Jane Morgan, shared with daughter Jane Gulley (nee Morgan). Avonview Cemetery, Bristol. The headstone has sadly collapsed and is now lying horizontally adjacent to the grave, and the inscriptions are difficult to read.

HARRY AND JANE'S CHILDREN:

1. Harry Morgan.

Harry was baptised at St. Philip & Jacob Church, Bristol, on 8th February 1891. At the time of his baptism the family were noted as living at Barton Hill, Bristol, and his father's occupation being recorded as being a Labourer.

Harry married twice. His first wife was Rosina May Rodbourn (born 8th December 1894, 238 Newfoundland Road, Bristol; died 2nd November 1929, Bristol, aged 34), who he married on 17th November 1915, at Emmanuel Church, Bristol. Harry's address was recorded as being 9 Alfred Street, Bristol, and his occupation shown as being a Barman. Rosina was living at 68 Kingsland Road, Bristol, with no occupation being recorded.

Rosina's father Mark was shown as being a licensee. Mark's wife Ada (who he married in 1916, following the death of his first wife Rosina Norman earlier that year) was the licensee of the Albion public house in Wellington Place, Easton Road, Bristol from 29th September 1913 until 1953.

The Albion Public House, Easton, Bristol.

They had two children:

- **Alice May Kathleen Morgan.**

She was born on 19th November 1916, Bristol. She married Charles Douglas Wintle (born 19th July 1911, Bristol; died 8th December 1967, Bristol, aged 56), on 26th December 1938, at St. Philip & Jacob with Emmanuel Church, Bristol. Alice's address on the marriage registration was shown as being 36 York Street, Bristol. Charles' address was recorded as being 9 Alfred Street, Bristol, with his occupation shown as being a Shop Manager.

They had two children.

She died on 20th June 1995, at 80 Conham Hill, Hanham, Bristol).

- **Queenie Dorothy Irene Morgan.**

She was born on 5th June 1920, in Bristol, and baptised at Emmanuel Church, St. Philips, Bristol, on 7th July 1920. The family address at the time was recorded as 23 Alfred Street, Bristol, and her father's occupation shown as being a Warehouseman.

She married Frederick Charles Parsons (born 17th April 1917, Bristol; died 3rd August 1995, Bristol, aged 78) in 1939, in Bristol. They had no children together. She died on 4th May 1972, in Bristol, aged 51, and was cremated at Arno's Vale Cemetery on 9th May 1972.

Frederick subsequently married Pamela Mary Bragg (born 5th December 1919, Bristol; died 21st June 2020, Bristol, aged 100) on 12th January 1973 at Bristol Registry Office.

Pamela was formally adopted by the Tambling family of Whitehall, Bristol in December 1937, taking the Tambling surname. She married Sidney James Dyer (born 4th October 1919, Bristol; died 25th May 1961, Bristol, aged 41), in 1941 and had one child.

Pamela died on 21st June 2020, aged 100.

The 1921 Census shows Harry and Rosina and their two daughters living at 23 Alfred Street, St. Philips, Bristol, where Harry worked as a warehouseman at Armours & Co., meat transporters, Small Street, Bristol.

Rosina sadly died on 2nd November 1929, in Bristol, aged only 34. She was buried at Greenbank Cemetery, Bristol.

Harry then married Lilian Ada Louisa Baker (born 16th July 1905, Bristol, died 21st August 1997, South Gloucestershire, aged 92) in 1931, at St. Paul's Church, Bedminster, Bristol, on 31st January 1931. At the time of their marriage, both Harry and Lilian were living at 33 Islington Road, with Harry's occupation listed as being a warehouseman. Lilian had been married before, to Albert Edward Mereweather (born 1902, Bristol; died 1926, Bristol, aged 24), but he passed away only a few years after their marriage on 21st April 1923 at St. Aldhelm's Church, Bedminster, Bristol. He was buried at Arno's Vale Cemetery, Bristol, in April 1926.

They had one child:

- **Joan Lilian Mereweather** (born 2nd April 1925, Bristol; died 1st May 2002, South Gloucestershire, aged 77).

Joan married twice, firstly to George Nicholls (born 1925, Bristol) in 1945, and subsequently to Philip Henry Eatherington (born 16th July 1909, West Bridgeford, Nottinghamshire; died 1979, Birmingham, aged 69), in 1949, in Kingswood, Bristol, with whom she had one child.

Harry and Lilian had no children together.

Harry died on 22nd April 1968, in Hanham, near Bristol, aged 77.

Lilian was buried at Mangotsfield Cemetery, Bristol on 28th August 1997.

2. Louisa Morgan.

Louisa was baptised at St. Lawrence Church, Easton, Bristol, on 6th March 1892. At the time of his baptism the family were noted as living at 8 Wellington Street, Bristol, and her father's occupation being recorded as being a Labourer.

She married Robert John McTavish (born 29th November 1891, Queenstown, Eastern Cape, South Africa; died 17th May 1958, Bristol, aged 66) on 21st November 1913, at Russell Town Congregational Church, Bristol.

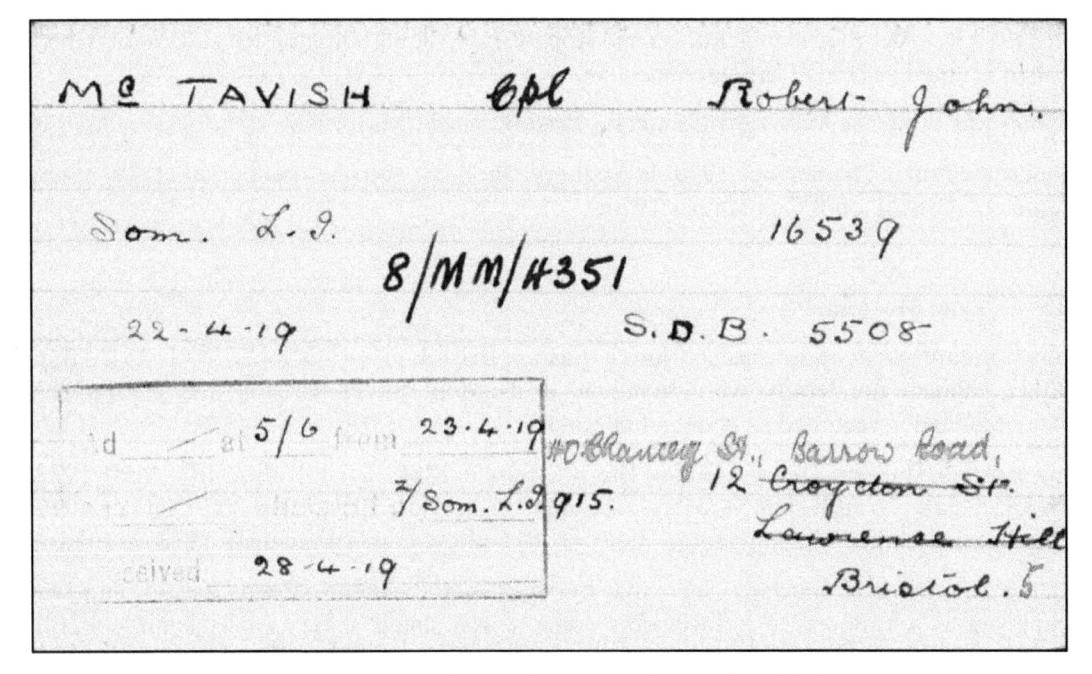

Robert John McTavish's WW1 pension record, showing his home addresses.

Robert served in the Somerset Light Infantry during World War 1.

He was eventually invalided out of the Somerset Light Infantry on 22nd April 1919, having had three toes amputated.

They had two children:

- **William Harry McTavish** (born 27th June 1914, Bristol).

William married Phyllis May Havens (born 9th March 1910, Bristol; died 2004, Bromsgrove, aged 93) on 11th April 1936, at Stapleton Holy Trinity Church, Bristol. William's address at the time was at 33 Islington Road, Bristol, whilst Phyllis lived at 652 Muller Road, Stapleton, Bristol. They had one child.

The 1939 Register shows the family living at 97 Mackie Road, Bristol, where William's occupation is listed as being a Stores Clerk at Aircraft Works.

William died on 11th July 1975, in Bristol, aged 61.

- **Jean Louisa Annie McTavish** (born 17th June 1920, Bristol).

Jean married William Harold Berry (born 6th March 1918, Bristol; died 29th April 1992, Bristol, aged 74) in 1938. They had two children.

The 1939 Register notes that Jean and William were living with Jean's parents at 33 Islington Road, Bristol, where William worked as an Aircraft Fitter.

Jean died on 5th June 2003 in South Gloucestershire, aged 82.

Louisa ran the Skinner's Arms public house in Pennywell Road, Easton, Bristol, for many years, maintaining the Morgan tradition. This is confirmed by the 1921 Census which shows the family living at this address, Louisa being noted as the licensee of the establishment.

The 1939 Register then shows Louisa and Robert living at 33 Islington Road, Bristol, where Robert is noted as being Carpenter and Joiner.

Robert was buried at Avonview Cemetery, Bristol, on 21st May 1958.

Louisa died on 3rd September 1970, in Sodbury, aged 78, and she was buried at Avonview Cemetery, Bristol, on 8th September 1970.

3.   Jane Morgan.

Jane was baptised at St. Lawrence Church, Easton, Bristol, on 14th October 1894. At the time of her baptism the family were living at 15 Harding Street, Bristol, and her father's occupation being recorded as being a Labourer.

She married William George Gulley (born 2nd June 1886, Bristol, died 19th April 1938, Lanark, Ottawa, Canada) at St. Mary's Church, Fishponds, Bristol, on 20th October 1917. They had one child, William George Henry (Bill) Gulley, born 29th January 1918, in Bristol.

At the time of their marriage, Jane was living at 641 Fishponds Road, Bristol, and was employed as a Tailoress. Her husband's address was stated as being 42 Channon's Hill, Fishponds, Bristol, and his occupation noted as being a private in the 2nd Canadian Regiment. He joined the 38th Battalion, Canadian Expeditionary Force, in Smiths Falls, Ontario, on 21st January 1915 (number 1263819 - also A10759). He transferred to the 2nd Battalion, C.E.F., on 25th August 1915 and was wounded on 25th or 26th September 1916. He was again wounded on 5th or 6th November 1917.

At the time of his enlistment, his details were noted as: trade as labourer; single; no current or previous military service; Church of England; height of 5 feet 6½ inches; chest of 34 inches fully expanded; fair complexion; blue eyes; dark hair.

(42nd) Smiths Falls, Regt'l No. A/O 759   Sworn in Jan. 21, 1915

ATTESTATION PAPER.
No.
Folio.

CANADIAN OVER-SEAS EXPEDITIONARY FORCE.

QUESTIONS TO BE PUT BEFORE ATTESTATION.
(ANSWERS).

1. What is your name? — William George Gully
2. In what Town, Township or Parish, and in what Country were you born? — Bristol, England
3. What is the name of your next-of-kin? — Mrs. Elizabeth Gully (Mother)
4. What is the address of your next-of-kin? — Fishponds, Bristol, England
5. What is the date of your birth? — 2nd June 1886 (29 years)
6. What is your Trade or Calling? — Labourer
7. Are you married? — No
8. Are you willing to be vaccinated or re-vaccinated? — Yes
9. Do you now belong to the Active Militia? — No
10. Have you ever served in any Military Force? — No
    If so, state particulars of former Service.
11. Do you understand the nature and terms of your engagement? — Yes
12. Are you willing to be attested to serve in the CANADIAN OVER-SEAS EXPEDITIONARY FORCE? — Yes

_____ (Signature of Man).
_____ (Signature of Witness).

DECLARATION TO BE MADE BY MAN ON ATTESTATION.

I, William George Gully, do solemnly declare that the above answers made by me to the above questions are true, and that I am willing to fulfil the engagements by me now made, and I hereby engage and agree to serve in the **Canadian Over-Seas Expeditionary Force**, and to be attached to any arm of the service therein, for the term of one year, or during the war now existing between Great Britain and Germany should that war last longer than one year, and for six months after the termination of that war provided His Majesty should so long require my services, or until legally discharged.

Date March 19 5.
_____ (Signature of Recruit)
_____ (Signature of Witness)

OATH TO BE TAKEN BY MAN ON ATTESTATION.

I, William George Gully, do make Oath, that I will be faithful and bear true Allegiance to His Majesty King George the Fifth, His Heirs and Successors, and that I will as in duty bound honestly and faithfully defend His Majesty, His Heirs and Successors, in Person, Crown and Dignity, against all enemies, and will observe and obey all orders of His Majesty, His Heirs and Successors, and of all the Generals and Officers set over me. So help me God.

Date March 19 5.
_____ (Signature of Recruit)
_____ (Signature of Witness)

CERTIFICATE OF MAGISTRATE.

The Recruit above-named was cautioned by me that if he made any false answer to any of the above questions he would be liable to be punished as provided in the Army Act.
The above questions were then read to the Recruit in my presence.
I have taken care that he understands each question, and that his answer to each question has been duly entered as replied to, and the said Recruit has made and signed the declaration and taken the oath before me, at Ottawa this 28 day of March 1915.

_____ (Signature of Justice)
JUSTICE OF THE PEACE IN AND FOR THE COUNTY OF CARLETON

I certify that the above is a true copy of the Attestation of the above-named Recruit.

_____ (Approving Officer)
Lt.-Colonel.

M.F.W. 23.

George Gulley's Attestation Paper, March 1915.

Sadly, Jane died on 16th February 1918, in Bristol, aged only 24, a victim of the Spanish Flu epidemic rife at the time. She was buried at Avonview Cemetery, Bristol.

William, a bricklayer by trade, emigrated to Canada with his son in 1921. They travelled on the Canadian Pacific vessel *'Empress of Britain'*, on September 22nd of that year, sailing from Liverpool to Quebec. William's occupation on the passenger list was shown as being a Fitter's Help, with his address being noted as being 42 Channon's Hill, Fishponds, Bristol.

William died in Lanark, Ontario, Canada on 19th April 1938, aged 51. His death certificate starkly advises that he 'dropped dead on street due to likely heart attack'.

An obituary for William appeared in the Canadian press later that day:

WILLIAM GULLEY DIES ON SMITHS FALLS STREET'

William G. Gulley, well known and highly respected resident of Smiths Falls, collapsed while walking on Beckwith Street here today, and died within a few minutes. Dr. W. A. Gray, coroner, decided that an inquest was unnecessary.

Deceased was born in Bristol, England, 50 years ago, but had resided in Canada since 1911, and was very well known in Smiths Falls. He had been employed with the Canadian Pacific Railway and the Frost and Wood Company, and more recently with local contractors.

His wife, the former Jane Morgan of Bristol, died some years ago, and he is survived by one son, William, of Smiths Falls, well known athlete and goaler with the Smiths Falls senior hockey team last winter.

Mr. Gulley was a World War veteran, having served with the 2nd and 38th battalions, C.E.F. in France and Belgium from 1914 to 1918. He was a valued member of Branch 95, Canadian Legion."

JANE AND WILLIAM'S CHILD:

- **William (Bill) George Henry Gulley.**

Son William left the United Kingdom for Canada with his father in September 1921 when 3 years of age.

He married Evelyn Gertrude Labelle (born 27th October 1916, Smith Falls, Ontario, Canada) on 27th September 1940, at Smiths Falls, Ontario, Canada. The wedding was reported locally:

'GULLEY-LABELLE'

"The manse of Westminster Presbyterian Church at Smiths Falls, was Friday afternoon, the scene of a quiet but pretty wedding of much local interest, when Rev. J. McB. Miller, the church minister, united in marriage Evelyn Labelle, daughter of Mr. and Mrs. James Labelle, Montreal, and William Henry Gulley, son of the late Mr. and Mrs. William Gulley, Smiths Falls. Attending the young couple were Mrs. Jack Vanexan, sister of the bride, as bridesmaid, and Burton Lorimer as groomsman.

Following the ceremony the young couple left by train for Montreal and points east, and on their return will take up their residence in Smiths Falls. Mr. Gulley is widely known in sporting circles of this district, a member of the Vico Softball Club, and star goalie of the Smiths Falls Brooklyn Braves Hockey Club in the Smiths Falls and District Hockey League."

William died on 4th March 1980 in Kingston, Frontenac County, Ontario, Canada. Evelyn died on 4th January 2008 in Bowmanville, Ontario, Canada.

William's obituary appeared in the Canadian local press on 6th March 1980:

'GULLEY, WILLIAM GEORGE'

At the Kingston General Hospital on Tuesday March 4th 1980, William George Gulley, Thomas St. West, Napanee, beloved husband of Evelyn Labelle, in his 63rd year, dear father of Mrs. John Coffey (Marilyn), Perth, and dear grandfather of Ryan and Tara. Resting at the Wartman Funeral Home, Napanee, with funeral service in the chapel on Friday March 7th at 10.30 a.m. Interment Hillcrest Cemetery, Smiths Falls at 1 p.m. Friends desiring may contribute to the Heart Fund. Visitations Tuesday 2-4 and 7-9 p.m.

DECLARATION OF PASSENGER TO CANADA.

S.S. Empress of Britain Class ___ 1921 Date of Sailing Sept 22/21

Inland routing ___ to ___ (STATE NAME OF RAILWAY)

582

1. NAME GULLEY WILLIAM GEORGE HENRY Age 3
   (PRINT IN BLOCK LETTERS, FAMILY NAME FIRST)
2. Sex Male. Are you married, single, widowed or divorced? Single
   If married, are you accompanied by husband or wife? If so, give name of husband or wife
3. Present occupation Nil   Intended occupation Nil
4. Birthplace Bristol   Race or people Eng
5. Citizenship British   Religion Presbyterian
   (IF PROTESTANT, STATE DENOMINATION)
6. Object in going to Canada   With Father
7. Do you intend to remain permanently in Canada?   Yes
8. Have you ever lived in Canada?   No   If you have, give Canadian address
   Port of previous entry ___ Date
   Port of departure from Canada ___ Date
9. Why did you leave Canada?
10. Money in possession belonging to passenger:
    (I am aware that I must have on my arrival in Canada the sum of $ —
11. Can you read? No   What language?
12. By whom was your passage paid?   Canadian Govt.
13. Ever refused entry to, or deported from Canada?   No
14. Destined to   Father Mr. W. G. Gulley
    Box No. 957 Smiths Falls, Ont.
    (IF JOINING RELATIVE, FRIEND OR EMPLOYER (1) STATE WHICH AND IF RELATIVE GIVE RELATIONSHIP (2) GIVE HIS OR HER NAME AND CANADIAN ADDRESS. (3) IF NOT JOINING ANY PERSON IN CANADA, GIVE YOUR OWN CANADIAN ADDRESS.)
15. By which Canadian railway are you travelling to destination?
16. Nearest relative in country from which you came
    Mr. G. Gulley   Grandfather
    (NAME)   (RELATIONSHIP)
    42 Channons Hill Fishponds Bristol
    (GIVE FULL ADDRESS OF SUCH RELATIVE)
17. Are you or any of your family mentally defective?   No
    Tubercular?   No   Physically defective?   No
    Otherwise debarred under Canadian Immigration Law?   No

Signature of passenger   W G Gulley

Sig. of Booking Agent   A. J. ___

William's Declaration of Passenger to Canada documentation, 23rd August 1921.

The headstone of William Gulley and wife Evelyn Labelle, Lanark, Ontario, Canada.

4. Frederick Morgan.

Frederick was baptised at St. Lawrence Church, Easton, Bristol, on 17th February 1897. At the time of his baptism the family were noted as living at 1 Berkeley Cottages, Bristol, and his father's occupation being recorded as being a Labourer.

He served with the Royal Navy during WW1, and his grandson John Moore provides a fascinating insight into part of his career:

"Frederick was a ship's rigger at the Albion dockyard and also a Royal Naval reservist when war was declared on 4th August 1914 by Britain, France and Russia after Germany refused to remove its troops from Belgium. Frederick was 17 and under-age when he possibly volunteered and joined the First Royal Naval division. The division comprised of 4 battalions each of 500 men, Drake, Hawke, Benbow and Collingwood.

It was Winston Churchill, as First Lord of the Admiralty's idea to create sailors who could fight on land, but because of poor training and near obsolete equipment were nicknamed "Saturday afternoon soldiers".

Germany referred to the Belgium invasion as "the race to the sea" to utilise Belgium ports to attack French ports such as Boulogne, Calais and Dunkirk and cut off supplies and troops from England. Ostend and Zeebrugge were also of strategic importance for cross channel attacks against Britain

The 2 Royal Naval divisions (8 battalions in total) were sent to Antwerp on October 6th to support the Belgian army in the impossible task of holding up the German advance. They were deployed in shallow trenches within sight of German observers. The British sailors had old breach loading Lee Enfield rifles against 174 German artillery pieces including 4 Super Howitzer siege guns (Big Berthas) that fired massive 16 inch/420 mm shells. After days of heavy bombardment it was decided to withdraw on 10th October to save the Belgian army and cross the River Scheldt at dusk. In the chaos of fleeing refugees and miscommunication, Commodore Wilfred Henderson never received the runner's message until 10.00 pm. By then it was realised that 3 battalions were cut off and when they reached the Scheldt at midnight the bridges were demolished and under German shrapnel bombardment. The troops crossed the river by small boats to rendezvous with trains but by then information was received that the Germans had destroyed the railway tracks at Moerbeke.

Frederick Morgan in RN Uniform, c. 1915.

Commodore Henderson then took the decision to march the 3 exhausted Hawke, Benbow and Collingwood battalions across the frontier to neutral Holland. During the 4 days of heavy shelling 57 were killed, 138 were wounded and for Frederick of Collingwood and 1478 others the war was over and 4 years of internment awaited. The sailors were initially held in Rabenhaupt military barracks in Groningen, North Holland but in early 1915 three large wooden huts were used as accommodation behind the barracks. To the Dutch, it was the Engelse camp (English camp) but to the internees it was dubbed HMS Timbertown. Henderson accepted Admiralty 'No Escape' orders to preserve Holland's neutrality.

The 3 battalions of Hawke, Benbow and Collingwood, led by Commodore Henderson were each allocated their own wooden hut. Each hut was 240 ft long by 60 ft wide and housed 500 men, whilst most officers stayed in hotels (1907 Convention).

It became clear that boredom would become the greatest enemy of the internees. Although regular route marches were a common sight around Groningen, some academic courses such as navigation and accountancy were available albeit sports, such as football, rugby and cricket which were much more popular. The most popular was football with each battalion fielding strong teams. A camp team played the Groningen team named 'Forward' in front of 3,000 spectators, paying 240 guilders which the British sailors won 7-2. Timbertown teams proved too strong for local teams and in November 1916 a camp representative team played Ajax of Amsterdam and came away with a very credible 1-1 draw, with Arnold Birch the Sheffield Wednesday keeper in goal. Trainer/coach Harry Waites returned to Holland after the war to make team Be Quick in 1920 and Feyenoord in 1924, Dutch National Champions.

Rugby was also popular and in April 1916 an "international" was played between English and Scottish internees at Leeuwarden in front of 2,500 spectators. The English team won 19-7 which included Frederick George Glassborow, who was Kate, The Princess of Wales' great-grandfather.

Fred Morgan's sport was swimming, and according to camp magazines was the one mile river race champion in 1915, 1916, 1917, and came second in 1918. My grandfather was the County water polo player in the newspaper article regarding the Morgans v Wrens football match. Fred swam for Barton Hill for many years.

Because of the Hague Peace Conference of 1907, officers were entitled to return home on leave. This caused resentment and increasingly cases of NCOs and other ranks were allowed to have "compassionate leave" with sick notes permissible from British doctors if close relatives were ill in the UK. There were over 100 interned sailors from the Isle of Lewis allowed up to 8 weeks leave to gather in the harvest as most of the island's able-bodied men were in other naval theatres of war. At the time of the 1918 Armistice, over 300 internees were in Britain. In fact my grandfather met my grandmother at Bath races around 1916 and had several bouts of "compassionate leave".

The British sailors were popular with the Dutch ladies and incredibly Timbertown was open to the public on Sunday's from 2 p.m. until 4 p.m. This led to courtships, some marriages and even pregnancies. Family legend has it, Fred had a Dutch girlfriend by the name of Sweenie Corbek as well as Charlotte Ham of Bath; could this be the reason he only came second in the river race in 1918? He had to choose between the 2 ladies after the war and it's there but for fortune that I support Bristol Rovers and not F.C. Groningen. Anyway 'Gashead' sounds much better than 'Groningenhead'!

He was working at Christopher Thomas's Soap Works, which many people will know as the red-brick Gardiner Haskins building in Broad Plain, Bristol, and in 1946 was severely scalded when a large vat of soap boiled over. He died of gangrene whilst convalescing at Portwey Hospital in Weymouth, 6 months after the accident."

Frederick married Charlotte Emily Ham (born 13th January 1899, Twerton, Bath) on 14th April 1920 at Russell Town Congregational Church, Bristol. The marriage register shows Frederick's occupation as a 'Shiprigger'.

The Census from 1921 shows their address as 30 Bolton Road, Bristol, and Frederick employed as a 'stager' at Charles Hill & Sons, Shipbuilders, Hotwells, Bristol – although it was also noted that he was 'out of work' at the time.

They had two children:

- **Winifred Lottie Morgan** (born 14th September 1921, Bristol; died 22nd December 1996, Bristol, aged 75).
- **Myra Jean Morgan** (born 2nd March 1931, Bristol; died 21st December 2011, Bristol, aged 80).

Frederick and his wife Charlotte with daughter Winifred, 1923.

The 1939 Register indicates that the family were living at 12 Croydon Street, Barton Hill, Bristol. Frederick's occupation was a Soap Boilerman.

Frederick died on 28th July 1946 whilst convalescing at Portwey Hospital, Weymouth, aged 49. He was buried at Avonview Cemetery, Bristol on 2nd August 1946. His home address at the time was 12 Croydon Street, Barton Hill, Bristol.

Wife Charlotte passed away on 21st January 1977 in Bristol, aged 78. She was buried at Avonview Cemetery, Bristol, on 27th January 1977.

FREDERICK AND CHARLOTTE'S CHILDREN:

1.   Winifred Lottie Morgan.

She married John Moore (born 18th December 1910, London; died 12th January 1996, Bristol, aged 85) by special licence on 19th October 1939, at St. Lawrence's Church, Easton, Bristol. The special licence was granted as John was serving in the army following the breakout of World War II.

They had two children.

It seems that she was planning to visit Hong Kong, according to the passenger lists from the P&O Vessel *'Chusan'* on a scheduled voyage from London to Yokohama on 21st December 1954; her name appears on the list, with her address shown as 12 Croydon Street, Bristol, but her details were crossed out – presumably due to cancellation of her plans.

Winifred and John separated and she subsequently married Harold Hulbert (born 1922, Bristol; died 2rd January 2018, Bristol, aged 98) in Bristol in 1964.

John lived at Kingsway, Bristol, for many years until the end of his life, and one of his jobs was working as a park patrol officer. On 16th March 1966 he discovered a person floating in St. Georges Park Lake, but despite retrieving him from the water and giving artificial respiration, the man sadly died.

Winifred died on 22nd December 1996 in Bristol, aged 75, and she was buried at Avonview Cemetery, Bristol, on 30th December 1996.

Harold's funeral was held on the 7th January 2018 and he was buried in the family grave at Avonview Cemetery, Bristol.

2.   Myra Jean Morgan.

Myra married Gordon Albert Bryant (born 27th May 1930, Bristol; died 26th September 2006 at the Bristol Royal Infirmary, aged 75) in 1953 at St. Gabriel's Church, Easton, Bristol. They had one child.

Gordon was cremated at South Bristol Crematorium on 6th October 2006.

Myra died on 21st December 2011 in Bristol, aged 80. She was cremated at South Bristol Crematorium on 6th January 2012.

The grave of Frederick and Charlotte, Avonview Cemetery, Bristol. Also of their daughter Winifred and son-in-law Harold.

CHAPTER 7.
THE FAMILY AND DESCENDANTS OF JAMES MORGAN.

James Morgan (1872-1935). Despite his naval uniform, there is no evidence to confirm he actually served in the Royal Navy.

James was born at 5 Tarr's Court, Lawrence Hill, Bristol, on 2nd February 1872, with his father's occupation recorded as a Labourer at Coal Works. He was baptised at Holy Trinity Church, St. Philips, Bristol, on 5th June 1872. His parents were recorded as living at Lawrence Hill.

He married Elizabeth Coles (born 10th May 1875, Bristol) on 24th May 1896 at St. Lawrence's Church, Easton, Bristol. They had seven children;

1. **Lilian May Morgan** (born 2nd July 1900, 1 Charlton Street, Lawrence Hill, Bristol; died 3rd February 1897, Bath, aged 86).

2. **Albert James (Bert) Morgan** (born 10th March 1902, 7 Eagle Street, Bristol; died 6th January 1953, Bristol, aged 50).

3. **Ivy Doris Irene Morgan** (born 5th March 1906, 79 Bellevue Road, Easton, Bristol; died 18th June 1992, Bristol, aged 86).

4. **Violet Matilda Morgan** (born 3rd Feb 1908, 79 Bellevue Road, Easton, Bristol; died 16th December 1968, aged 60).

5. **Ethel Maud Morgan** (born 22nd July 1910, 168 Church Road, Redfield, Bristol; died 27th May 1960, aged 49).

6. **Gilbert Thomas Morgan** (born 4th January 1912, 168 Church Road, Redfield, Bristol; died 6th May 1975, aged 63).

7. **Grace Eveline Alice Morgan** (born 21st July 1915, 168 Church Road, Redfield, Bristol; died 4th June 2004, aged 88).

The 1901 Census indicates that the family lived at 16 Charlton Street, Bristol. James was described as being a Master Pork Butcher, and living with wife Elizabeth and 9-month old daughter Lilian. Two lodgers lived with the family at this time, Oliver and Jack Malpas, Oliver being a Seaman and Jack a Labourer at Chocolate Works.

Stop me and buy one – James Morgan posing as an ice-cream salesman!

A charabanc outing from the Rising Sun, probably around 1914 or 1915. James Morgan in front of the charabanc on the extreme left, with four of his children on his right. Note his name on the pub sign at the top of the photograph.

James Morgan at the bar of the Rising Sun. Photograph probably taken at the same time as the one overleaf.

Interior of the Rising Sun, landlord James Morgan on the right, with his brother John (Jack) Morgan on the left.

The 1921 Census provides a great deal of information about the family. James continued to be the landlord of the Rising Sun, but most of their children had found local employment. Lilian was working at Mardon, Son & Halls in Victoria Street, a well-known box manufacturers as a 'Cardboard Box Maker'. Albert was working at Charles Hill & Sons, Cumberland Road, shipbuilders, as a Boiler Maker, and Ivy a 'Learner Cardboard Box Maker' along with her elder sister at Mardon, Son & Halls. All other children were still at school, but James's wife Elizabeth's brother Harry Coles was living with the family as an out-of-work Labourer, and Lillian (Lily) Jarrett was employed by the family as a servant.

The Rising Sun was a popular public house in the Redfield area of Bristol, and although there were numerous other public houses in the vicinity it was certainly well used. James was a great pigeon-racer and was a regular participant in local races. He was also an excellent swimmer, and along with some of his brothers was a regular attendee at Barton Hill Swimming Baths.

James Morgan and his racing pigeon cages at the back of the Rising Sun, Church Road, Redfield, Bristol.

James and Elizabeth Morgan pose in front of his Morris Oxford saloon, late 1920s.

James Morgan at the back of the 'Rising Sun', Redfield.

Research of the family archives has revealed a very sad and poignant letter to his daughter Ivy, written a few months before his death. One can easily imagine how he spoke, judging from the way he wrote. The 'bonny girl' referred to is my mother, Barbara. The letter, written in pencil, is difficult to read, but has been transcribed as below:

JAMES MORGAN
C WARD
SOUTHMEAD HOSPITAL
11/3/35

Dear Daughter,

I received your kind letter today Monday. I was glad to hear that you are very well also the baby and I am proud to hear it is a bonny girl. Well Ivy I regret to say I am very bad indeed and they can do no more for me, my head is so bad. I cannot hardly write this letter. Well Ivy I want to ask you one thing, my time is short and I want you to promise me that you will look after her when I am gone. I know my time is short, my eyes are so bad I can hardly see. Ivy don't forget what I want I want you to go and look after your mother. I and your mother have done our best for you all, your mother has been a very good wife and I only wished years ago that I was going to be laid up like this. We threw our money away. Now don't forget look after your money. Now I have suffered this year or two. Now my dying wish is that you must look after your dear mother, she is breaking up. Now God bless her now don't forget my wish that is my last wish. This would be a great help to your mother.

You can see by my writing how bad I be. Well my wish to you look after your mother. I want you to write by return and let me know if you will do all my wishes.

Well you never sent me no kisses in your letter now kiss your mother for me and don't forget to look after her when I am gone. The days so far passed me by now don't forget to send me a letter by return. Now don't forget what I have asked you to do, don't let anybody put a hand on her, she is good. Now don't forget to remember me to George and Joy and God will bless you if you look after your mother. Now God bless you I shall never see any of you again I am too ill. Now cheer up and God bless you. With all love for you.

Dad x

Kisses for your mother

xxxxx

Ivy Morgan with daughters Barbara (left) and Joy (right) on the day of James Morgan's funeral, 10th July 1935.

James passed away on 6th July 1935 at Southmead Hospital, Bristol, and was buried at Avonview Cemetery, Bristol, on 10th July 1935, in the Morgan Family grave.

Following James' death, his widow Elizabeth took over the running the pub. However, a few interesting events came to light over the next few years; one, in 1937 made the local press:

"The loading of beer and food into a motor-coach outside the Rising Sun public-house, Church Road, St. George, Bristol, for a "diddle 'em club" outing, led to the appearance at Bristol Police Court on Monday of the licensee, Mrs. Elizabeth Morgan, charged with supplying and selling liquor out of hours and with aiding and abetting Albert Trutch, secretary of the club, to commit an offence by taking away liquor from that public-house, with which he was charged.

Mr. A. C. Caffin, prosecuting, said that at 8.40 a.m. on July 3rd a police sergeant saw two men carrying a case of beer from the public-house to a motor-coach. Trutch was with the two men. The officer stopped the coach as it was about to move off, and found five cases containing 12 flagons of beer each. "I asked Trutch who was in charge of the liquor, and he said he was. We call ourselves the Rising Sun Diddle 'em Club. The liquor is not paid for yet, but it will be when we get back. What we do not drink we will take back, he said," stated the sergeant.

Celebrating the King's coronation at the Rising Sun, 1937. Landlady Elizabeth Morgan in the centre, with daughter Violet on the right. The gentleman on the left is Reginald Cole, husband of daughter Lilian Morgan.

Mrs. Morgan, the licensee, told him that they had done it for 29 years. That particular party had been on a trip from that house for the last 10 or 12 years, and they had always taken liquor. The beer had been paid for the night before.

Mr. W. Ireland, defending, asked the sergeant if it were not a fact that that of thing was done all over the city, to which the officer replied that that was so, but it was very difficult to detect, as the people arranging them used subterfuge.

Mr. Ireland said that his clients had no idea that an offence had been committed. All that Mrs. Morgan had to do to comply with the law was to keep a delivery book at the house.

He produced an order for food and beer for the outing, and said that while that did not strictly comply with the law, it could be used as a check by the police. And that, he said, was all the police required. They admitted that a technical offence had been committed. Mrs. Morgan said that before the sergeant came, a police constable was there while they were loading up the coach with beer.

"The police constable said that he wished he was going with us" she said, and added that she had shown him the receipt for the payment for the beer.

After a retirement, the magistrates (Mr. E. Brookhouse Richards and Mrs. E. Robinson White), dismissed the case against Mrs. Morgan on payment of £2 costs.

The case against Trutch was also dismissed.

On Monday 6th February 1939, the local press reported that:

"A presentation of a chiming clock was made to Mrs. Elizabeth Morgan, retiring hostess of the Rising Sun Hotel, Redfield, from the customers.

Mrs. Morgan and her late husband (a well-known Bristol sportsman) between them held the licence for 30 years, and some years ago secured second prize presented by the Bristol Brewery Georges' and Co. Ltd., in the competition for the best-kept hotels".

Replacing Elizabeth as the landlord of the pub in February 1939 was Arthur Stanley Hodge, the husband of James' and Elizabeth's youngest daughter Grace, thereby keeping the establishment within the family.

The Rising Sun public house with Arthur Stanley Hodge displayed as the landlord.

The 1939 Register revealed that Elizabeth was living at 38 Victoria Avenue, Bristol, with Henry Donaldson, a Sales Representative for Cash Machines, her former servant at the Rising Sun, Lily Jarrett, and her married daughter Violet Matilda Webber.

She was mentioned in the local press on 7th October 1939 when it was reported that:

"Elizabeth Morgan (64), of 38, Victoria Avenue, Redfield, sustained a scalp wound and concussion when she fell downstairs early this morning. She is detained at the Royal Infirmary."

Elizabeth married William Edwin Stokes (born 3rd October 1976) at St. Mary's Church, Fishponds, Bristol, on 3rd May 1943.

Sadly, William died on 28th August 1946, and was buried at Avonview Cemetery, Bristol on 31st August 1946. William was by all accounts a friendly and personable man, and was always very formally known as 'Mr. Stokes' by family members.

The wedding of Elizabeth Morgan and William Edwin Stokes, St. Mary's Church, Fishponds, 3rd May 1943.

Elizabeth Morgan died on 20th August 1963 at 61 Queen's Road, St. George, Bristol, the home of daughter Grace and husband Arthur Stanley (Stan) Hodge.

She was buried at Avonview Cemetery, Bristol, on 23rd August 1963 in the Morgan family grave alongside her first husband James, mother Mary Ann, sister Mary Ann and brother Henry amongst other family members.

The Morgan family grave at Avonview Cemetery, Bristol.

It is interesting that her death certificate shows her name as Elizabeth Stokes, but she is buried under her first married surname of Morgan on the family grave, no doubt due to a family request.

JAMES AND ELIZABETH'S CHILDREN:

1.   **Lilian May Morgan.**

Lilian was baptised on 5th August 1900 at St. Philip & Jacob Church, Bristol. Her parents' address was vaguely recorded as 'Lower Easton' and her father's occupation noted as being a Carter.

She was the subject of an interesting press report published on 13th April 1910:

"Yesterday, at Bristol County Court, before his Honour Judge Austin and jury, there was action tried in which Lilian May Morgan, by James Morgan, her father, sued Joseph John

Ballard for damages she had sustained. The plaintiff lives with her parents at 168, Church Road, St, George, and the defendant lives at 1, Old Holly Lodge. St. George.

Mr. Weatherly (instructed by Mr. W. H. Brown), appeared for the plaintiff, and Mr. Waite (instructed by Messrs Tuckey and Clifton) appeared for the defendant. There were damages claimed for injuries sustained by the plaintiff by reason of the negligence of the defendant or his servants or agents or workmen in suffering the water chute of a tenement and premises situated at 178, Church Road to be insecure, that the fastenings which should have supported it failed to do so, and it fell on the plaintiff, and she sustained injuries.

Mr. Weatherly, in his opening, said the plaintiff was about eight years old, and on the 26th of September last was calling, as her practice was, at the house of a sweep named Abraham, for a little girl, her friend. She was standing at the door, and between the two cottages there ran down a chute to carry off the water from the roofs, and upon the top of the chute was a snow box or head. That head of the chute fell on the head of the child, and she suffered very considerably. From September to December she was unable to go to school. He asked for reasonable damages.

Dr. Mainland was the first witness called. He said he practised in Stapleton Road. On the 27th September he was called to see the child. That was the day after the accident, and it was at her father's residence. He had attended the family before. He found a contused wound on the head just at the junction of the back with the top of the head, and extending backwards about two inches in length, and nearly quarter of an inch deep.

The wound had been stitched when he saw it. After three or four days' attendance he removed the stitches, then found the depth of the wound a little more. The child also suffered from a shock, and was pale and distressed, and her system generally had run down. She was allowed to be present in school, but did no lessons. At present she suffered from malnutrition. His charges up to the present time had been five guineas.

Mrs. Matilda Hudson, who lived on the opposite side the to the plaintiff, proved that on the day in question the child was standing at the door of Mr. Abraham, and the top of the chute fell on the child. Someone picked her up and took her to her father.

Lilian May Morgan was called, and stated that she called at the house to see Daisy Abraham, that they might go to chapel, as it was Sunday. James Morgan, licensee of the Rising Sun, Redfield, St. George, father of the child, gave evidence of the expenses incurred through the accident to the child.

Evidence was given by Mr. Williams, who had collected rents for the defendant, as to the complaints made respecting the state of the roof and chute at the house of Mr. Abraham.

Edward Abraham stated that he was a weekly tenant of Mr. Ballard. He proved seeing the child after the accident, and stated that he had complained about the state of the roof, but not of the snow box.

Frank Meeds, plumber, stated that he examined the house on the Tuesday following the accident, and found the chute in a bad state. He considered that the head had not been painted for ten years. He thought the head had been cracked for some years. It might have lasted if the nails had not come away.

This was the case for the plaintiff.

Waite contended that there was evidence to go to the jury that the owner, who was the defendant, agreed to do the repairs to the house. And further, when the house was let, there was ground for supposing the house was out of repair.

His Honour said at present the only question of fact for the jury was one of damages. Mr. Waite said his contention was that at the time the houses were let, the premises were not out of repair, and witnesses would be called to show they examined them in April last and found them in good order.

Joseph John Ballard (the defendant) was called and said there were three houses in Church Road, and they were in good repair. Abraham had lived there for some years. He employed two men named Lewis and Fox to see after the repairs of his different houses.

Cross-examined: When complaint was made he had the repair of the roof of Abraham's house carried out, examined the plaster to which the head of the chute was fastened and found it was all right. He could not account for the fall of the head; he had no control over the weather. He thought the head fell through the wind.

Samuel Fox gave evidence of having carried out repairs to the houses of the defendant. The snow-box at the house in question was safe, and the mortar in good order.

Re-examined; he kept about 60 houses of Mr. Ballard in repair.

The evidence of another employee of the defendant was also taken, and was to the effect that when some new horizontal chuting was put to the house in question, the snow-box was tested and found secure.

The learned counsel addressed the jury for their respective clients, after which His Honour summed up carefully. He said the plaintiff might have sued Abraham as the occupier, for he was bound to keep the house in good condition as regarded by the outside public. The reason he was not sued was that he was a chimney sweep. Ballard, as the owner of the property, was worth more.

The occupier was *prima facie* liable. If their minds were in doubt on the balance, it was their duty to find for the defendant.

The questions put by his Honour to the jury were.

(1) Was there any agreement on the part of Mr. Ballard's repair?

(2) Was the snow-box in a dangerous condition in 1904?

The jury retired to consider their verdict, and after a short absence returned into court and answered both in the negative, which amounted to a verdict for the defendant."

Lilian married Reginald Stanley Cole (born 26th January 1902, Bristol; died 1st April 1964, Southmead Hospital, Bristol), on 8th September 1928, at St. Lawrence's Church, Easton, Bristol.

Lilian's address at the time of marriage was recorded on the marriage certificate as being 12 Croydon Street, Barton Hill, Bristol. Reginald was living at 112 Easton Road, Bristol, and his occupation recorded as being a Railway Worker.

The 1939 Register records the family living at 253 Church Road, St. George, Bristol, where Reginald's occupation is noted as being a Centre Lathe Hand.

Lilian died on 3rd February 1987, in the Bath area, aged 86.

They had three children:

- **Ronald Reginald J. Cole** (born 13th June 1929, Bristol; died 2001, Bristol, aged 71).

Ronald married Patricia Herbert in 1971 and had no children. Patricia had previously been married since 1952 to Arthur William Youell (born 1931, Reigate; died 12th August 1959, Bristol, aged 28), and they had one child together.

- **Terence John Cole** (born 30th April 1932, Bristol; died 10th August 1983, Bristol, aged 51).

Terence married Patricia Rose Pritchard (born 22nd August 1936, Bristol) on 20th Oct 1956 in Bristol.

They had no children.

- **Elaine Margaret Cole** (born 5th August 1937, Bristol, died 1st January 2014, aged 76).

Elaine married Leslie Thomas Reginald Garland (born 1933, Bristol; died 3rd June 2016, Bristol, aged 83) on 5th August 1957, in Bristol.

They had four children.

Leslie was a keen sportsman and played cricket for Syston Cricket Club and ran the Syston United under-14 football team.

The wedding of Elaine Cole and Leslie Garland, 5th August 1957.

2. Albert James (Bert) Morgan.

Albert was baptised on 30th March 1902 at St. Philip & Jacob Church, Bristol. His parents' address was recorded as Easton Road, and his father's occupation noted as being a Carter.

Albert married Rosalie (Rose) Lily May Vincent (born 16th April 1907, Bristol; died 10th October 1987, Bristol, aged 80) on 25th February 1946 in Bristol.

Albert died on 6th January 1953, at Southmead Hospital, Bristol, aged 50. At the time of his death, Albert was living at 8 Robert Street, Barton Hill, Bristol.

Rosalie gave a brief insight into life at the Twinnell House flats in Barton Hill in a newspaper article from 7th October 1974:

"Mrs. Rosalie Morgan (66) lived at Aiken Street all her life, until widowed, when she went to a bedsitter flat at Butler House, St. George. Mrs. Morgan, who now lives on the ground floor at Twinnell House, said; "My dear, it was lovely, really lovely up there.""

"But then my daughter and her husband separated and she and her little boy needed a home so we got this flat. When she gets her divorce I'd like to go back to Barton Hill – perhaps a little bedsitter flat again but it's got to be where there are no steps or stairs because of my hip."

Albert (right) and his sister Ivy, c. 1920.

Mrs. Morgan has had more painful operations on her hip than she can almost count but she had limped out to the entrance to be in a bit of sun and see the people passing by."

They had one child, Margaret Rose Morgan (born in 1947, Bristol, who married twice; firstly to Gordon A. Gay (born 1937, Bristol), with whom she had one son, and then to Keith W. Cullum (born 1944, Bristol).

Margaret died on 26th April 2008, in Bristol, aged 61. She was buried at Avonview Cemetery, Bristol, on 7th May 2008 in her parents' grave.

The grave of Albert and Rosina (Rose) Morgan and their daughter Margaret, Avonview Cemetery, Bristol.

3. Ivy Doris Irene Morgan.

Ivy was baptised on 25th March 1906 at St. Philip & Jacob Church, Bristol. Her parents' address was vaguely recorded as 'Lower Easton' and her father's occupation noted as being a Carter.

Ivy, aged 15, with long hair.

The family group at the wedding of Ivy Morgan and George Aldridge. Picture taken at the Rising Sun.

The wedding of Ivy and George. Photograph taken at the Rising Sun public house, Redfield.

She married George Arnold Aldridge (born 22nd October 1900, Bristol; died 3rd September 1986, Manor Park Hospital, Bristol, aged 85) on 25th April 1927, at St. George Parish Church, Bristol. Both were living at 46 Clouds Hill Avenue, Bristol, according to the marriage certificate, and George's occupation shown as being a Bricklayer.

They had two children;

- **Muriel Joy Aldridge** (born 11th November 1929, Bristol).
- **Barbara Rose Aldridge** (born 5th March 1935, Bristol Royal Infirmary, Bristol; died 21st May 2013, Robinson House, Stockwood, Bristol, aged 78).

A son (Graham) was apparently stillborn, around 1927.

The 1939 Register shows the family living at 13 St. James' Churchyard, Bristol, where George was landlord of the Carpenter's Arms public house.

The Carpenter's Arms (left), 13 St. James' Churchyard, Bristol.

George was trained as a bricklayer and during World War 2 was involved in building the Mulberry Harbour used for the D-Day landings in 1944.

Ivy was trained as an Air Raid Patrol (A.R.P.) Warden during the early part of the war, based at the Carpenter's Arms.

The family moved many times, moving out from the centre of Bristol during the early part of WW2 (1941) in order to escape the German bombing of the city.

Other homes were subsequently occupied; Coronation Road (Downend), Maywood Crescent (Fishponds), Park Place (Upper Eastville), Hill Street (St. George), Hawkesbury Road (Fishponds), Beaufort Court (Downend), and finally St. Clements Court (Soundwell).

George died on 6th September 1986 at Manor Park Hospital, Bristol, aged 85, following a stroke and 'essential hypertension'. He was cremated at Canford Cemetery, Bristol, on 9th September 1986.

Ivy died in Bristol on 18th June 1992, at Frenchay Hospital, Bristol, aged 86, the cause of death being recorded as Carcinomatosis (Cancer) and Carcinoma of Ovary. She was also cremated at Canford Cemetery, Bristol.

Both Ivy and George's address on their death certificates were recorded as 44 St. Clements Court, Soundwell, Bristol.

Canford Crematorium, Bristol, where Ivy and George were cremated.

Eldest daughter Muriel (known as Joy) married John Colin Anderson (born 4th March 1927, Bristol; died 5th February 1995, aged 67) in Bristol on 28th June 1952 in Bristol, and they had three children.

John was an astute businessman and keen sportsman, and was Chairman of Bedminster Cricket Club and Bath City Football Club at various times.

Youngest daughter Barbara married Kenneth Bennett (born 5th November 1931, Bristol; died 25th February 2014, Frenchay Hospital, Bristol, aged 82) on 3rd March 1956 at St. George Parish Church, Bristol.

Barbara's address on the marriage certificate was shown as being 61 Queens's Road, Bristol, the home of her Auntie Grace and Uncle Stan, no doubt to allow her to marry at the church of her choice.

Her occupation was shown as being a Chemist's Assistant, as she was working at the Kingswood branch of Boots at the time. Kenneth's address was shown as being 96 Bishopsworth Road, Bristol, and his occupation shown as being a Carpenter.

The wedding of Barbara Aldridge and Kenneth Bennett, 3rd March 1956, St. George Parish Church, Bristol.

L-R: Ray Jenkins (Best Man), Mary Ann Bennett, Isaac Bennett, Kenneth Bennett, Barbara Aldridge, George Aldridge, Margaret Morgan (bridesmaid), Ivy Aldridge (nee Morgan).

They met when both were members of the Avon Road Club, a cycling club based in Bristol. They lived their entire married life at their house in Maple Avenue, Hillfields Park, in the Fishponds area of Bristol.

They also had three children.

Barbara worked for many years as a shop assistant at the local Spar supermarket, and also undertook work for the BBC audience research panel before finding a clerical job at Manor Park Hospital, Fishponds.

She even took (and indeed passed) the Radio Amateur Examination, obtaining call sign G7HOJ during the 1980s, as well as learning to drive.

Kenneth worked in the carpentry and shopfitting industry for many years, working at Colston Shopfitting in Soundwell and then forming B.T.B. Design & Construction in Hanham, before setting up his own business (K.B. Woodcraft) in the 1970s. He became area shopfitting manager for Rediffusion in Bristol during the late 1970s and then set up another shopfitting business (B&S Shopfitting Services) in the early 1980s.

Following this, Kenneth worked at the Skill Centre at Oldbury Court, Bristol, teaching carpentry, a job which he continued at the young offenders' centre at Eastwood Park, near Bristol. He then worked briefly at Horfield Prison, Bristol, and finally working repairing bicycles at Fred Baker and Bits-Z-Cars in Bristol. He also taught carpentry at Brunel

Technical College in Bristol, and obtained his City & Guilds Medal in carpentry, recognising him as one of the best in the country.

Barbara died on 21st May 2013, aged 78, at Robinson House, Stockwood, Bristol. She was cremated at Westerleigh Crematorium, Bristol, on 6th June 2013.

Family group picture, 1970s. L-R: Kenneth Bennett, Barbara Bennett (nee Aldridge), Grace Hodge (nee Morgan), Ivy Aldridge (nee Morgan), Arthur 'Stan' Hodge and George Aldridge.

A photograph of Ivy (right), husband George, and sister Grace (left).

4. Violet Matilda Morgan.

Violet was baptised on 23rd February 1908 at St. Philip & Jacob Church, Bristol. Her parents' address was vaguely recorded as 'Lower Easton' and her father's occupation noted as being a Carter.

Violet married Albert James Webber (born 4th July 1907, Hanham, Bristol) at St. George Parish Church, Bristol on 19th December 1932. According to the marriage certificate, Albert was living at 3 Hill Street, Bristol, and was working in the Royal Air Force.

Violet was living at 46 Clouds Hill Avenue, Bristol, with no occupation recorded.

The wedding of Violet Morgan and Albert Webber, 1932. Photograph taken at the 'Rising Sun' in Church Road, Bristol.

They had one child, James.

Albert joined the Royal Air Force in 1927, working as an 'Aircrafthand Storekeeper' having previously worked as a Grinder at the Douglas Works in Kingswood, Bristol.

His home address on his RAF documents from that date was recorded as 7 Furber Road, St. George, Bristol.

The 1939 Register shows Violet living with her mother at 38 Victoria Avenue, Bristol, sharing the house with the Rising Sun employee Lily Jarrett. Albert was no doubt serving with the RAF at the time.

Albert and Violet ran the Rising Sun public house in Redfield, Bristol, for a short time in the early 1950s, continuing the family involvement in the establishment.

Violet and son James, 1947.

A slightly later photograph of Violet and James.

Violet died on 16th December 1968, in Bristol, aged 60. Albert subsequently married Lily May Palmer (born 16th February 1910, Hampshire; died 2002, Bristol, aged 92) in Bristol, in 1970.

Albert Webber and Lily May Palmer.

Albert died in 2000 in Taunton aged 92. He was cremated at Westerleigh Crematorium, Bristol, on 25th April 2000.

5.   Ethel Maud Morgan.

Ethel was baptised on 14th August 1910 at St. Philip & Jacob Church, Bristol.

Her parents' address was recorded as 168 Church Road, Bristol (The Rising Sun Public House) and her father's occupation noted as being a Publican.

Ethel married John (Jack) William Davidson (born 15th February 1906, Bristol) on 24th January 1931, in Bristol.

Ethel Maud Morgan (1906-1960).

They had five children, all born in Bristol:

- **Graham John W Davidson** (born 28th May 1931, died 15th February 2011, Bristol, aged 79).

- **John Michael Davidson** (born 5th May 1933, died 21st September 2017, Bristol, aged 84).

- **Geoffrey Davidson** (born 25th May 1936, died 7th June 2001, New Zealand, aged 65).

- **David James Davidson** (born 17th September 1938).

- **Janet Elizabeth Davidson** (born 2nd October 1940).

John ran a radio and cycle shop for many years, located at Mina Road, St. Werburgh's, Bristol, but the shop was not a financial success, and the assets were sold by auction in early 1939. A press report of the time stated that:

"Davidson said he was employed as a house decorator up to November 1935, then purchased a shop and dwelling house at Mina Road, Bristol, for £450, which he raised on a mortgage. He commenced business, without capital, as a radio and cycle dealer.

He had four petrol pumps installed subject to hiring agreements. Because the service pipes went under the shop and dwelling house, they were prohibited from living there, and they rented premises next door for five years at £65 per year.

In February, 1936, in addition to the petrol business, he commenced to sell wireless sets and bicycles on hire-purchase. A large number of his customers defaulted in hire-purchase payments, and the finance company collected the sets from defaulters and left them with him.

Later he signed a promissory note for £258 14s 9d, the amount of arrears due to the company. He owed the company £304, and subsequently a writ was issued for that amount, and costs.

The examination was closed."

John (Jack) Davidson's Radio and Cycle Shop, Mina Road, Bristol.

The 1939 Register shows the family now living at 88 Windermere Road, Thornbury, Bristol. John is noted as being an Aero Engine Inspector, with Ethel undertaking unpaid domestic duties.

A lovely photograph of Ethel on the family's motor cycle.

A Davidson family group. John (Jack), wife Ethel, and children David, Janet and Graham.

John (Jack) Davidson with wife Ethel and daughter Janet.

Ethel died on 27th May 1960 aged 49, and she is remembered on the Morgan family grave at Avonview Cemetery, Bristol.

The inscription on the Morgan Family Grave, Avonview Cemetery, Bristol.

John subsequently married Doris Kathleen Watts (born 16th July 1915, Weston-super-Mare; died 2000, South Gloucestershire, aged 84) in Bristol in 1960.

Doris had previously married Howard George Derby Stokes (born 16th December 1915, Bristol; died 2nd December 1959, Bristol, aged 43), on 31st July 1937 at Holy Trinity Church, Kingswood, Bristol.

They had one child together, Maureen Doris Stokes (born 18th December 1941), who married Kenneth Walter Ashmead in 1961, at the same church as her parents.

Maureen died on 12th September 1998 in Bristol, aged 56, with Kenneth passing on 10th October 2014 in Bristol, aged 78.

John Davidson died on 13th March 1968, in Bristol, aged 62.

6. Gilbert Thomas Morgan.

Gilbert was baptised on 4th February 1912 at St. Philip & Jacob Church, Bristol. His parents' address was vaguely recorded as 'Redfield' (although it was certainly the Rising Sun Public House on Church Road) and his father's occupation noted as being a Publican.

Gilbert had an interesting life growing up in the Redfield area, and described those times in an article written later in his life.

It gives us a glimpse into what life must have been like in Bristol in the 1920s - a time which saw extremes of poverty and wealth. His home was the Rising Sun pub in Church Road, Redfield, but his working day was spent as a page boy at the Royal Hotel, Bristol, near College Green and Bristol Cathedral. The hotel is still operational and now known as the Royal Marriott Hotel.

He recalls:

"In 1926 I lived a life in two worlds. For by day, at the hotel, I made personal contact with film stars, actors, millionaires, famous aviators, commercial travellers and professional tipsters. But by night, in east Bristol, I experienced the blue, smokey atmosphere of a spit and sawdust public house, a place which happened to be my home. Here and there was a bar spittoon, and a gas jet was used to seal bottles in the 'bottle and jug' with red wax.

Our way of life was very different in those days, and I saw much poverty among my good friends and neighbours in Derby Street, St. George.

Comparing our back street struggle for the very necessities of life with the soft lights, sweet music and plush carpets of the hotel, I felt I was living a Jekyll and Hyde existence.

From the pub window in the early morning, I could see women queuing up outside the pawnbrokers shop opposite. Clutched closely to their white laced cotton pinafores were white sheet bundles tied at all four corners. These women also wore their husband's caps, but to add a feminine touch they pushed an oversized steel hat pin through the top.

Those were the days of the dreaded means test, and unemployment was rife. Groups of men would stand idly on street corners, their only possession a packet of Woodbine cigarettes. But this was also the era of the Bullnose Morris car, the lamplighter crystal set, the tin trumpeted gramophone, the barrel organ and radio stations 5WA Cardiff and 2LO London.

This was still the age of the smithy - the clanging, dancing hammer on the anvil, and the fumes from burning horses' hooves. Cockle-sellers in Welsh national costume would roam the streets, their cries of 'cockles!' mingling with the melodious rumbling of a side street barrel organ. Kids would be in the streets playing conkers, kicktin, monkey tops, bedlam, hoops and skipping.

A young Gilbert Morgan in page boy uniform.

They also swapped or exchanged cigarette cards known as 'generals'. There was also a wonderful series of *'Do You Know'* and *'Cries of London'*. A weekend chore for them was polishing knives, forks and spoons on a scouring board. The sweet shop on the corner sold aniseed balls, humbugs and halfpenny gobstoppers that changed colour with every few sucks.

Wire-rimmed glasses and spectacles came from the sixpenny bazaar. A cry of 'ripe bananas' came from barrow boys, and weekend joints were sold by butchers at Saturday night giveaway prices. Horse dealers trotted their horses up and down the side streets under the watchful eye of would-be buyers, and sheep and cows, being driven from the market to the slaughterhouse, would dirty the streets.

An occasional escaped bull would run amok, causing excitement and scattering pedestrians in all directions. My playground, St. Georges Park, was where many ex-professional soccer players - such as Billy Coggins, Walt Jennings and Ted Hathway - booted red rubber gaskin balls about on the grass.

Even Bob Hope, in later life America's king jester, sought pleasure in the park. He, like many other youngsters, fished for tiddlers in the lake and quenched his thirst from the chained copper cup water fountain at Park Crescent.

But each morning I left this world behind me as I boarded a tram to the Centre to take up my duties - a long 12-hour day working at the hotel. Alongside the docks, by the city Centre, was ex-Bristol and England rugby player Sam Tucker. By day a foreman docker, he would stand on a box and select his men for the day's work. Hundreds more, with cigarette in mouth, would miserably disperse to idle away yet another day of unemployment.

At the top of Park Street was the Princes Theatre, destroyed in the Blitz of 1940. Pauline Frederick, the silent film star and stage star, made an appearance there in the late 1920s after a two-week run of The Wandering Jew featuring that very famous actor Matheson Lang. It was Miss Frederick's manager who offered me a film test at the Fox Studios in Hollywood. It was all very exciting - until my parents objected and dashed forever my hopes of seeing Charlie Chaplin, Jackie Coogan, Ruth Roland, Tom Mix and William S. Hart in real life.

The Royal Hotel, College Green, Bristol.

My wages at the hotel were six shillings a week, but tips gave me an average of £2 per week. At Christmas the kindly chairman of the board of directors handed me a gift of two brand new half-crowns (25p)

Bert Hinkler and Captain McIntosh, two famous aviators of the time, often joked with me. One day they even signed my autograph book. I remember seeing Yehudi Menuhin, and I became friendly with Will Hay's son, who often accompanied his father.

When a famous film star tried to make her presence in the city a secret, it was no mystery to me how it became known to Bristol readers. Old Bill Hooper, at the Princes Theatre stage door, was a well-known personality. Known as Larry Lynx, he obtained good information about horses from stage personalities. His tips seldom failed.

On classic race days, such as the Derby or Lincoln, I would pluck a pigeon from Dad's racing loft and transport it to the hotel in a box. I had a pigeon post operating. Gambling of any kind was forbidden in the pub, so the gent's toilet was used, with bets often written on the back of a cigarette packet.

Mamoud, a Derby winner, proved one of Bill's certs.

My autograph book was stuffed with names - Yehudi Menuhin, Larry Gains, Layton and Johnstone, George Formby, Houdini, Nellie Wallace, Ella Shields, Henry Ainley, Richard Tauber, Talbot O'Farrel, G. S. Elliot, Kreisler, Mona Vivian, Flotsam and Jetsam and many others. But the book, just like the Princes Theatre, was burned in the Blitz. Now, those big names are just a memory."

One lovely story about Gilbert, related by one of his grandsons, was that he entered a competition during the 1930s that a 'Guinness Stout' campaign was running. They wanted a new slogan and he suggested *"Guinness Gives You Strength"* but he did not win. However new posters and beermats started to appear using *"Guinness For Strength"*, which he was not happy with - he felt cheated out of his £5 prize money.

Gilbert insisted he saw a ghost once at the top of the stairs of the Rising Sun pub. Gilbert was climbing the stairs one evening and saw a dark figure stood at the top of the stairs, and as he looked up at it just disappeared. He then climbed the rest of the stairs and there was no sign of anyone up there – although one does suspect that this might have been a prank on him, pulled by another family member!

An early picture of Gilbert Morgan (L) with sister Grace and their parents James and Elizabeth.

Wedding photograph of Gilbert and Betty, 29th July 1937. Taken at the back of the 'Rising Sun' in Church Road, Redfield, Bristol.

He married Florence Elizabeth (Betty) Rogers (born 24th December 1916, Bristol; died 21st July 2011, Bristol, aged 94) on 29th July 1937, at St Matthews Moorfields, St. George, Bristol. Gilbert's address was recorded as 168 Church Road, Redfield (The 'Rising Sun') and his occupation shown as being a Telephonist. Florence's address at the time was 4 Albert Street, Bristol, with no occupation recorded.

Gilbert was another keen footballer, playing for the Morgan Family football team when required.

Gilbert continued the family tradition of running Public Houses by becoming a short-term landlord of the "Wellington Arms" at 4 Wellington Place, Clifton, from October 1937 until sometime in 1938. Sadly the venture was not a success and his career as a landlord ended at that point.

The 1939 Register shows Gilbert and Betty living at 21 Kingsway, a street they would live in for the rest of their lives. Gilbert was recorded as being a 'Clerk at Aeroplane Works', and Betty undertaking unpaid domestic duties.

They relocated to 85 Kingsway after the war.

On 11th May 1953, Gilbert was featured in the local newspaper:

"Out for a walk on Syston Common, Mr. Gilbert Thomas Morgan, 85 Kingsway, Two Mile Hill, heard a report which sounded like a rifle shot.

Rounding a corner he saw milk pouring from a bullet-hole in the side of a milk-churn outside Mill Farm, Syston Common. While the farmer was being called, Mr. Morgan put his finger in the hole preventing any further wastage until the milk could be transferred to another churn.

Inside the damaged churn was a bullet. Staple Hill police were called, and are investigating.

Staple Hill police do not associate this incident with the report from a Kingswood man that last week he and his fiancée were fired at while walking at Hanham."

The Wellington Arms, date unknown. Now a private dwelling.

As previously mentioned, Gilbert was a keen member of the Morgan family football team, and he became involved in local football in the area. In fact in a letter published in August 1954 he was ahead of his time in highlighting the issues within the amateur game, a situation which still continues to this day:

"Mr. G. T. Morgan, 85 Kingsway, Kingswood, who says he is the Bristol representative of West Ham United, has written to me and below I give extracts from his letter:

English soccer is faced with a graver problem than the need for a new look training programme for professional clubs, and that is the decline in influence of amateur football. Amateur club secretaries have to scratch round to find money to buy new shirts and other match kit. This is not peculiar only to the West Country but England as a whole.

Our breeding grounds everywhere are dying a slow death. Better amateurs will lead to better professionals and if we give the amateur game more encouragement, we shall be doing something worthwhile and helping to put English soccer back on its pedestal."

Gilbert had built up an excellent relationship with West Ham United F.C., setting up a club for youngsters between the ages of 9 and 11 called 'West Ham United Juniors". Proof of his work with the club came in a poor-quality photograph and press report from September 1954:

"Young Roger Bennett, under the watchful eye of the coach, G. T. Morgan, demonstrates to his colleagues of West Ham United Juniors how to approach the ball for a free-kick before the trial match at the Kingswood Training Ground.

Mr. Morgan has formed West Ham United Juniors from boys between 9 and 11 years from all parts of Kingswood. He is to coach them and let them watch as much senior football as possible."

It appears that the club did not play in any local leagues but played a series of friendly matches against local clubs and charity matches in the Bristol area, including one against the Bristol City Ladies' Supporters team.

The club was visited by the West Ham Manager, Ted Fenton, along with England international Harry Hooper in January 1955, when the league club were in Bristol to play Bristol Rovers in a Division 2 fixture.

The club received plenty of interest both locally and nationally, and two of its players, Roger Bennett and Roger Lane, appeared on the BBC's 'In Town Tonight' on 12th February 1955.

The latter raised a few eyebrows when asked about the predicament of having broken one of his bootlaces; he simply replied that he "replaced it with one from Mum's corsets".

The club's secretary was Maureen Morgan, one of the daughters of Gilbert and Betty, and one of the players was one of their other sons, Peter, who later played for the Morgan Family team.

The West Ham United Juniors team meet Ted Fenton and Harry Hooper of the West Ham United league team. Gilbert's son Peter Morgan is receiving words of advice from Harry Hooper.

The club continued until 1960, when following interest from the Bristol City F.C. Manager Peter Doherty, the name of the club was changed to Bristol City Wasps.

In 1955, Gilbert wrote a fascinating letter to the *'Bristol Evening Post'*, mentioning plenty of local landmarks and history which may have passed many people by:

"How many Bristolians know that on the three-and-a-half-mile walk alongside the Avon between Netham and the Chequers at Hanham, there is a ferry reputed to be one of the oldest in the land?

Mr. Gilbert T. Morgan, of 85 The Kingsway, set out with his three children this week to walk this stretch of the Avon to find out all he could of the historical features on either side of the river and to talk with the folk who live there. A member of the famous Morgan football family, who ran their own football team for years and raised large sums for Bristol hospitals with the charity games they organised and played in, Mr. Morgan is a scout for West Ham United.

One of his complaints about Bristolians is that they do not know enough about their city and flock readily to the seaside or country when in or very near the city are interesting walks. "In the old days, the paths along the river between Brislington and Hanham used to be thronged with people on fine summer evenings. Now one only sees children playing in the river, a few fishermen and a handful of walkers" he says.

"We had an afternoon packed with interest" says Mr. Morgan. "We saw some wonderful scenery and some items of genuine historical interest. Barges moored alongside the St. Anne's Board Mills first attracted their attention. Over 30 years ago they had quite a different cargo to carry. Once a year, children from the local Sunday school were towed up river by a tug boat. Hanham Mills was a kiddies' paradise in those days"

Then came the Blackswarth Road-St. Anne's ferry, reputed to be among the oldest ferries in England patronised by monks many centuries ago. King Henry VII crossed the ferry on his way to church at St Anne's, Pilgrims walked down Blackswarth Road and crossed this ferry on their way to St Anne's Chapel and Holywell.

Some things mystified Mr. Morgan. What is the history of the building whose frontage can be seen from the water's edge of the Avon? It is set in the ground at the side of the Avonview Cemetery. It may be a bath house, probably of 18th-century origin. The water wells up from the sandy floor.

"At the bottom of Strawberry Lane, St. George, we found a kiln. It was very small in comparison with those used in present day pottery work.

The history of the kiln was interesting. A gentleman named Anthony Amatt, who was born in Derby, built two kilns on this site of which only one is now visible. This all happened in 1808 and he sold his pottery for years from a handcart to local residents. The last use for the kiln I was told was as a home for pigeons"

Many Bristolians believe Troopers' Hill was the scene of a big battle many years ago, and took its name from such an event. This is not so, according to Mr. Morgan. Back in 1600 this hill, with its small chimney stack at the top, was known as Truebody's Hill, and alternatively as Harris Hill. It was within the King's forest (which was to give Kingswood its name), and stone lifted from this place was used to build the Wesleyan Memorial Church at White's Hill, St. George. Up through the centre of the hill from the river, there was at one time an underground tunnel to the stack to dispose of the fumes from the old copper works which once stood near the Bristol end of where William Butler's works now stand.

In 1894 the River Avon overflowed its banks and great floods occurred. Mr. Morgan and his family found the level recorded on the office wall at Butler's.

The river bends sharply at Conham Hall, and here is a second ferry to be found on the walk. Since 1846 it has been taking people over to the tea gardens on the Somerset side of the river. Just beyond Conham is the quarry from which in the old days, metal ore was mined. But there is no ore produced there now. Quarrying was a big industry in this part of the valley, and between Brislington and Hanham there were once eight quarries. And so the Morgans passed on to Hencliffe Woods, past picturesque riverside cottages, and to Hanham Lock, the Chequers, and its famous ferry which in olden times belonged to the Abbey at Keynsham."

In 1959, Gilbert made an attempt to reform his beloved "West Ham Juniors" football club which had become defunct a few years previously. In typical fashion, he used the local press to publicise his plans:

"A school for soccer stardom is being formed in Bristol by a former scout for West Ham United.

The man behind the school is Mr. G. T. Morgan, 85 Kingsway, Kingswood – one of Bristol's famous footballing family – who is inviting players between 12 and 14 and who have footballing ability, to write to him at his home. All he wants at the moment is their age and position on the field.

Mr. Morgan said that the name of the school will be West Ham Juniors and that they will wear a strip in the 'Hammers' colours. He added that the boys he is particularly interested in are sons of professional or part-time footballers.

This year West Ham Juniors will be content with friendly games but, said Mr. Morgan, it is hoped to arrange games with Continental sides which are visiting this country at Easter."

He was always an enthusiastic letter-writer and many of his compositions with regard to local history continued to appear in the local press. One such letter, looking back on the Redfield district of Bristol, appeared on 22nd December 1966:

"Gone are the tipplers, the tumblers and the racing pigeons that hovered and fluttered over Derby Street, Redfield. Gone too, the humble dwellings and the people of many generations who lived there. Here down this street existed really true comradeship. Everyone shared another's troubles and misfortunes. Literally they were one.

Gone are the white-laced pinafores and women wearing their husbands' caps with a long steel hatpin through at the top; the rattle and rumble of the tramcars and the chinkle of glass marbles along the gutter. Gone are the gas-lit streets and the lamplighter, the Welsh cockle-seller in national costume, that occasional swop of cigarette cards, the ringing note of steel hoops along the pavement, the horse and cart and the chant of "Will, Will, whip behind".

It is with regret that I found my birthplace at the Rising Sun, Redfield is awaiting demolition. Over 200 years old, the Rising Sun was kept by my people. For more than 40 years it was a hive of sports - soccer teams, quoits, darts, tug o' war and racing pigeons. My father James was a high ranking name in the pigeon world. His pigeons did war service in the First World War and flew north to Lerwick in the Shetland Islands, some 606 miles and on the South Road to San Sebastian, in Spain.

With the closing of the Rising Sun I feel the loss of something dear to me."

In addition to his historical work, it would appear that Gilbert was very much a keen inventor; in fact he invented a new-style numeral for identifying individual houses. Basically a fluorescent stick-on numeral which he called 'Florie', he claimed it would meet the need for modern colour schemes prevalent at the time. He explained:

"After experimenting over many months with colour, scores of adhesives, weather changes and other factors, I have succeeded in maintaining a fluorescent colour for the numerals over a long period."

The numerals could be attached to the freestone on the right of the door (the best position for a house number) in a second, and no screws are drilling were required. Some houses in the area used these numerals, but it is not known how successful they were elsewhere.

Gilbert worked at the BAC in Filton and was also a shop steward; he was very keen to become involved with social activities, and captained the Bowling team. He was featured in the *Bristol Evening Post*'s 'Green 'Un' sports newspaper on 5th July 1958.

> GILBERT MORGAN, of 85, Kingsway, Kingswood, who skippered Bristol Aircraft to victory in the rinks contest at the B.A.C. sports day competitions last Saturday.

Gilbert Morgan, 1958.

The same year, he reached the fifth round of the Weston-super-Mare Open Bowling Tournament, only narrowly losing to a strong Welsh entrant, T. J. Owen.

By the early 1970s he was still heavily involved with youth football, and with his relative Les Garland he helped to create a new under-13 team at Syston, near Bristol. The local press recorded his work on 25th August 1971:

'RAGS TO RICHES'

"Take a load of jumble, a field of stubble, a dozen 13-year-olds, some guiding adults, and what have you got…..a football club.

That's all it took out at Webb's Heath, Warmley, to create a new junior side to be called Syston United. The youngsters gathered the jumble while the adults, led by farmer Jim Dursley, tackled the stubble.

The lads, organised by planner-in-chief Les Garland, raised over £13. Gilbert Morgan, of Kingsway, Kingswood, who told me of Syston United, recalls back in the 1940's, a group of youngsters at Barton Hill were given 11 sugar sacks by their manager Jack Beese.

Their parents cut them into shirts, and then had them dyed. The team became known as Sugar Bag Juniors.

Perhaps the Syston lads, who have entered the Bath and Bristol Sunday League, will become known as Jumble Sale United."

An evocative photograph of Gilbert and Betty.

He became heavily involved with the Concorde project, and in 1974 he was featured in the *'Western Daily Press'* when he started to compile a history of the Company from the Bristol Boxkite leading up to Concorde. He had been off work due to ill-health but worked on this 'Hall of Fame' during his time at home.

The feature read:

'GOING SUPERSONIC'

Mr. Morgan's one-man Hall of Fame.

While the might of the British Government and the giant aircraft industry battle over the life or death decision of Concorde, Mr. Gilbert Morgan has made his own contribution to the cause.

Mr. Morgan is not a Government minister, nor can he command a vast trade union following.

To most people he is just one of the thousands of workers who have helped build the supersonic aircraft; a small cog in the giant wheel that has made Concorde a world leader.

But now 62-year-old Mr. Morgan has started his own one-man fight against the huge forces that want Concorde destroyed.

And he is a firm believer in building for the future with Concorde.

So, when ill-health struck, and Mr. Morgan had to down tools as BAC worker and shop steward, his efforts for Concorde did not stop.

He spent patient hours at his home in Kingsway, Kingswood, Bristol, preparing a special dossier of the aircraft which led up to Concorde's feat of technology.

"I thought of compiling a history of the Bristol Aeroplane Company and British Aircraft Corporation when I first went off work sick. I wanted something to do, and this kept me enthusiastic", said Mr. Morgan, a shop steward of the Association of Professional and Executive Staffs.

In his history of aircraft, Mr. Morgan writes: "It can be said that Concorde is the great great grandson of Boxkite, the first aircraft to be built in Bristol."

"The cancellation of Concorde would mean that the final curtain would come down on all future aircraft built in Bristol."

Mr. Morgan runs through the entire history of Bristol planemaking, from the days of the 1910 Boxkite, just six years after the Wright Brothers' first flight.

What is now the massive BAC, was then housed in a few sheds and houses on two acres of land in Filton, Bristol.

"From the start, the Bristol company took a leading position among aircraft manufacturers," says Mr. Morgan.

He lists the Bristol Fighter F2B, which was launched in 1916, the M1C monoplane and the Braemar bomber as some of the fighters which helped Britain to win World War One.

"At the outbreak of war in 1939, Bristol was making a major contribution to the RAF's growing strength. From that day forward, Bristol aircraft and engines were constantly in action."

Finally, Mr. Morgan's Hall of Fame reaches modern technology, and the Olympus high-thrust engine, now used the RAF Vulcan bombers.

"Take a walk down the first 50 years of the Bristol Planemaker's Hall of Fame, and ask how would Britain have fared without this industry during two world wars," he says."

Gilbert died on 6th May 1975 in Bristol, aged 63, and was buried at Avonview Cemetery, Bristol, on 9th May 1975. Betty died on 21st July 2011 in Bristol, aged 94, and was buried alongside her husband.

The headstone displays Gilbert's work as a scout for West Ham Football Club. Their son James is also remembered on the headstone.

Gilbert as featured in the 'Hall of Fame' article from 17th June 1974.

The grave of Gilbert and Betty Morgan, along with their child James Michael, Avonview Cemetery, Bristol.

GILBERT AND BETTY'S CHILDREN:

- **James Michael Morgan** (born 15th November 1937, Bristol died 1st December 1938 in Bristol aged only 7 weeks).

James was buried at Avonview Cemetery, Bristol, on 5th December 1938. He is commemorated on both the Morgan family grave and also on the grave of his parents.

- **Maureen Elizabeth Morgan** (born 27th December 1939, Bristol; died 14th September 2010, Bristol, aged 70).
- **Gillian Anne Morgan** (born 15th August 1943, Bristol).
- **Peter Gilbert Morgan** (born 12th February 1947, Bristol; died 13th January 2023, Bristol, aged 75).

Peter was very active in promoting the music of Eddie Cochran and was President of the Appreciation Society (West Country Branch) for many years.

He followed in his father's footsteps with plenty of his letters being published in the local press, mainly dealing with his beloved rock'n'roll hero, but also trying to highlight the lack of youth facilities and TV programming in the area.

He regularly campaigned for a memorial to Eddie Cochran in Bath and Chippenham, where the singer was sadly killed, and he wrote numerous articles about the singer for specialist magazines. He also wrote sleeve notes for many of Eddie Cochran's posthumously-released LPs.

In 1984, however, his dreams of erecting a statue to his hero were dashed when expected funding did not materialise; the *'Bristol Evening Post'* carried the news:

"Peter Morgan's dream of putting up a statue of his rock'n'roll idol Eddie Cochran has been shattered.

Peter, a 37-year-old Rolls-Royce Clerk, started a memorial fund two years ago. But he is nowhere near reaching the £5,000 needed for the bronze statue, and the support he had hoped for from record companies, music publishers and the music press was not forthcoming.

He is arranging the return of the £160 he has collected."

Another interest of his was the Girls and Boys Life Brigade in Kingswood, Bristol, of which he was the founder, and he helped to raise money for them to run a Bugle Band. He was proud of his achievements in this work and even wrote to the Queen, telling her of his success; he was very pleased to receive a reply from a member of the Royal Staff at Windsor Castle, wishing the band all success.

He was also a talented footballer, playing for various local sides and the Morgan family team in the 1960s. He also supported Bath City for many years, and was also a keen supporter of Somerset County Cricket Club.

He was buried at Avonview Cemetery, Bristol, on 22nd February 2023.

- **Philip James Nelson Morgan** (born 4th July 1948, Bristol; died 12th October 2020, Bristol, aged 72).

Philip married Valerie J. Brown (born 19th March 1956; died 31st May 2015, Bristol, aged 59) in 1977, at St. John's Church, Chipping Sodbury, near Bristol. They had three children.

He was a great fan of Elvis Presley, and often recorded himself singing many of his songs. He also thoroughly enjoyed ghost-hunting, something which he no doubt got from his father; apparently his father Gilbert saw a ghost at the top of the stairs of the 'Rising Sun' pub when he was young, which disappeared into thin air when he approached it.

He loved to play snooker and pool, and was regularly to be found at local clubs and pubs, playing against his friends and children.

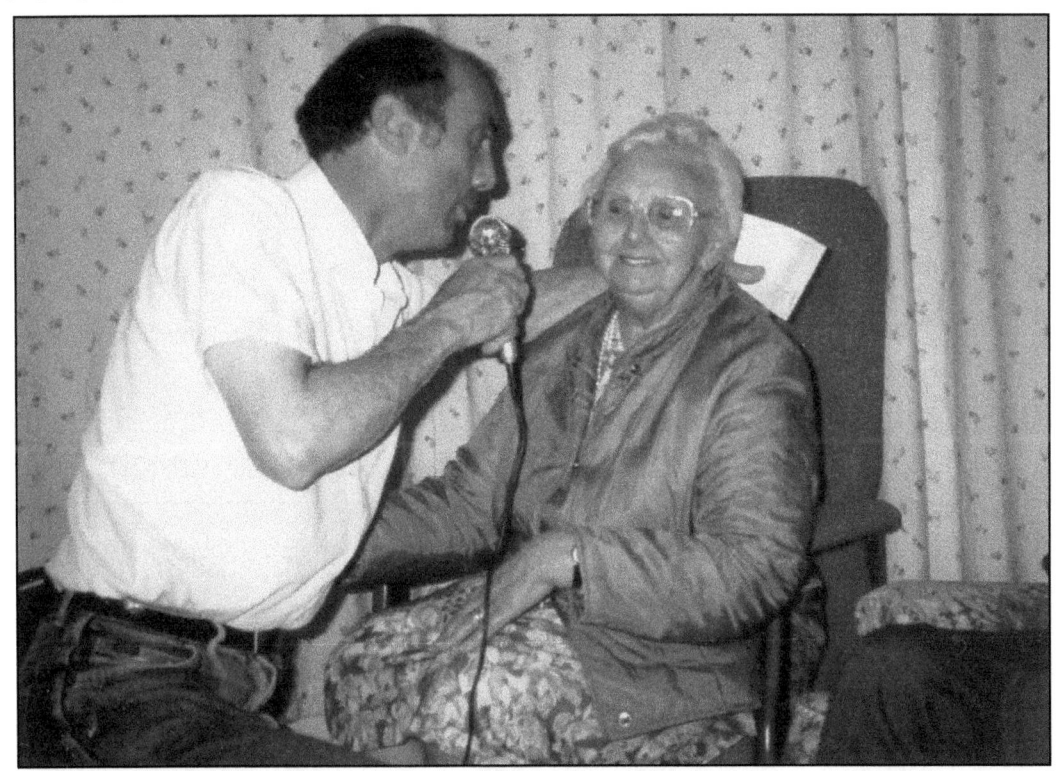

Philip Morgan serenading his mother Betty. Photograph courtesy of Philip's family.

7. Grace Eveline Alice Morgan.

Grace married Arthur Stanley Hodge (Born 12th February 1914, Bristol; died 23rd March 1984, Bristol, aged 70) at St. Ambrose Church, Whitehall, Bristol on 27th September 1937. Both Grace and Arthur were living at 253 Church Road, Redfield, at the time of their marriage. This was also the address of Grace's elder sister Lilian.

Arthur was better known as 'Stan' in the family, and as 'Uncle Stan' to many of us.

Grace on the beach with nieces Joy and Barbara, early-mid 1930s.

The wedding of Grace and Stan, St. Ambrose Church, Whitehall, Bristol, 27th September 1937.

They had no children.

By the time of the 1939 Register, Grace and Stan were living at 168 Church Road, Bristol, better known as the Rising Sun public house, where Stan worked as a 'Leather Finisher and Victualler'. Stan took over the running of the Rising Sun from that year when his mother-in-law Elizabeth Morgan decided to retire.

For many years in the 1960s and 1970s, Grace ran 'The Wool Shop' in Church Road, which regularly acted as a meeting point for family members in the area, with plenty of tea and biscuits (or cake) being made readily available in the back room of the shop.

The family home was at 61 Queen's Road, St. George, Bristol, and was a regular location for family gatherings and Christmas parties over the years. As many of Grace's family lived in the immediate neighbourhood, her home was an obvious choice as a family meeting place, and she was a particularly friendly and welcoming host.

Grace's mother, Elizabeth, also lived there for the final years of her life.

Stan died on 23rd March 1984 in Bristol, aged 70, and was buried at Greenbank Cemetery, Bristol, on 26th March 1984.

Grace died on 4th June 2004, at the Bristol Royal Infirmary, aged 88. She was cremated at Westerleigh Crematorium, Bristol, on 10th June 2004.

The Wool Shop, Church Road, Bristol.

Grace with one of her great-nieces, St. Georges Park, c. 1967

Grace and Stan in later years.

CHAPTER 8.
THE FAMILY AND DESCENDANTS OF JOHN (JACK) MORGAN.

John was born at 5 Tarr's Court, Lawrence Hill, Bristol, on 10th February 1874, with his father's occupation recorded as a Stoker at Coal Works. John was baptised on 22nd April 1874 at Holy Trinity Church, St. Philips, Bristol. His parents' address was recorded as Tarr's Court, Bristol, and his father's occupation noted as being a Fireman.

John (Jack) Morgan (10th February 1874-1944).

John (sometimes known as Jack) married Sarah Tranter (born 20th January 1872; died 1st February 1951, Bristol, aged 79), on 25th November 1894 at St. Luke's Church, Barton Hill, Bristol. They had seven children:

1. **John Morgan** (born 21st April 1895, Bristol; died 24th October 1959, Bristol, aged 64).

2. **George James (Nicky) Morgan** (born 18th December 1896, Bristol; died 10th April 1977, Bristol, aged 80).

3. **William Henry Morgan** (born 20th July 1898, Bristol; died 17th May 1971, Bristol, aged 72).

4. **Reuben Edward Morgan** (born 22nd November 1904, 16 Tichborne Street, Barton Hill, Bristol; died 20th July 1983, Bristol aged 78).

5. **Lillian Rosina Morgan** (born 18th September 1908, Bristol; died 2002, St. Austell, aged 93).

6. **Florence Beatrice Morgan** (born 30th September 1910, Bristol; died 4th January 1992, aged 81).

7. **Alice Violet Morgan** (born 25th April 1918, Bristol; died 14th November 2007, Bristol, aged 89).

The 1901 Census shows Sarah and her three eldest children living at 5 Tichborne Street, Barton Hill, Bristol, along with Sarah's mother Amy Tranter and Sarah's brothers Reuben, Amy and John. Sarah shown as working at the time as a Cotton Spinner.

By the time of the 1911 Census, John had returned and the family had moved down the road to 16 Tichborne Street, Barton Hill, Bristol. The whole family was recorded as having occupations, John being an out-of-work Labourer at the Gas Works, son John being a Chocolate Cream Maker, and son George being a Soap Packer at the local Soap Factory. A lodger by the name of Ada Lewis, a Cotton Spinner, was noted as living with the family at this time.

By 1921, the family were still at the Barton Hill address of 16 Tichborne Street, John recorded as being a Dock Labourer, and son George a General Labourer at John Lysaghts Galvanising Works, a well-known local employer,

The family made the local papers on 22nd August 1933, when it was reported that:

"John Morgan (59), of Tichborne Street, Barton Hill, Bristol, was fined £2 and ordered to pay 30 shillings costs at Bristol Police Court yesterday for keeping a betting house. His son. John Morgan, Jr. (39), of Andover Road, Knowle, who was accused of aiding and abetting was discharged, the magistrates saying they would give him the benefit of the doubt.

Police officers gave evidence keeping observation on the father's house at Tichborne Street, and seeing a number of people go there. Subsequently the police raided and searched the house, and a number of horse-racing betting slips and football coupons were found. John Morgan Sr. admitted the charge, but his son denied the accusation against him, stating that his presence at his father's house was in the course of ordinary visits."

The 1939 Register shows the family still at 16 Tichborne Street, Barton Hill, where John had found employment as a Dock Labourer, Sarah undertaking domestic duties, George employed as a Dipper in the Metal Trade, William a Builder's Labourer, Reuben a Tinker in the Metal Trade, and Alice a Cardboard Box Maker.

John died on 3rd November 1944, at Snowdon Buildings, Bristol, aged 70, and was buried at Avonview Cemetery, Bristol, on 10th November 1944.

Sarah died on 1st February 1951, aged 74, also in Bristol, and was buried alongside her husband on 8th February 1951. She received an obituary in the *'Bristol Evening Post'* on 2nd February 1951:

'MRS. S. MORGAN'

"Mrs. Sarah Morgan (75), on 16 Tichborne Street, Barton Hill, whose death has occurred, was the mother of four well-known footballers.

Her husband, the late Mr. Jack Morgan, was also a footballer, and four of her six nephews played professionally for various clubs.

Mrs. Morgan had lived in the same street all her life."

JOHN AND SARAH'S CHILDREN:

1.   John Morgan.

John was baptised on 10th January 1897 at St. Philip & Jacob Church, Bristol. His parents' address was vaguely recorded as 'Barton Hill', and his father's occupation noted as being a Labourer.

He served as a private in the Norfolk Regiment during WW1 (service number 28634) and his home address during his time of service was recorded as 16 Tichborne Street, Barton Hill, Bristol. He was discharged on 24th August 1917, and it was noted he was suffering from 'Otitis Media', inflammation of the middle ear, attributed to his war service.

He was another talented footballer and was first noticed playing for Fishponds City in a match against Bristol City in the 1917/1918 season. In fact he scored the winning goal for the Fishponds team in a 1-0 victory, and signed for Bristol City shortly afterwards.

Bristol City Football Club, 1919-20. Johnny Morgan 3rd from right, front row.

He married Alice Lily (Lillian) Allen (born 1st December 1893, Bristol; died 3rd January 1980, Bristol, aged 86) on 20th October 1919, at St. Paul's Church, Bedminster, Bristol.

The wedding of John Morgan and Alice Allen, 20th October 1919.

At the time of their marriage, John was living at 29 Philip Street, Bristol, and Alice at 37 Essex Court, Bristol. John's occupation was listed as being a Footballer.

The 1921 Census reveals that John, Alice and Edna were living with Alice's parents, George and Alice Allen, at 29 Philip Street, Bedminster, Bristol. Also recorded on the Census was Victor Raymond Allen, shown as the youngest son of George and Alice (Alice's parents) but in reality he was the son of their daughter Alice. Inspection of Victor's birth certificate confirms the mother as Alice Lilian Allen, a Tailoress, of 23 East Street, Bristol with no mention of the father's name. It would appear that Victor was brought up by Alice's parents.

Victor was born on 14th September 1913 at 23 East Street, Bristol, and married Alice Irene Hughes (born 8th October 1910, Knowle, Bristol; died 11th April 1982, Bristol, aged 71).

They had two children:

- **Raymond A. H. Allen** (born 1940, Bristol; died 7th November 2016, aged 76).
- **Rita Edna Miriam Allen** (born 10th November 1944, Bristol; died 8th January 2010, Bristol, aged 65).

It is nice to see Rita named after her half-sisters Edna and Miriam. She was featured in the local newspapers on 6th August 1963 when she became the 5,000th bride at St. Barnabas Church, Knowle, Bristol in 25 years.

Victor's baptism information from 9th October 1913 at St. Paul's Church, Bedminster, is interesting as it names his father as Hubert Allen, with his mother correctly recorded as Alice Allen. One would suspect this may not be correct as 'Hubert' was not named on the birth certificate, and the name was possibly a ruse to obtain permission from the church for the child to be baptised.

By all accounts, Victor led an 'interesting life' and appeared in the local newspapers on a regular basis:

19th May 1947: At Weston-super-Mare Magistrates Court, Victor Raymond Allen, of 6 Firfield Street, Totterdown, Bristol, was jointly charged with Harold Wills, of 401 Wells Road, Totterdown, Bristol, and another man at present unknown, with breaking out of a dwelling-house of Tom Rees Jones, St. James' Street, Weston-super-Mare, after having stolen an attache case, deed box, a quantity of personal papers and about £56 in money – together valued at £250.

They were remanded until May 30, bail being allowed in personal sureties of £50.

The accused had been brought before the Magistrates the previous evening, when Detective-Constable Overy (Flax Bourton) stated that following a report that some persons had broken out of the Globe Hotel, St. James' Street, Weston-super-Mare, he met the Weston-Bristol train at Flax Bourton.

He questioned the accused in a compartment, and they accompanied him to Flax Bourton police station, where he charged them.

Police Superintendent H. J. Baker said there were further enquiries to be made relating to a third man and the property, only a small amount of which had been recovered.

16th May 1956: "That's a bit stiff sir", protested a Knowle West man to the chairman of the magistrates, Mr. S. W. Evans, after he had been fined £5 in Bristol today for stealing tea at Avonmouth Docks.

Victor Raymond Allen (42), 29 Torrington Avenue, pleaded guilty to a charge which related to 8s 3d worth of tea which had fallen out of damaged packing cases. He explained that he had had a poor week's wages and thought in the circumstances it was a "shame to let all that tea lying on the floor. I was hoping to get away with it, but unfortunately was challenged".

Det-Insp. George Cox said that Allen had been sent to prison for burglary, nine years ago.

24th December 1965: Victor Raymond Allen (51) of Torrington Avenue, Knowle, was fined £10 with £2 2s costs in Bristol today when he admitted stealing a half bottle of whisky worth £1 2s 6d from Sainsbury's.

Victor died on 16th June 1995, in Bristol, aged 81.

Returning to the 1921 Census, John's occupation was shown as a professional footballer at Bristol City Football Club, Ashton Gate.

Official records held by Bristol City F.C. confirm that he played in 7 matches during the 1917/18 season, scoring 10 goals, 5 in friendly matches, and 5 in the Bristol County Combination League. As mentioned earlier he signed for Bristol City after appearing against them for Fishponds City earlier that season.

In the 1918/19 season he played in 10 League (Bristol County Combination) matches and 24 friendly matches during the 1918/19 season, scoring 12 League goals and 15 friendly goals, including three 'hat-tricks'.

On 1st February 1919 he scored against local rivals Bristol Rovers in a 2-2 draw; his goal being recorded as: "Morgan gave the City the lead with a magnificent header, this goal being the best of the match."

Details of his appearances are shown in the table below:

Date	Team played	League	Goals
LEAGUE MATCHES			
9 March 1918	Bristol Rovers	Bristol County Combination	1
30 March 1918	Royal Engineers (Portbury)	Bristol County Combination	4
20th April 1918	Royal Engineers (White City)	Bristol County Combination	0
12 October 1918	Royal Engineers (White City)	Bristol County Combination	3
19 October 1918	Royal Engineers (Portbury)	Bristol County Combination	1
2 November 1918	Tractor Depot	Bristol County Combination	3
9 November 1918	RAF Filton	Bristol County Combination	1
16 November 1918	Bristol Dockers	Bristol County Combination	0
7 December 1918	Royal Engineers (Portbury)	Bristol County Combination	1
26 December 1918	Bristol Rovers	Bristol County Combination	0
8 February 1919	RAVC	Bristol County Combination	0
15 February 1919	Bristol Dockers	Bristol County Combination	3

| 21 April 1919 | Bristol Rovers | Bristol County Combination | 0 |

FRIENDLY MATCHES			
23 March 1918	RFA Larkhill	Friendly	2
29 March 1918	Bristol Rovers	Friendly	1
1 April 1918	Bristol Rovers	Friendly	1
11 May 1918	Cardiff City	Friendly	1
14 September 1918	Bristol Rovers	Friendly	0
21 September 1918	Douglas Brothers	Friendly	1
28 September 1918	RAF Reading	Friendly	1
5 October 1918	Bristol Rovers	Friendly	2
26 October 1918	Bristol Rovers	Friendly	0
23 November 1918	RAF Yate	Friendly	1
30 November 1918	Bristol Rovers	Friendly	0
14 December 1918	Timsbury Athletic	Friendly	1
21 December 1918	Douglas Brothers	Friendly	2
25 December 1918	Bristol Rovers	Friendly	1
4 January 1919	Ex-Servicemen	Friendly	2
11 January 1919	BC Aero Company	Friendly	0
18 January 1919	Fishponds City	Friendly	1
25 January 1919	Wedlocks XI	Friendly	0
1 February 1919	Bristol Rovers	Friendly	1
1 March 1919	Horfield United	Friendly	0
8 March 1919	Bristol Rovers	Friendly	1
15 March 1919	Wedlock's XI	Friendly	0
22 March 1919	Bristol Dockers	Friendly	0

29 March 1919	Ebbw Vale	Friendly	0
2 April 1919	Bristol Rovers	Friendly	0
5 April 1919	Bristol Rovers	Friendly	0
18 April 1919	Bristol Rovers	Friendly	0
3 May 1919	South Mid Field Amb.	Friendly	0
10 May 1919	Bristol Rovers	Friendly	0
24 May 1919	Bristol Rovers	Friendly	1

One interesting comment appeared after the match against RAF (Yate) on 23rd November 1918; it was reported that "Morgan, who was due play for West Ham, turned out for City as he missed his train."

It could be that this missed train may well have changed the course of his football career.

It was reported in the local press in May 1919 that he had signed for Bristol City for the following season:

"Bristol City and Bristol Rovers' directors are both finding their players extremely coy with regard to signing on for next season, and especially does that apply to players who were professionals in the service of the clubs in pre-war days.

Notably is that the case with Bristol City who, however, have signed J. Morgan, who was their chief goal-scorer in the season just closed."

He later signed for Caerphilly Town and then Bristol Rovers but seemingly never made a first team appearance for the latter. With around 100 players 'signed on' by the club (including amateur players), the lack of first-team opportunities wasn't unexpected. However, he played for and captained the Morgan Family football team in later years.

They had two children:

- **Edna Lilian Kathleen Morgan** (born 6th September 1920, Bristol; died 15th December 1996, Bristol, aged 76).
- **Miriam Morgan** (born 21st March 1927, Bristol; died 22nd November 1996, Bath & N.E. Somerset, aged 69).

The 1939 Register reveals that the family were living at 7 Andover Road, Knowle, Bristol, where John is listed as being a Police Guard at Whitchurch.

After the war he was noted as living at Hilltop House, 265 Redcatch Road, Knowle, Bristol.

It was reported in the local press on 12th September 1959 that John had been taken ill:

'JOHNNY MORGAN IN HOSPITAL'

"Johnny Morgan, of Hilltop House, 265 Redcatch Road, Knowle, Bristol, who is now at Frenchay Hospital, played for Bristol City in Charity Cup games and friendly matches during the First World War.

In 1918-19, with 25 goals in 17 games, he was their top scorer, completing a couple of hat-tricks.

On occasions he also played for Bristol Rovers for whom later his younger brother Jerry was a most useful inside-forward. John Morgan also captained the famous Morgan Family team."

Sadly, John died on 24th October 1959, in Bristol, aged 64, and he was buried at Avonview Cemetery, Bristol, on 28th October 1959.

John's passing was reported in the *'Bristol Evening Post'* with a detailed (if partly inaccurate) obituary.

'A FOOTBALLING MORGAN DIES'

"The death today of Mr. John (Johnny) Morgan, who played as a professional for both Bristol City and Bristol Rovers in the 1920s, recalls one of Bristol's most interesting football matches.

It took place during the war*. Mr. Morgan, one of the footballing Morgan family who were able to turn out a complete football side, took part in a challenge match with the Brown family, who included Ald. Kenneth Brown, former Lord Mayor, at outside-right.

The game was in aid of the *'Evening Post's'* section of Bristol's Own Fund. It was a thriller. Fans who saw it still talk about it today.

Mr. Morgan died at his home, 265 Redcatch Road, Knowle.

The funeral will be on Wednesday (11.30 a.m.) at Avon Vale.

'The Traveller' writes: Morgan, the strong and forceful forward, played for Caerphilly in the Welsh League after leaving City to join Rovers.

In season 1918-19, his best for the City, he scored 24 of their 101 goals in war-time football. Morgan completed a couple of hat-tricks.

In that season, his partner on the left wing was generally Joe Harris. Behind him was Bert Neesam. Johnnie Morgan was a member of the well-known family of footballers who lived in Bristol East. The members of that family did much for local charities in representative matches.

The other members of the Morgan family who played against the Rovers** were Tom, William, Dave, George, Harry, Douglas, Freddy, Reuben, Arthur and Gordon.

Billy Wedlock was referee and the linesmen were Sam Tucker and Steve Sims."

**The match actually took place on 8th December 1937.*

***A typographical error. The team should have been the Browns.*

Alice died on 3rd January 1980, also in Bristol, aged 86, and she was buried alongside her husband in Avonview Cemetery on 8th January 1980.

John Morgan in a relaxed pose.

The grave of John and Alice Morgan, Avonview Cemetery.

JOHN AND ALICE'S CHILDREN:

- **Edna Lilian Kathleen Morgan.**

Edna and Dennis Morgan and family. Date unknown.

Eldest daughter Edna was baptised at St. Luke's Church, Bedminster, on 22nd September 1920. Her parent's address was recorded as 29 Philip Street, Bristol, and her father's occupation noted as being a Footballer.

She married twice; firstly to Albert Edward Roy Kingdon (born 25th February 1920, Bristol), whom she married in 1942, in Bristol. They had one child. She then married Dennis Morgan (born 1st July 1919, Bristol), and together they had four children.

Albert Kingdon died on 21st January 1981, in Southampton, aged 60. Edna herself died in 2005 in Bristol, aged 75, and husband Dennis died in 2005 in Bristol, aged 85.

- **Miriam Morgan.**

Youngest daughter Miriam married an American (surname Frankum), in the USA. There is a 'Miriam Morgan', a shop assistant from Bristol amongst the passenger lists for the liner 'Queen Elizabeth' sailing from Southampton to New York on 7th September 1948, arriving at New York on 12th May 1948. Her final destination is noted as being St. Louis, Maryland, and it is likely that this would be the correct person.

However, this marriage did not last and she returned to the UK around 1950. She subsequently married Brian Trevor Jenkins (born 12th June 1927, Bedminster, Bristol) in 1952. They had two children.

Miriam died on 22nd November 1996, in the Bath & North East Somerset area, at the age of 69. Brian died in 2022 at the age of 96.

2. George James (Nicky) Morgan.

George was baptised on 10th January 1897 at St. Philip & Jacob Church, Bristol. His parents' address was vaguely recorded as 'Barton Hill', and his father's occupation noted as being a Labourer.

George (known throughout his life as 'Nicky', never married. He was another talented footballer, turning out regularly for the Morgan Family football team.

The 1939 Register shows him living at home with his parents at 16 Tichborne Street, Barton Hill, Bristol, where his occupation shows him as being a 'Dipper in the Metal Trade'.

He died on 10th April 1977, in Bristol, aged 80.

3. William Henry Morgan.

William was baptised on 14th August 1898 at St. Philip & Jacob Church, Bristol. His parents' address was vaguely recorded as 'Barton Hill', and his father's occupation noted as being a Labourer.

William also never married. He similarly appears on the 1939 Register living with his parents at 16 Tichborne Street, Barton Hill, Bristol, where his occupation shows him as being a Builder's Labourer.

On 26th January 1957 he was injured in a road accident which was duly reported in the local press:

"A cyclist, William Morgan (58) 16 Tichborne Street, Barton Hill, Bristol, was in collision at Bath Bridge, Bristol, today with a van and was taken to B.R.I. with an injured left knee."

He died on 17th May 1971, in Bristol, aged 72, and was buried at Avonview Cemetery, Bristol, on 21st May 1971.

4. Reuben Edward Morgan.

Reuben was baptised on 14th December 1904 at St. Luke's Church, Barton Hill, Bristol. His parents' address was recorded as 16 Tichborne Street, Bristol, and his father's occupation noted as being a Labourer.

Reuben made an appearance in the local press in August 1931:

"Through catching his hand in a machine at Messrs Lysaght's, Feeder Road, on Saturday, Reuben Morgan, of 16 Tichborne Street, Barton Hill, Bristol, received injuries to two fingers. He was taken to the Bristol General Hospital by the St. John Ambulance and detained."

He also appears on the 1939 Register living with his parents at 16 Tichborne Street, Barton Hill, Bristol, where his occupation shows him as being a 'Tinker in the Metal Trade'.

He married Nellie Emily Holbrook (born 8th May 1904, Bristol) in 1953, in Bristol. They had no children.

Nellie had previously been married to Christopher Henry Benden (born 18th October 1901, Bristol) and their marriage took place on 8th May 1926 at St. Matthew Moorfields, Bristol. They had three children together:

- **Irene May Benden** (born 1927, Bristol; died 2nd November 2019, aged 92). She married Royston F. Burr in 1947 in Bristol, and had one child.
- **Edna Lillian Benden** (born 15th March 1930, Bristol). She married Arthur J. Jones (born 14th March 1930, Bristol) in 1950 in Bristol, and had two children.
- **Kenneth William Benden** (born 26th November 1931, Bristol; died 1997, Bristol, aged 65). He married Brenda June Jenkins (born 5th May 1933, Bristol; died 1977, Bristol) in 1953, in Bristol. They had four children.

Christopher died in 1951, in Weston-super-Mare.

Reuben and Nellie lived at 135 Whitefield Road, St. George, Bristol for many years.

In common with many other members of the Morgan family, Reuben was an avid pigeon racer until late in his life. He gets a mention in an *'Bristol Evening Post'* report from 15 July 1975:

"Thousands of valuable racing pigeons have disappeared after bad weather hit one of the biggest races in the Bristol and West pigeon-fanciers' calendar. The full extent of the disaster may not be known until the end of the week, while fanciers still wait hopefully for stragglers.

But only a few of the 2,300 birds released from Thurso the North of Scotland on Saturday have arrived in their lofts. Fancier Mr. Reuben Morgan (71) of Manor Close, Speedwell, said: "It was a disastrous race. In Bristol about 250 to 300 birds are in, but are very, very, shabby."

"These birds were the cream. It is a terrible loss. I had three birds racing worth about £75 and none of them have returned"

He was a keen football follower, and contributed many times to the local press with his views on local football, and Bristol City F.C. in particular.

He died on 20th July 1983, in Bristol, aged 78. Nellie died at Frenchay Hospital, Bristol, on 24th September 1990, aged 84.

5.   **Lillian Rosina Morgan.**

Lillian was baptised on 7th October 1908 at St. Luke's Church, Barton Hill, Bristol. Her parents' address was recorded as 16 Tichborne Street, Bristol, and her father's occupation noted as being a Labourer.

She married James Alfred Walters (born 18th September 1908, Bristol; died 1983, Bristol, aged 77) on 21st December 1929 at St. Luke's Church, Barton Hill, Bristol. At the time of their marriage, both Lillian and James (probably better known as 'Alfred') were living in Tichborne Street, Barton Hill, Lillian at number 16 and James at number 12. Lillian's occupation noted as being a 'Corset Passer', whilst James was employed as an Electrician.

There is some confusion over the name of Lillian's husband; the baptism register and the death register has his name as 'Albert James Walters', whilst the marriage register states 'James Alfred Walters'.

The 1939 Register has Lillian and James living at 36 Abingdon Road, Bristol, James still employed as an electrician, but Lillian now undertaking unpaid domestic duties.

Lillian died in 2002 in St. Austell, Cornwall, aged 93.

They had two children:

- **Jean Margaret Walters** (born 13th October 1930, Bristol; died 31st October 2009, Newquay, Cornwall, aged 79). Jean married William John Clinton (born 1931, Bristol; died 2001, Truro, aged 70), in 1950, in Bristol. They had one child.
- **Maureen L. Walters** (born 30th June 1936, died 31 March 1965, Frenchay Hospital, Bristol, aged 28). Maureen married James E. Fowler (born 1935, Bristol), in 1956, in Bristol. They had one child. Maureen was cremated at Arnos Vale Cemetery, Bristol, on 6th April 1965.

6. Florence Beatrice Morgan.

Florence was baptised on 19th October 1910 at Christ Church, Barton Hill, Bristol. Her parents' address was recorded as 16 Tichborne Street, Bristol, and her father's occupation noted as being a Labourer.

She married Donald Gilbert Luther (born 18th February 1911, Bristol; died 17th December 1997, aged 86) in Bristol in 1936.

The 1939 Register shows the couple living at 34 Northend Avenue, Kingswood, Bristol, with Florence being shown as 'Beatrice' on the document.

They had two children.

Florence died on 4th January 1992 in Bristol, aged 81.

7. Alice Violet Morgan.

Alice was baptised on 15th May 1918 at St. Luke's Church, Barton Hill, Bristol. Her parents' address was recorded as 16 Tichborne Street, Bristol, and her father's occupation noted as being a Labourer.

The 1939 Register shows Alice living at home with her family at 16 Tichborne Street, Barton Hill, where she found employment as a Box Maker, Tobacco.

Alice married Leslie Stanley James (born 20th March 1915, Bristol) in 1941, in Bristol. They had four children.

Leslie died on 11th November 1975, in Bristol, aged 60, whilst Alice died on 14th November 2007 in Bristol, aged 89. She was buried at Avonview Cemetery, Bristol, on 23rd November 2007.

CHAPTER 9.
THOMAS MORGAN.

Thomas was born on 18th January 1876 at 5 Tarr's Court, Lawrence Hill, Bristol.

He was baptised on 27th September 1876 at Holy Trinity Church, St. Philips, Bristol. His parents' address was recorded as Tarr's Court, Bristol, and his father's occupation noted as being a Labourer.

He sadly died the following year on 31st May 1877, at Tarr's Court, Bristol, and was buried on 3rd June that same year at Greenbank Cemetery.

CHAPTER 10.
THE FAMILY AND DESCENDANTS OF THOMAS MORGAN.

Thomas was born on 25th March 1878, at 1 Barnett's Court, Lawrence Hill, Bristol, with his father's occupation recorded as working for a Hat Manufacturer.

He was given the same name as his elder brother who tragically died young, and was baptised on 11th November 1878 at Holy Trinity Church, St. Philips, Bristol. His parents' address was recorded as Barnett's Court, Bristol, and his father's occupation noted as being a Fireman.

Thomas Morgan (1878-1944)

He married Lillian (Lily) Rosina Langford (born 16th October 1885, Bristol; died 17th July 1952, Bristol, aged 66) on 1st December 1904 at The Emmanuel Church, Bristol. Both Thomas and Lillian were living at 48 York Street, Bristol, at the time of their marriage.

They had one daughter, Doris Rosina Morgan, born on 12th August 1906, in Bristol.

Thomas became the landlord of the Apple Tree public house in Rose Street, Temple, Bristol, in August 1905, although this was a short-lived tenancy. He subsequently moved on to become the landlord of the more lucrative Weaver's Arms public house in Barton Hill in 1907.

On 23rd September 1908, Thomas appeared in the local press following proceedings at the Bristol Police Court:

"The first case taken was against Thomas Morgan, licensee of the Weaver's Arms, Great Western Street, Barton Hill, who was summoned for selling intoxicating liquor to a boy under the age of 14, in an open vessel. The mother of the boy (Mary Ann Meredith), was summoned for sending the child for the liquor. Mr. H. R. Wansbrough defended the licensee.

Inspector stated that on Friday, September 4th, whilst at Barton Hill, he saw a small boy carrying a jug, leave the Weaver's Arms. On seeing witness, the lad attempted to run away, but was stopped by a sergeant, who accompanied witness, and asked his age. He said he was 15, and gave his address. They followed him home, and his mother stated the lad would be 14 years old on November 8th, and admitted she had sent him for beer. They then returned to the Weaver's Arms where the licensee admitted serving the lad, and stated he had been previously informed that the boy was over 14 years of age. He further said he had asked the boy his age.

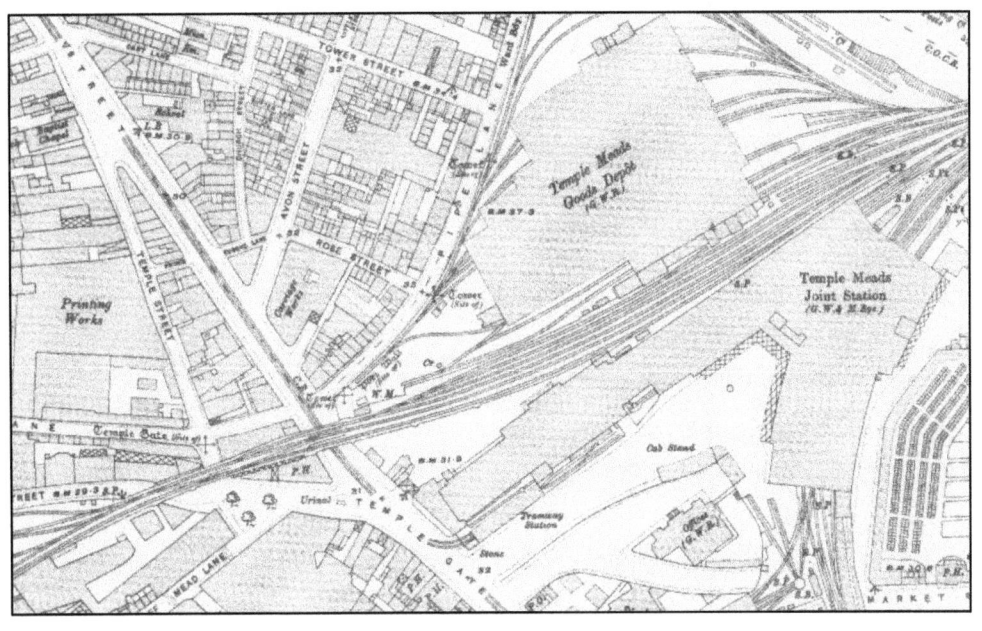

Rose Street, as shown on a map of Bristol c. 1930. The street can be seen in the centre of the map, between Pipe Lane and Avon Street.

Mr. Wansbrough pointed out that the licensee had taken all the reasonable steps a man could take to ascertain the age of the boy. He had asked Meredith his age, and said he was gone 14 and going on 15. He had made it a practice to always inquire into the ages of youthful customers, and he (Mr. Wansbrough) contended it was not a case in which the licensee could be convicted.

Morgan went into the witness box, and replying to a question from the Clerk (Mr. Braithwaite) said it was customary to use judgment as to the age of boys when they came to be served, and in the present case the boy did not appear to be 14 years of age.

The Chairman (Mr. Humphries) pointed out that it would have been better for everyone if the boy had been brought to the court, so that they might judge for themselves how old the boy looked.

Mr. Wansbrough said he was not defending the woman, and the attendance of the boy was nothing do with him. Mr. Humphries remarked it might have strengthened Mr. Wansbrough's case nevertheless.

The defendant Meredith pleaded guilty to having sent the boy, adding that the reason why the boy was not present, was that she did not like to keep him away from his work. Evidence was given by three witnesses who had heard the licensee ask the boy his age prior to serving him, and the bench, in fining the woman 5 shillings, including costs, pointed out she at least, could have had no doubt as to the boy's age.

As regards the licensee there might possibly be some doubt, and the case would be dismissed. They thought, however, that the police had done right in bringing forward the case."

The 1911 Census reveals the family were living at 11 Maze Street, Barton Hill, Bristol, which is the address of the Weaver's Arms public house mentioned above. Thomas was landlord of the establishment at the time, and a servant (Florry Turner) is also noted as living with the family.

Thomas was called up for the 6th Auxiliary Petrol Coy, a section of the Royal Army Service Corps (Mechanical Transport) on 8th March 1917, being issued with the rank of Private and with service number 299878.

His service record shows that he had already enrolled in the Army Reserves on 10th December 1915, and when he entered active service in 1917 he was working at the military camp at Fovant, Wiltshire and then on dockyard duty before leaving service on 25th June 1919. He was medically examined at Boulogne, France, confirming that he did not suffer from any disability due to military service.

His character reference makes for entertaining reading:

1. How has he been employed in the Army?

    Lorry Driver.

2. Sobriety.

    Good.

3. Is he reliable?

    Yes.

4. Is he intelligent?

    Yes.

5. Has he shown any special aptitude for particular employment in civilian life?

    No answer.

The family were still running the Weaver's Arms by the time of the 1921 Census, and two servants were living with them; Winifred Desborough and Kitty Giles.

Between 1927 and 1931 Thomas was landlord of the Post Office Tavern, Staple Hill, details of which can be found in ***Appendix 3.***

By the time of the 1939 Register, it is noted that Thomas and Lillian lived at The Clarence public house, 60 Chelsea Road, Easton, Bristol, where Thomas is described as being a Licensed Retailer. Thomas was landlord from 1931 until his death in 1944, when Lillian took over.

The Weaver's Arms, Maze Street, Barton Hill, Bristol (right of centre).

Group photograph of some of the clientele of the Weaver's Arms outside of the pub. Date unknown.

A Morgan family group from the early 1930s. Thomas Morgan on the left of the top row, with sister Alice at the left of the front row. Thomas's brother James on the extreme right of the front row.

The Clarence public house, Chelsea Road, Easton, Bristol.

As mentioned earlier, Thomas died on 19th January 1944, in Bristol. He was buried at Avonview Cemetery, Bristol, on 24th January 1944, close to the Morgan family grave.

The memorial of Thomas Morgan on the Langford family grave at Avonview Cemetery, Bristol.

Lillian remarried in 1947 to Ernest Meredith (born 16th July 1891, Lancaster), but died on 17th July 1952 in Bristol. She was buried on 22nd July 1952 next to her first husband at Avonview Cemetery, Bristol. However, her surname appears on her grave as Morgan and not Meredith. Her probate record states that she was indeed married to Ernest Meredith and lived at 'The Clarence', 60 Chelsea Road, Easton, Bristol; however her effects were left to the Midland Bank as trustee and executor.

The headstone of Thomas Morgan and Lillian (Lily) Morgan, Avonview Cemetery, Bristol.

DAUGHTER OF THOMAS AND LILLIAN:

Doris Rosina Morgan.

Doris was baptised on 4th September 1906 at Emmanuel Church, St. Philips, Bristol. Her parents' address was recorded as Rose Street, Temple, Bristol (the Apple Tree public house), and her father's occupation noted as being a Beer Retailer.

Daughter Doris married George Henry James Hill (born 1st December 1900, Bristol) on 7th November 1927 at Holy Trinity Church, Bristol. Doris's address at the time was recorded as being at the Post Office Tavern, Staple Hill, with George residing at 8 Stanley Street, Bristol (although the street name is indistinct on the certificate). He was employed as a 'Cigarette Operator'.

The 1939 Register shows the family living at 8 Albert Crescent, Bristol, with George being employed as a Licensed Victualler, and Doris undertaking unpaid domestic duties.

Doris died on 18th July 1971, in Bristol, aged 64, whilst George died on 5th May 1983, at 2 Bifield Gardens, Stockwood, Bristol, aged 82.

They had two children, both born in Bristol:

1. **Mavis Barbara Hill** (born 30th September 1930; died 27th June 1973, 258 Badminton Road, Downend, Bristol, aged 42.).

Eldest daughter Mavis married Frederick A. Surr (born 1930, Swindon), in 1955, in Bristol. They had five children.

2. **Eileen Myrna Hill** (born 11th October 1938; died 25th June 1988, 65 Hetherington Road, Charlton Village, Middlesex).

Youngest daughter Eileen married twice; firstly, in 1960 in Bristol to Michael G. Savage (born 1936, Bristol), and then in 1968 in Richmond-upon-Thames to Bryan James Rosling (born 26th August 1924, Huddersfield). She had no children from either marriage.

Bryan died in Middlesex in 1988, aged 63.

CHAPTER 11.
THE FAMILY AND DESCENDANTS OF FLORENCE BEATRICE MORGAN.

Florence was born on 19th September 1880 at 1 Barnett's Court, Lawrence Hill, Bristol, with her father's occupation recorded as working as a Labourer at Coal Works.

She was baptised on 15th June 1881 at Holy Trinity Church, St. Philips, Bristol. Her parents' address was recorded as Barnett's Court, Bristol, and her father's occupation noted as being a Labourer.

Known in the family as 'Florry', she married John McGoldrick (Frederick) Dawes (born 27th May 1882, 23 Winsford Street, Bristol; died 20th October 1926, Bristol, aged 44) on 27th May 1900 at Moorfields St. Matthew's Church, Bristol. They were both living at 12 Albert Street, Bristol, at the time of their marriage.

They had one child, Ernest Frederick Dawes, born in Bristol on 18th November 1900.

The 1911 Census reveals the family were living at 55 Croydon Street, Barton Hill, Bristol, where John's occupation is stated as being a Baker.

By 1921, the family were living at 44 Goodhind Street, Bristol. John was employed at Charles Hill Shipbuilders, Albion Dockyard, in Bristol, working as a Galvanised Sheeter. Florence had 'household duties' whilst son Ernest was an apprentice with his father at Charles Hills.

John died on 20th October 1926 aged 44, in Bristol. He was buried at Avonview Cemetery, Bristol, on 25th October 1926.

Florence could be found on the 1939 Register, living at 7 Bean Street, where she lived with her son Ernest.

Florence died in on 8th November 1956, in Bristol, aged 76. She was buried at Avonview Cemetery, Bristol, on 14th November 1956.

FLORENCE'S AND JOHN'S CHILD:

Ernest Frederick Dawes.

Son Ernest was baptised at St. Lawrence Church, Easton, Bristol, on 16th December 1900. His parents' address was recorded as being 55 Croydon Street, Bristol, and his father's occupation noted as being a Baker.

He married Adelaide Florence Pocock (born 21st June 1899, Bristol; died 24th June 1970, Bristol, aged 71) on 3rd April 1926, at Holy Trinity Church, Bristol. They had no children. At the time, Ernest was noted as living at 7 Beam Street, Barton Hill, Bristol, and Adelaide at 8 Stanley Street, Bristol.

The family lived at 8 Stanley Street, Easton, Bristol, for a time, before the 1939 Register lists them as living at Eltham House, Clifton Place, Bristol, where Ernest was listed as being an Engineer Borer and an A.R.P Warden.

Ernest took over the running of the 'Lord Raglan' public house in Stapleton Road, Bristol, from his uncle Albert Stephens, in 1953.

Adelaide was buried at Avonview Cemetery, Bristol, on 29th June 1970.

Ernest subsequently married Alice Kate Marsh (born 10th July 1909, Bristol) in Bristol in 1976.

Ernest passed away on 25th August 1994, again in Bristol, aged 93. Alice died on 1st September 2001, in Bristol, aged 92.

CHAPTER 12.
THE FAMILY OF ALICE MORGAN.

Alice was born on 8th July 1881 at 29 Catherine Street, Barrow Lane, Bristol, with her father's occupation recorded as working as a General Labourer.

Alice was baptised on 19th March 1884 at Holy Trinity Church, St. Philips, Bristol. Her parents' address was recorded as 29 Catherine Street, Bristol, and her father's occupation noted as being a Labourer.

She married Albert James Stephens (born 27th November 1883, Bristol; died 30th December 1960, Frenchay Hospital, Bristol, aged 77) on 10th July 1904, at St. Lawrence's Church, Easton, Bristol. They had no children.

The 1911 Census indicates the Alice and Albert were living at 79 Belle Vue Road, Easton, Bristol, where Albert's occupation was listed as being a General Stores Dealer, with Alice assisting in this role.

Albert and Alice Stephens (right) with James and Elizabeth Morgan. Date unknown.

> POULTRY. BIRDS. DOGS. &c.
>
> GRAND Pedigree AIREDALE PUPS; cheap. Sire ex Hatter's Double; dam ex Dalmeny Duke.—Apply Stephens, Lord Raglan, Stapleton Road, Bristol.

Evidence of Albert Stephens' breeding of Airedale Terriers.

By 1921, the couple were living at 121 Stapleton Road, Bristol, better known as the Lord Raglan public house, were Albert was the landlord. Albert bred Airedale terriers, and numerous advertisements appeared in the local newspapers looking for suitable homes for them, such the one displayed above from February 1924.

Another photograph of Albert Stephens (right) with wife Alice next to him. On the left are James Morgan (Alice's brother) and wife Elizabeth.

Albert Stephens at the wheel of the charabanc outside of the 'Lord Raglan', Stapleton Road.

The 1939 Register shows the couple still living at the 'Lord Raglan' where Albert continued to be the licencee.

Alice died on 16th April 1940, in Bristol aged 56, of cancer. She was buried at Avonview Cemetery, Bristol, on 22nd April 1940.

Albert was buried at Avonview Cemetery, Bristol, on 4th January 1961. His last known address was 71 St. Nicholas Road, St. Pauls, Bristol.

CHAPTER 13.
THE FAMILY AND DESCENDANTS OF CLARA MORGAN.

Clara married Daniel Foley (born 1st October 1888, Bristol; died 27th March 1961, Bristol, aged 72) on 19th April 1908 at St. James' Church, Bristol. At the time of their marriage, both were living at 7 Priory Place, Bristol, where Daniel was described as being a Collier.

They had four children, all born in Bristol:

1. **Doris Lillian Foley** (born 2nd August 1909; died 1987, Bristol, aged 77).
2. **Daniel Leslie Foley** (born 14th January 1914; died 7th March 1986, Bristol, aged 72).
3. **John Albert K. Foley** (born 1st October 1922; died 1987, Pontypool, aged 64).
4. **Beryl Eileen Foley** (born 1928, Bristol; died 7th September 1937, Bristol, aged 9).

The 1911 Census shows the family living at 13 Bright Street, Russell Town, Bristol. Daniel is shown as being a Galvaniser, whilst Clara is employed as a 'Tailoress Machinist.'

By 1921 the family had moved to 81 Twinnell Road, Bristol, where Daniel's occupation had changed to working at the saw mills at John Lysaght Ltd., another well-known local company in Bristol.

Clara sadly took her own life on 24th February 1937. The official family line was that she was depressed after the death of her daughter Beryl that same year, but investigation has revealed that Beryl actually died after her mother's suicide, ruling out that supposition.

A press report of the time stated:

'LAST AFFECTIONATE NOTE LEFT TO HUSBAND'
Tragedy of Woman Who Took Own Life.

A note, written in terms of deep affection, addressed to her husband by a woman who had taken her own life, was produced, but not read, in the Bristol Coroner's Court yesterday. The inquest was on Clara Foley (51), Twinnell Road, Stapleton Road, Bristol, who was found lying in a lane off Twinnell Road suffering from injuries to the throat.

Dr. W. M. Capper said Mrs. Foley was dead on her arrival at the Bristol Royal Infirmary and death was due to shock and haemorrhage following a cut throat. Daniel Foley, Twinnell Road, said arriving home he found his wife absent. His sister told him that something was the matter at the end of the road, and as his wife was not in very good health, he became worried. He then saw the note addressed to him and discovered that his razor was missing.

Alice Brice, of Twinnell Road, said she saw Mrs. Foley go into the lane pulling something from her pocket.

"Thinking something was wrong I ran towards her, but before 1 reached her she fell down and I found her bleeding from a wound in the throat. Nearby was a razor."

A verdict of "Suicide while of unsound mind" was returned.

Clara was buried at Avonview Cemetery, Bristol, on 2nd March 1937.

Daniel remarried in 1938, to Rosina Maria Sampson (nee Cook, born 10th May 1892, Bristol; died 14th June 1977, Bristol, aged 85), but they had no children together. The 1939 Register shows them living at 32 Daventry Road, Bristol, with Daniel's son John and one of Rosina's two daughters from a previous marriage, Violet Sampson.

The last known address for Daniel and Rosina was 107 Kenmare Road, Bristol.

CLARA AND DANIEL'S CHILDREN:

1. Doris Lillian Foley.

Doris was baptised on 22nd August 1909 at St. Philip & Jacob Church, Bristol. Her parents' address was recorded as being in 'Barton Hill' and her father's occupation noted as being a Labourer.

She married Clifford Ronald White (born 11th April 1909, Bristol; died 8th June 1969, 4 Woodcote Road, Fishponds, Bristol, aged 60) in 1937, also in Bristol. They had no children.

The 1939 Register shows the family living at 239 Forest Road, Fishponds, Bristol, where Daniel's occupation is noted as being a Baker's Roundsman.

Doris died in 1987, in Bristol, aged 77.

2. Daniel Leslie Foley.

Daniel Leslie Foley married Florence Beatrice May Howard (born 13th May 1921, Eastville Workhouse, Bristol; died 8th September 1993, 122 Chessel Street, Bedminster, Bristol, aged 72) on 12th August 1939, in Bristol. They had two children:

- **Sheila Foley** (born 1940, Bristol).
- **Judith M. Foley** (born 19th July 1943, Bristol; died 2007, Taunton, aged 63). She never married.

The 1939 register shows the family living at 81 Twinnell Road, Bristol, the former home of Daniel's parents. Daniel's occupation was described as being a 'Time Keeper'.

Daniel and Florence subsequently divorced, and Daniel then married Doreen Muriel Bowman (born 13th February 1920, Bristol; died 16th March 1979, Bristol, aged 59) on 11th May 1946 at Trinity Methodist Church, Fishponds Road, Bristol. The marriage certificate shows Daniel living at 11 Selkirk Road, Kingswood, Bristol, with his occupation recorded as being a Timekeeper at Airways Company. Doreen was noted as being a Clerk Typist, living at 15 Summerleaze, Hillfields Park, Bristol.

The certificate also shows an interesting entry in the 'Condition' section, where it states that Daniel was "formerly the husband of Florence Beatrice May Foley, formerly Howard (spinster) from whom be obtained a divorce."

They had no further children. Florence subsequently married Robert Frederick Base (born 13th May 1921, Bristol; died 22nd February 1992, Bristol, aged 70) on 22nd June 1946, in Bristol, and they had two children.

Daniel died on 7th March 1986 at Downside Nursing Home, Clifton, Bristol.

3.   **John Albert K. Foley.**

Third child John Albert K. Foley (known as Jack) married Mary Kathleen Parkhouse (born 14th December 1924, Bristol; died 29th June 1995, Abergavenny, aged 70) on 2nd June 1952, at St. Patrick's Church, Pilemarsh, Bristol. They had no children.

John died in 1987 in Pontypool.

4.   **Beryl Eileen Foley.**

Their youngest child Beryl sadly died on 7th September 1937, in Bristol, aged only 9. She was buried in the family grave at Avonview Cemetery, Bristol, on 10th September 1937.

Service card for Beryl Foley, 1937.

CHAPTER 14.
IT WAS ALWAYS SUMMER.

These are the written memories of Ivy Doris Irene Morgan, daughter of James Morgan and Elizabeth Coles, transcribed exactly – although some minor grammatical errors have been corrected.

When I was four years of age I was taken to Lawrence Hill to start school. It was in Russell Town Avenue. My father's sister took me (Aunt Clara). She was a kindly person with projecting teeth and her hair tied behind in a bun. After seating me in a stand like a small football stand she stood by and watched. One minute she was there, next minute she was gone back to the little house in Bright Street where she lived with her mother Tilly (or Matilda), my Gran. Oh didn't I cry, they could not stop me. I was taken from one class to another. One kind teacher offered me a slice of cake but oh no, I wasn't having any. You see this was a Church School and belonged to Russell Town Church but I was in an unknown place. My home was nearly a mile away near the entrance to St. George's Park.

Come summertime I was taken to the top of some dark stone steps and who should come up but my mother. I think she was as glad to see me as I her. I was to remain at home a while. You see there were 2 sisters younger than me, Violet and Ethel, and an elder brother Bert, and another sister Lily six years older than me. My brother and I were very near and dear, both of us March-born, me 5th March, him the 10th. In the next 10 years, two more children were born, making it a total of seven children; Gilbert, 6 years between us, and Grace, another girl, 10 years between us.

The children of James and Elizabeth Morgan. Photo taken c. 1915 at the back of the 'Rising Sun'. Left to Right: Violet, Ethel, Albert, Lilian, Grace, Gilbert, Ivy.

My parents James Morgan and my mother Elizabeth (Coles) were both hard working. Having previously bought a little grocers shop in Bellevue Road, Easton, they branched out to Redfield and were renting a pub from Georges Brewery and there we were in our own little world surrounded by back to back streets and amongst the poorest people I know. At the time there was Easton Road Pit, Whitehall Pit, Deep Pit, Speedwell Pit and so on.

I remember my father getting up to open the pub doors at 5 o'clock in the morning for the miners to come in and sit around the huge fire and a funnel saucepan in the grate to warm their porter or old beer, and oh dear, their faces were black like the coal they dug, and they were all so pitifully thin. If mother had a bit of meat left over she would cut off some slices of bread for these men and they got their pocket knives out and with the meat and a raw onion, it must have been as milk and honey. What with the pitch pine sawdust my father was spreading over the floor and in the spittoon, it was a smell I have never forgotten.

Opposite our home, the 'Rising Sun', there was a haulage firm, Hemmings. The owners were very nice posh people and they had a telephone, a tall one; I think it was the only one I ever saw at my young time of life. In front of their yard was a horse-shoeing forge run by a Mr. Bundy and his son, who lived nearby in Roseberry Park. It was all horses in those days and Bristol Corporation was one of their main customers. It was so nice in winter to see the horses being shoed and the fire alight.

Just a little way up the road next to St. George's Park gates was another man. 'Joe Tinner - Farrier' was his name in big letters. He used to pop in to our pub sometime and he had a fair moustache and his little villa was behind the forge where now there is a ladies and gents convenience.

Saturday nights outside Mr. Bundy's, Cheap Jacks would come and teeth extracted if required and a coloured man would sell his own-made toothpaste in a round box. Crowds of us children would gather around. There were no youth clubs or discos in those days.

We enjoyed our own games swinging around lamp posts, whip and top, pottle, hop scotch or the boys would run down hills on home-made planks with wheels attached from babies' prams. Some of the older boys would line up and make a line each one on the back of a boy in front. I did not care too much for this game.

Then Mondays it was Band of Hope at Bethesda Chapel. We would be told about the evils of strong drink and shown scenes of drunkards by magic lantern but it used to make me feel awful because my father kept a pub. Then I joined night school for 3 winters. Gym was taught, millinery dressmaking by Miss Bateman and the headmaster was Mr. Pickles. All so kind and we paid 1/- per winter to enrol but St. George Grammar School was really grand and I think many of the day scholars went on to make their name in life.

When I was 5 years old I went to Redfield Council School in Avonvale Road with my brother Bert. My first teacher was Miss Nott and she had a round red jovial face. In our classroom was a large fireplace and a guard was around the front of it. I learned my letters very well and was the first to read *"The cat sat on the mat"* from the blackboard. In the windows would be flowers in season in 2lb jam jars. We all loved to pick flowers for our teacher. At playtime we would mingle with the older girls on the other side of the playground but the little privvies (no flush) would smell awful. Boys and girls would go in but of course we were very young and noticed really that girls weren't any different to boys. We would join in rings and sing *"Ring a Ring of Roses"* or *"Here we go Gathering Nuts in May"* and then a teacher would come out with a big hand bell and we would get in line and march to our classrooms.

There were no trade unions then. Some teachers would ride by cycles or use the tram cars but I am sure they radiated love and care to us and we would fight to hold their hands and walk out of school a little way when the day was over.

At 8 years old I went into the big school. The First World War had begun and my first teacher, Mrs. Spiller's husband, was killed in action. He was not too young either. I often wonder if she married again. One half of the big school was for boys. Mr. Kempster was headmaster. He rode every day in from Redland. The girls' headmistress was Miss Bolwell and she was short with pince-nez glasses on a cord. I am sure she was more like a man. One teacher took us for sewing, one for history, one for singing and painting, and another for sums and writing.

I received an attendance certificate and a good report on leaving which my youngest daughter has been given by me. I left able to knit, sew my own underwear by hand and trained in cookery and housewifery for 3 years. I wonder today if this happens. Today it is outings by coach to zoos around London and other places, how that helps them I wonder? Swimming was held after school for 1 hour, one day a week at Barton Hill Baths and we would walk there and back in twos. Perhaps that is why our generation called geriatrics owing to our age have lived so long I wonder?

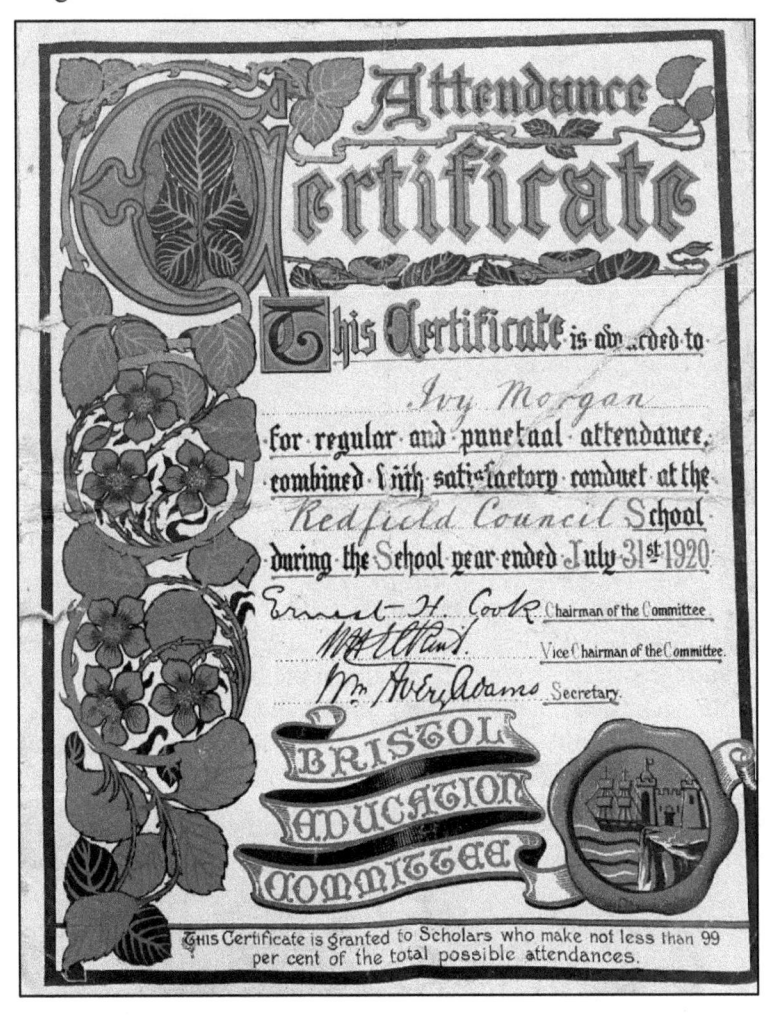

Ivy's school leaving certificate from 1920.

Now in the summer we would go down Blackswarth Road near the park gate past Derby Street, Stanley Road, Lewin Street and Grindell Road to the river where we could be ferried across ½d each way. Where we waited for the rowing boat there was some waste hilly land called Donkey's Hill. There roamed a couple of cows and a nanny goat. A couple of cottages lay nearby. We used to play war games, the girls were the nurses when the boys fell or supposed to be injured. At the top overlooking us was Avon Vale* Cemetery. It always seemed to me that one day it would topple over into the road below leading to Crews Hole.

*No doubt Avonview Cemetery.

Silas Hopes, Blacksmith, close to St. George's Park. Silas was distantly related to Ivy via the Williams family.

When we crossed the ferry there stood a house where St. Anne's Board Mill is built now. We could buy a big jug of homemade lemonade for 1d, enough for 4 or 5 cups, one cup for each one of us. Then into the woods. We would paddle in the brook in the woods with our shoes or boots around our necks tied together. There was a huge black pipe which we would try to see how many times we could make it across. I can hear now the laughter and happy children's voices.

Some Sundays after Chapel (Methodist) I would make a little journey through the woods and sit on a stile and make up little verses or poems. Alone I would be, and somehow this I know today would be silent meditation or inner to a place of the soul just God and myself and I know also I never walked alone and some kind of happiness was bestowed on me to follow me on the path of life.

Sometimes the Chapel would organise a ramble to Mrs. Beese's Gardens at Conham and there again we would go across in the ½d ferry. Of course this would take place in a holiday time and I remember we would sing hymns on our return journey home; *"Now The Day is*

Over", "One More River to Jordan" and *"We Shall Meet in the Sweet Bye and Bye"*. Then Wednesdays, Bristol East Band would play in St. George's Park and couples would dance in pairs all around the path outside the covered bandstand. I loved to watch them. The men wore straw boaters and the girls had long hair with large bows of ribbon tied at the back.

I also remember where the bowling green is now, a balloon moving off up into the sky with Queen Mary and King George VI printed outside. While I watched, sorry to say a boy came along and stole my medal of their likenesses which all schoolchildren had been given for the coronation of the good King and his Queen. I had it pinned in my pinafore which was decorated with beautiful lace frills.

Sometimes too my brother Bert would take me to the lily ponds at Speedwell to get tadpoles. Sad to say the buttons came off my liberty bodice which held up my pretty drawers and I walked all the way home one day with them off so I would not ever go again and really I never did.

Now every year there would be Lansdown Races and our pub being on the main road we were able to see the racegoers returning home, if they had a good day at winning they would throw coins mostly ½d and 1d pieces to the crowds lined along the pavement, but the main event was a kind of wagonette pulled by a donkey with a woman's lace open drawers on its front legs – oh. The laughter and happiness this would cause, perhaps one day this could be done for a charitable cause but leaving out the Bath Races.

Beese's Tea Gardens, St. Anne's.

At Sunday School, Tudor Road off Devon Road, Whitehall, was where sister Lily, brother Bert and I attended (my younger brother and sister went to St. Leonard's Church), we would pay in 1d on Sundays to go to Weston super Mare for the Sunday School outing by brake and horses. I think we paid a total price of 1/- including tea. I know when we arrived I would always make for the arcade to buy mother a cup and saucer with 'A Present from WSM' in gold letters or a view painted on it. Our tea was taken in a Methodist Chapel Hall and was usually a bun and a large slice of sultana cake. Mr. Russ, who was in charge, always said Grace to God before we started tea. Straight after the homeward journey began we would sing *'When the Fields are White with Daisies'* and *'All Things Bright and Beautiful'* all the way home. But when we got to what they called the Roddy we would all get out and walk to the top as the load was too much for the horses to pull. Then when we drove through a certain byway we would shout *'Whip Away Will'* and the driver would pass the apples down on our heads but apples never mattered to me. Usually a small child would have nodded off to sleep and I would not disturb it as it would be in my arms.

Now where Queens Road, Jubilee Road and Malvern Road are today, that was waste land and it belonged to a Mr. Cousins. There was a big gate and so far in was a pond, not too big. Our Lily and Bert would go up there with other boys and girls. One day they took me. I was about 4 to 5 years of age. There were apple trees in there and of course you can guess what would happen. But on the day they took me, off came our boots and we paddled in the water. Suddenly Mr. Cousins appeared, everyone got away except me. I was too small and young to run fast. Anyway he asked my name and he waited for me to put on my boots and he caught hold of my hand and took me outside the gate. He was a kind man, I know that now, and I never went there again. That gate led out to where my sister Grace lives today (Queens Road).

Now at about my early day of life we would always hear of very young babies dying before their first year of life. Mostly it was measles and whooping cough and fits that ended their miserable days. Many a time I have gone in a house in Derby Street to go up the bare rickety stairs to see a little white coffin with a child still and silent.

One day a girl with me said; "You touch its hands" (and how cold and stiff it was). But beside that fleas would be on its forehead. It was the finest thing in the world years later to know how these back to back houses were demolished. Yet with it all the people who lived in these houses were of one accord. They were all good neighbours. One poor old soul would take parcels to pawn at Mr. Swaish's pawn shop when they were hard up. One day sad to say she was killed while crossing the road. I expect they missed her terribly.

A Mr. Phipps, a market gardener at St. George had a beer off licence at the bottom of Derby Street and when the vegetables were brought from the market garden he would employ the strongest woman who wore sack aprons to bundle them up in his yard at the back where there were big double gates. May White, a girl who lived next door and whose mother worked there, would often throw us a carrot or a turnip to eat. I never told my parents but that was part of the fun in those days.

There was another shop on the other corner where they made toffee apples (½d each). I really loved biting these till they would sometimes break off the sticks and finish up on the ground.

On Good Fridays boys and girls would gather around a baker's shop next door to the Rising Sun (our home) with their mothers' washing baskets with a handle each end. Come about 6 o'clock in the morning, Bert, Lily and I would sit in the wide window sill of our bedroom to see their baskets being filled with the really hot cross buns. The children would go around the streets shouting *"one a penny two a penny hot cross buns (ringing a bell), if you don't like then give them to your sons"*.

Many a poor boy or girl made a few shillings this way and enjoyed this so much. Today trade unions say it's wicked for scholars at 16 to help clean their schoolrooms and get £1/hour. Who do they think they are?

The social revolution is now on their side and not the English families who are doing this to firms who employ them and the people have holidays abroad, cars, and own their own houses. They are better off today than the small firms who employ them.

Now we 3 older children would be sent to Mr. Browns the bootmaker who had a boot shop over what mother would call the second bridge. This would be from the Lawrence Hill coal depot to the Co-op stores near the "Glass House" public house kept by a Mr. J. Hollister.

When we arrived at Mr. Brown's (who by the way was a member of the Easton Road Salvation Army), we would be taken to the back of the shop to a leather-covered long seat and a man would come and measure our feet for our boots made of real glacé kid. They would come to about 4 inches below our knee and were always black. We could choose buttons or lace-ups. I preferred buttons.

The Glass House, Lawrence Hill.

The family of Mr. Brown was a son and 3 daughters. The older daughter always had a bag of sweets in her pocket and we would be asked to take one. I remember too when there was a funeral of a Salvation Army member a band would march at the head of the funeral and the women behind the band would have wide white sashes over one shoulder to the waist. They would walk very slowly to the tune which I think was called the death march.

I remember when my grandmother died us children wore black armbands on the day of the funeral to Avonview Cemetery. Today we are told people grieve over the passing of a loved one for a long time but in those days this was not so. I wonder if our love of Chapel and Church and being taught the faith as a natural thing. It was a wonderful consolation which comforted people and we would know that all was well for the loved ones.

Now after I had been in the big school at Redfield Council about a year or so some poor children were able to have boots suppled to them by paying 1d a week. They were up to the ankle and thick leather. Also they could go to the Barton Hill Settlement each dinnertime and have a free bowl of soup and bread. You see as I have said the people were very poor indeed and the Poor Law office in Avonvale Road would open each day for people to get a ticket to buy articles of food. As I have said before although this happened, the people of Bristol East were workers; they grew most of their own vegetables, and in those days there were no refrigerators in butcher's shops. The people would wait till last thing on a Saturday night and then meat would be sold off cheap and it was a Godsend. A Mr. Frankcom I remember was very well loved and respected as he had his butcher's shop opposite the Rising Sun.

Now around that part of Church Road where I lived were three Bartons; each had about 4 or 5 little cottages. One was where Taylor's Builders Yard is today, one just before the Public House called the Fire Engine, and one on the other side of the road. I knew all these people and where Church Road Post Office, Redfield now stands there too were a few cottages, but they were burnt down about 1908. A Mr. Ballard owned most of the little cottages in these Bartons and he lived across St. George's Park. He was found dead one morning in the Park (from a seizure) by the miners coming home from a night shift. Mother always says he was a mean landlord and the properties were poor.

At these times it was stone floors and often I have gone with a girl I went to school with to buy sand to sprinkle on the stones downstairs to be absorbed with the dampness. Also the lavatories were wooden seats and oh dear, a bucket of dirt was outside to sprinkle over the awful contents after using. One by one they moved out and down to Roseberry Park and Lyppiatt Road.

Now opposite these roads was a pub called The George & Dragon. Still there today. Beside the pub was a lane called George & Dragon Lane. A one-legged man on crutches used to make bread in one place there and three cottages were on the other side. One woman in a cottage used to go around selling fish. She had three children and brother Bert was friendly with the brother of them. Two girls made up the three.

At the top of the lane was a street called Clifton Street. Many a morning I had to drag sister Violet screaming through this street. The people used to come out and say poor Violet, but it was because she would not go to school. The headmistress (Miss Hallett) locked her in a cupboard one day. I ran home and told my father. He kept her home a long time after this. In fact they forgot all about her. But Miss Hallett was angry about me telling Dad and she kept me by her desk all morning after and would clap her hands together right in front of my face. I was afraid after that to tell mother or father.

Now in our hall at school were two large honours boards. When a girl or boy went on the Grammar School their name was written there in gold letters. A girl in my class, Ann Yeadon, a fair girl with plaits over her shoulder did very well I remember. Also when the 1914 war ended my father collected and sent a nice sum of money for the names of past scholars who were killed in action to be inserted on a roll of honour in the hall.

Church Road in the 1900s. St. George's Park entrance to the left.

Now I will tell about the coal wharf at Lawrence Hill. It was by the Earl Russell public house and led to the back of the railway station. There was Cookson and Osborne, Mills, Hunters, Hemmings and others. In the winter, boys and girls would be able to hire a cart – the back would slide up to enable the coal to be tipped out. The charge of the cart for hire from the coal merchants would be 1d and bag of coke 6d. Although my parents bought their coal by the ton at about 28/- to £1 14/- a ton. I always loved to go down with someone and help to push it back. Mind you these carts were always taken back to the Wharf and Dad always said the best coal was from the Forest of Dean. It would burn slow and bright and last a lot longer than the other kind.

Now the other side of the Earl Russell was a clothing factory called 'Dicky Parsons'. I would go with the others and watch the women in summer when the doors were held back. You see they made the uniforms for the brave soldiers in the 1914 war.

Sometimes I would have to go for my father to a shop (house really) where they sold shellfish and butter and cheese. Always mother gave me a basin and I was to ask for 4d worth of mussels and "mind they give you some liquor on them". Also ½lb of butter stamped out with a swan as they used the wooden boards and shaped the butter round for the swan to be stamped on.

On the way home from the shop in Morley Street past Russell Town Church was some waste ground and at time a fair would be used by show people and I always stood watching them setting it up. The lovely doll people on the roundabout who moved when the music began and the twisted brass long poles with the horses and bears and ostrich figures going up and down was a sight to behold.

There were swings, hoop-la and a bearded lady in a tent. One time I paid 1d in a sideshow and saw a large spider's web with just a lady's head in the middle. Many a night I woke up seeing this thing in my dreams but of course it was done by trickery.

Now just before you got to Lawrence Hill station there were four or five shops. I remember one, a fishmonger and greengrocer kept by a Mr. Carter, a very fat man, and next door was a shop called Suttons Dining Room. He had faggots and peas and potatoes keeping warm in the window. My sister Lily would send me there with a very large jug to buy some when she was fanciful. She called it 'Daddy Sutton's' but I have heard his son was Randolph Sutton the variety star.

Then coming near home on the other side before you got to St. Matthew's Church was a lane called Dove Lane and there was a public house on the corner, the Dove Inn. My mother and father later bought two houses off Mr. Verrier, a magistrate. These were at the top of Dove Lane (Victoria Avenue).

The Dove Inn, Church Road.

Further on nearer home was the Westminster Bank. My father said a ghost appeared there sometimes called P. P. Bereton who had shot himself in the old days before the bank was built. Also there was a dairy (Didham's) where the milk would cascade down into a large receptacle. Also cream was made and the milkman would deliver the milk twice a day, calling; "Bring out your jugs to the front door!"

My husband has told me one day he ran in and dipped his fingers in the cream and a policeman chased him and caught him. He loves to tell about this, he was let go he said because he wet his trousers!

Now my husband was born in Mary Street facing the St. George's Hall Picture Palace. Next to it was a wide door for the St. John's Ambulance Station. As his mother had such a large family (12 children) they moved to a new larger rented house at the bottom of Cloud's Hill Avenue. Summerhill School was in the next street being built and his father helped to build the stone-built excellent school.

At dinnertime my husband would get out his roller skates and go down past the Rising Sun to get chops at 10d a pound and 1½d worth of all sorts for a stew. At night he would go up to the Conservative Club opposite the Park Picture House and help clean it. Saturdays all day he worked for Mr. Taylor the grocer at the top of Cloud's Hill Avenue. Deliver groceries, clean out the shop at night and he would get home to his mother about 12 o'clock with a part of a loaf and some boiled ham with 5/- wages.

His mother gave him a 3d piece and he knew the money was needed because there were five younger ones and he was the seventh child born, six were older ones and a couple worked in Fry's the chocolate factory.

Now when it was our summer holidays, St. George's Park was our playground. Sometimes an older strong girl would hire a tub boat and row us around the lake. Of course we had to give her our pennies. The children around the lake would run around and call out "go on, Nellie" to the girl who rowed us.

Then we would have roly-polys down from the top path and bare feet was the order of the day. Mother would say "someone come down at 4 o'clock and fetch some tea for a picnic". Needless to say we would keep asking the men who had watch chains "is it 4 o'clock?" hours before time. I think our Lily fetched it. A large jug of tea (about a quart) with plenty of milk and sugar and a whole new cottage loaf sliced and spread with raspberry jam. Didn't we tuck into it! At evening we would go back home with daisy chains in our hair and around our necks and some tall shivery shake grasses for my mother. She would put them in vases over the fireplace in the kitchen.

An evocative picture of Lawrence Hill, c. 1910.

Now there was a family of barge-owners called Ashmead. They lived in Beaufort Road past Avonview Cemetery (which part belonged to Phipps Market Gardeners at one time). By the house was Lamb Hill and Strawberry Lane. Some very lovely cottages lay around and I have read that at one time a pottery was there. But I cannot remember this but I knew a man who lived at the bottom who told my parents his house was haunted and a ghost wandered in his garden by the well. In past times lots of the older houses had wells. There was one in the Rising Sun cellar, also a tall pump around the back garden. A big toad lived around the well of the pump and my mother thought the world of it. My oldest brother was fond of animals, he kept rabbits, white mice and bantam fowls.

Entrance to St. George's Park with children of the time.

Also there was an old lavatory in one corner of the yard. No cistern and if one went out at night without a light you would see dozens of cockroaches all sizes covering the floor and some on a plank seat of the lavatory. My father asked George's Brewery could it be demolished. The man in charge of these matters was a Mr. Savory (this was a very unsavoury matter I think!).

Now Avonvale Road began at Redfield where Bethesda Chapel starts. Go past Redfield School a little up was Chappell Allen or the Stay Factory, as the people then called it. It was a very large building in Victoria Avenue. Facing the factory was Pile Marsh Road and further up was Grindell Road. Now in the first house there lived a family called Grindell. They were horse dealers and the house was medium size with a large sideway into a yard and side stables. Now opposite was a large field called Grindell's Field where the horses would roam. As a child I remember two old cottages in this field. My great uncle Ike Williams lived in one and attended the horses etc. If you looked up the wide fireplace in his cottage you could see the sky. When I was about six years of age on the Boxing Day we had awful winds and during the night both cottages blew down. They were rehoused in nearby Orchard Square and other girls and myself would go the field and pile up the stones from the cottages. They were yellow and black large stones not brick like the houses around. Sometimes we would go the field to see a balloon go up.

Facing Grindell's was Netham Road, and if you travelled down the end there was a Public House *(Beak's - actually called the Waggon & Horses, where the Beak family were landlords between 1886 and 1944)* and beyond this the large Imperial Chemical works. This awful place smelling of sulphur employed quite a lot of men. I used to go with a girl called Nellie Coombes to take her father's dinner wrapped in a red handkerchief. It would be bread and cheese and two large pickled onions and Nellie would have a pint of old beer put into her empty bottle carried from her house to the Beak's Public House. Sometimes her father would cut an onion in half to share between us. Surely this stuff they made they must have breathed in because the powder going down pipes would drop out here and there. It would not be allowed today (by the unions of course).

There was always a big furnace going a few doors up. There were piles of coke around it. Travel further down we would come to Netham Bridge over the river heading to Brislington and Marsh the opposite way. I never cared much for these parts of Redfield. Coming back turn left was a large Cooperage where my Uncle Tom Fuller was foreman. They lived nearby in Avon Park and Cooperage Road was the next street down. This part of Avonvale Road led to the cotton factory at nearby Barton Hill. My mother was proud when she told us she worked there on leaving Castle Green School and had four looms. She told me all those little streets leading off Avonvale Road were built for the cotton workers and a man named Moss came down from Manchester to be in charge of the weavers. In her day it was called the Backfields but when I married in 1927 it closed down and I believe they manufactured silk stockings or viscose so named.

My Dad's brother kept a pub (Weaver's Arms) at the corner of Factory Street leading to Maze Street where Barton Hill Baths were situated. All around these parts lace workers were employed on the railways. One had to go down Day's Road and Day's Bridge leading to Barrow Road, on to Lawrence Hill so on to West Street and Castle Street where Bristol Castle was built many hundreds of years before. My mother's family lived around these parts in Ellbroad Court where she says it was haunted. They would sometimes hear chains clanging at night in the bedroom. As I was growing up my mother would tell me of people she knew and would say the lived outside the gate (of the Castle I presume). People in her time say 'outside' or 'within' the gate to show the way.

My husband has told me that when he was 16-17 years of age, he left Fry's chocolate factory to work for the railway. His work was to go around the district knocking up drivers and firemen for their time to be ready to take a train out, this was mostly at night. His mother would give him a rice pudding baked hard in an enamel dish to eat when he was hungry. He said perhaps one train would be due to go out at 1.30, the next 2.15 or later and many a night he has stayed in a doorway in Queen Anne Road at Barton Hill. He said one man (a driver) was always very kind to him and gave him a steaming cup of tea with lots of condensed milk in it. I think he never forgot it. But his job was hard so he went into the building industry.

Now when I was about 14 or 15 a large fairground was set up where the boys played football in St. George's Park. It was in aid of the Labour Party. A man, a Mr. Milton, who later on became Lord Mayor of Bristol with his wife, played a large part in this event. It was here that Billy Butlin had a hoopla stall etc. Charlie Heal the showman had the merry-go-round, revolving cars. Roger's also were there with children's roundabouts and Pruett's also. I loved to go over the top in Pruett's overboats. Mrs. Milton ran a shellfish stall and would say they all had a birth and death certificate.

The Heal's family were good sportsmen. They all had blue eyes and were good looking and worked very hard. The mother of the family had a beautiful caravan and would look out at all that was taking place. My father became friendly with some of the family. Now we know Billy Butlin went on to build a holiday empire for people's enjoyment. I wonder if the Roger's and Pruett's are still going about to the fairs today.

Now once a year my father would take a charabanc party to Wickwar. A month before the event a large notice would go up in the long bar to say "A-nutting we will go". About 9 o'clock on a Sunday morning off they would go for cob nuts. My mother really hated this event. She would supply boiled beef sandwiches and beetroot, and of course there would be flagons of beer. About 1-30, ½ hour before closing time, they would be back and a merry lot they were! *"Nellie Dean"* would be sung and *"Don't Go Down the Mine, Dad"* and *"Dreams Very Often Come True"*. But the main thing was it was all orderly and enjoyable getting away for a few hours. Also another event saved up for was Cup Final day. The men would go from Lawrence Hill station and again mother provided refreshments. The last time Dad had this outing was 1924, the year I got married. He always said the Barber at London gave him a Monkey Gland. I think he had the hot towel treatment and he was sold some face cream. But of course my father could always tell a good story. He worked hard and he played hard but my mother it was no play hard – with it all she lived 25 years longer than dear father.

Now I am unable to finish my true story without mentioning the pony and carts being driven in from Hanham and Kingswood and round about on a Saturday morning with people selling poultry, rabbits, vegetables, and fruit. Also the "cow heel and tripe" man and his wife with a 2-handled cart. They always wore white overall coats. Also the Welsh cockle woman. She would come around on weekdays with her tub on her head calling "cockles". Evenings there would be a German band of three and they passed till one played alone. Then there was the Irish woman and her son with a little organ to be played with five fingers. Her son would collect the money. Also the shoe black who holding the brushes in his hand back to back would play *"Men of Harlech"*. Also a match-seller called Gwennie who would kick her height for one penny. She was about seven feet tall. At the end of it wall was a dedicated minister at Moorfields Mission. He would pray in the parlour at the funeral of a loved one before the person was taken to Avonview Cemetery to be interned. Before this, we would sing a hymn.

The Hope Pole Inn, Redfield, Bristol.

And in the background of shadows was Nurse Green with her blue veil head dress and white collar and cuffs and navy cape. She would call to any home who requested her services. Everyone paid 1d per week into a fund for her services. Mother would tear up anything white and newly washed to give her for bandages. She lived in Avon Vale Road next to a bakers shop opposite Hop Pole Inn (see previous page).

Again I remember we would go to Winstanley Street at Barton Hill to have our clothes made by a dressmaker, Miss May. She had an apprentice and a large table and scissors and a huge pin cushion. We would have silk dresses in summer and velvet in the winter. Also I loved to wear an indigo double-breasted coat and dress costume called serge. This lady truly worked very hard in her trade. I never knew her charges for making our clothes but I expect that's why father would sometimes get cross when pub trade was quiet.

My two brothers had suits from Coles & Pottow in West Street or "The Batch" as it was sometimes called. I think they were sold ready-made.

As we grew out of our clothes mother would pack them in a black Italian cloth apron and send us to various people she knew. They were always so grateful for them.

My Dad also was a sportsman and we had a team of Morgans, cousins and others who would play football games for charity. One team was the Comrades of the Great War. Others followed, such as the Browns (11 sons).

My uncle Jack Morgan had a large family and had been in the Boer War. On his return he worked for Bristol Corporation. When I had whooping cough he managed to bring along a tar cart that was used to repair the roads. I was taken up a ladder and held over the fumes. I suppose it was meant to dispose of the whooping cough but it was a dreadful ordeal for me I can tell you.

Also, a piece of tar rope was tied around my neck, it itched dreadfully. If we had colds we were put to lie between our parents at nights. I never slept, I was so very hot and thirsty but it seemed to do the trick and we were better after.

Saturday mornings we would have to line up in the kitchen for a spoonful of Brimstone and Treacle. I never minded this really. Saturday night the boiler was lit. Mother used it for washing the clothes, boiling hams and Christmas puddings.

On our Saturday bath nights, water would be bailed out and we would bath in front of the kitchen fire. A handful of soda was put in and didn't we have shiny faces after! But mother always had a bottle of glycerine and rosewater for us to dab on our hands and faces after. Always before getting into bed we said our prayers kneeling down ending with God bless mother, God bless father and all the little children, Amen.

Sister Lily, Bert and myself were brought up in the Methodist Church but the younger ones attended St. Leonard's Church in Blackswarth Road. But I am glad I was a Methodist because John Wesley went out to the people to preach God's holy words. The church is not so relaxed with its creeds and rectals over and over again.

Next to where the Fire Engine public house was situated was a lane heading into Cossham Road, called The Wicket. I would go with a girl after school through this lane and on to Beaufort Road and Strawberry Lane to a little cottage. The girl, Laura, who lived in Derby Street, would carry a large jug and buy barm for her mother. I have been told it was used to make wine or some drink or other.

The Fire Engine, Church Road, St. George, Bristol.

Some of the fathers of girls I went to school with would be outworkers for Woodington's Boot Factory, St. George. After school was over the boys or girls would push hand carts to the factory (it was uppers they called them) made in sheds in their gardens and where they lived. I suppose they were attached to the soles of the boots or something – I never really found out. Today nothing like this is allowed by law.

In the summer a man and woman would come around the back streets with a horse and lorry. There would be a small roundabout set out for the very young children (about 3 or 4 years old) to have a ride for ½d a time. Then before they moved on the woman would sing a song. I will remember *"The Sunshine of your Smile"* and *"Let the Great Big World Keep Turning"*. I believe these people were from Ireland but I will always remember she had a wonderful voice and with a few pence from those around on they would travel.

Also there were Italian organ grinders with lovebirds as they called them, in a cage, attached near the handles next to the organ. The birds would be trained to pick a small message of love for anyone for 1d.

Truly now I am so very old, the pleasures of my childhood I recall over and over again. There were not two kinds of people, no-one was envious of the other, all went about their daily tasks whatever it was they had to do.

Again there were the knife grinders and scissor sharpeners with the wheel and band and they would put their foot on a pedal to turn the wheel and a little water would drop down from time to time.

My mother and father had a horse and open cart and would drive around the local villages selling crockery which he obtained from a pottery somewhere and the cart would be full of straw to prevent breakages. My father's parents – little is known but I believe the family came across from Wales before the 1851 Census. Their names were Morgan and Williams but St. Philip & Jacob's Church, Old Market, holds a lot of our family records.

Now the odd grocery shops, mostly on street corners, would sell milk, ladled and measured into your jug. Liquorice bootlaces, jars of gobstoppers, shapes ½d each, shrimp or mint flavoured, also firebricks (made from coal dust, ½d each). Also bring your own cup, a 1d of mustard pickle would be measured out from a large glass gallon jar on the counter.

Woodington's Boot Factory.

Of course the milkman would come around twice a day, also the rag and bone man, you would be given a windmill made of paper or a balloon for what you brought out. Most people in the little houses had oil lamps to light at night and at bedtime candles would be used. One old lady near the Barton above us caught herself on fire early one night and was burned to death. My father rescued her but she was dead when he put her down. Her husband used to go around mending umbrellas.

Next door was a chimney sweep and next again a rag and bone shop. There were always rabbit skins hanging in the doorway, ½d was the price given for these.

Below us was a fish and chip shop. You could get ½d worth of chips in newspaper and I did hear that a cat fell in the pail where the flour and water mixture was and it caused quite a bit of fun. Then there was a small house where the old man would make up ointment for different rashes (ringworm) and cough mixture (infirmary) and mother would get a mixture of seven oils for us to rub on our chest for colds. It was always kept near our kitchen range during the winter. Also daisy powders for headaches and different things for catching flies. One was a brown square, you put in a saucer of vinegar on a window sill or a long pull-out one to hang from the ceiling, Also Mrs. Gillman had a little sweet shop and sold home-made ice cream from a pail packed around with ice. We could sit on a form in the shop and suck it off a glass short cane.

Also there was Tom Herbert the greengrocer. He always had a bowlful of winkles in the doorway and you could buy a bag of these for 1d.

Across the street was a cycle shop (nearer park), a little house where a very old lady and gent lived. He had been in the Crimean War and I believe they were gentle folk come down in the world. He wore a velvet smoking jacket and pillbox hat with a tassel. His wife was very tiny and always wore long cameo ear-rings and must have been so beautiful in her early days. I used to cut up wool and rags to make rugs. She earned a little money from the Heritage whatever that was. Their names were Mr. and Mrs. Page.

Next door was Hills the butcher. Bladders of lard were always hanging in the window. He had a slaughterhouse in the Barton at the back and after school Nellie Coombes and I would often sneak around the back and see a beast killed and hung up.

Also there was an outhouse where pigs were kept waiting to be killed. Rats would come out from holes in the stonework and eat away at the pig food. Good job it's more hygienic today (1980).

Hills the Butchers, Church Road, Redfield, Bristol.

Church Road shops, Redfield, Bristol.

I feel all this is in the past yet as plain as it was then it is to me now. Mr. Smart next door sold sweets, toys and comics. I always remember the wooden Dutch dolls with black painted hair. Also for one penny we could buy a game of snakes and ladders or Comic Cuts with a skinny man on the front looking out of prison railings with arrows on his suit!

Next door was a large grocers. The owner looked like King George V but I think his wife was a Belgian, very tall and a florid face. Once I took a silver threepenny piece off the till in the bar and went over and bought 12 long liquorice sticks. The moment I got home, mother was waiting and as she know she had not rung up the money the missing one was the culprit – me. I remember them all looking at me just saying nothing except mother. That was the first and last time I ever did such a thing. It was a lesson in life. Thou shalt not steal (from the Bible).

When Sir Billy Butlin died, the papers stated he started his career with a hoopla stall so I was right. Also, John James, who had his shop above the Rising Sun (our pub). He never forgot his humble times and is now doing all he can for boys and girls of poorer parents in our town.

I have cause to be so grateful to my parents who always worked so hard for us. The only smart thing Dad wore was when he went out to the pictures with mother on a Tuesday afternoon - then he would put on his short gabardine coat with black velvet collar and bowler hat, and carry his silver mounted umbrella on his arm. The rest of the week it would be an old pair of grey trousers and cotton shirt with no collar. God bless him.

One family that stood out on Church Road was the name Verrier. A road facing the Redfield Methodist Chapel was named after one man who was a magistrate. His house was near Dr. Foss, Clouds Hill House. If a person objected to having a young child vaccinated against small pox he would give a note to say granted. The law in those days was a child should have this done but 1980 as today I write this it is a thing of the past.

Another Verrier was a tailor and a good one too, with double breasted indigo suits on display in the window. Again another had a sweet shop next to the higher grade school and I believe there was a daughter. As we grew up and went off to work my Dad bought three houses off Mr. Verrier the magistrate for about £500. Gosh, it's hardly believable. One was in Morse Road, and another two in Victoria Avenue. One (number 40) was blown up in the 1940 air raids on Bristol. By then my dear father had died and my mother had gone there to retire. Lucky she was out on the Good Friday but persons each side were killed.

I guess this is about all I can remember about my young days. At fourteen I left school. Brother Bert was employed by Cable Boot Shop, Castle Street. Sister Lily was employed by Mardon Sons & Hall, box making. I wanted to be a dressmaker, but was sent to work with Lily who was 20 by then. Mother gave me 7½d a day, that was my tram money. I'd return to Old Market, and dinner was had in Owen's Faggot Shop, Old Market. I would have just sausage and mash, with a cup of tea and piece of bread. Later I would go the works' dining room in winter where you could have cottage pie and potatoes, cabbage and ½d for a cup of cocoa. In summer I would go with other girls to Temple Church and we would sit under the trees and each cheese sandwiches and perhaps a piece of mother's cake or a bar of chocolate.

It was there I met my first boyfriend George A – I did not marry him but another George – George Aldridge. Two fellows, same initials!

We would alight from our tram in Old Market Street and wend our way to Tower Hill, turn the corner, over St. Phillips Bridge, past Avon Cold Storage, Counterslip where there was a paper bag factory (Bennetts) down to Georges Brewery. Then Temple Back past Temple Church and Shakespeare Inn, and Neptune's Statue across the road past Todd's Clothing factory and DCL Yeast Company. Somehow the yeast company always had an awful death smell like the cheese shop in Temple Back. We always pinched our noses on going past this dirty-looking shop.

Looking back today although it is all so different, office blocks, insurance offices and the like, in those days it was a joy to see the various shops. Byzantine windows, coloured lights. Two shops stand out – Wil-Sam-Mor wallpaper shop and Oliver's Bar, where you could get a large glass of port wine of 6d and before you crossed over to Bristol Bridge, a second-hand bookshop and opposite Gaskell and Chambers who sold brass and wooden barrel taps. On the corner the very resplendent Georges Brewery Offices and opposite at Redcliffe Street was Robinsons where you could watch the 1lb paper flour bags being made. This fascinated me.

Old Market Street, Bristol.

On bonus days about March, the girls would spend some of their money in Oliver's Bar and return drunk to work. We would hide them behind stacks of boxes to sleep it off. By the way, another well-known rough public house was The Posada just after crossing Bristol Bridge. It was a haunt of factory workers from Wills in Redcliffe Street, Huddon's cigar factory, Robinsons and Fry's Chocolate factory in Pithay.

Little did I know after I married we would come to live in the city. We took the Carpenters Arms at 13 St. James' Churchyard, and my dearest parents put money down for us to better ourselves in this world. We did very well, working 12 hours a day, 7 days a week and repaid my parents in just over a year.

While living there 2 girls, Joy and Barbara were born. We knew little rest until they started school. Joy attended St. James School until 9½ years of age and later Barbara went to St. Gabriel's High School or Convent School run by catholic sisters. We paid 4 guineas for Joy and 3 for Barbara per term and paid for all books.

George had 2 cars (Fords) one after the other and then came the war and air raids. George and I left the pub and moved out, taking mother with us (her house was bombed) to Coronation Road, Downend. The girls went to local schools. George was called up for jobs for the War Office – Cirencester, Fairford, Chippenham, Down Ampney, Lechlade etc.

Then at short call to Portsmouth where 3 Mulberry Harbours were built and he worked on them with others for the Government. As invasion day drew near he returned to Bristol and was sent to Avonmouth loading ammunition boats (he received danger money for this). He made friends with American soldiers etc. Many a piece of meat or some fruit he was given because rations were so small.

One night he did not return home until 3 o'clock in the morning. I was so alarmed. He was driven home in a jeep by a Yank. As I opened the front door our brave men were setting out from Lyneham and other places and flew over our house heavy and loaded with bombs. I can hear the drone today. Come 7 o'clock came the news – This is D-Day. I ran upstairs to George – the girls were awake and I said we are bombing the Germans. All the little ammunition boats and others were there at Avonmouth and the next minute they were gone. Oh dear God I pray never our grandchildren will ever go through such times. My dear brother Gilbert was in this war in Italy but returned safe.

The Carpenters Arms, St. James' Churchyard in the 1920s when Ivy and George were in residence.

And now I am an old lady. George is still with me at 80 years of age. We get on each other's nerves sometimes as we are in an Anchor Housing flat, 86 people on different floors just ending our life in the time God has given us. It's no pleasure to live to be old. We are very independent and my dearest wish is that no more such places as this are built. They call it sheltered housing but I say this as my mother said years ago "never give up your home and live with others". We never thought in this day and age such places would be. It's all on a posh style but really it's like 100 Fishponds Road* where I used to visit an old lady. It's like a chapel of rest.

*100 Fishponds Road was the location of the Eastville Workhouse, close to Eastville Park.

No matter, I will finish. It's nearly the time "The day thou gavest Lord is ended". So be it. We both will walk one day in God's heavenly light.

I will now conclude. If, after reading this, tear it up if you like but do not grieve. Remember hell is what others make for you on this Earth. So be happy, live your lives to the full and be of good cheer.

Au Revoir.

Mother.

CHAPTER 15.
ECHOES FROM THE PAST.

These are further written memories from Ivy, recorded in an exercise book towards the end of her life, and reproduced in full.

My interest was first aroused when a notice of article was in our *'Bristol Evening Post'*. It said that people from the Caribbean had put in a bid to buy Holy Trinity Church, Trinity Road, between St. George, Bristol to Stapleton Road, Eastville. They had bought it and it was going to be a community centre. But – that the graves in the churchyard were causing a voodoo and people would not attend and they would have the graves removed.

Holy Trinity Church, Bristol.

Now I do understand the money was from a grant of three given from our Government to do this (but the Caribbeans wanted a car park for persons to attend and would remove headstones and do this). This shocked me because to come to Bristol and do this sort of thing from their country of origin was wrong, although the church had so very few parishioners was there not, some other use was made of it than this; how about a school or market etc. This place of worship was a landmark. I am not against a coloured person in any way, we are all God's children.

The outcome was on going past the Community Centre (as it was now called) were beer casks and rubbish strewn all over the entrance to the place. Then last month in our evening paper was a picture of piled up gravestones waiting to be carried away from the Centre. Also a notice inserted regarding persons who had loved ones and ancestors buried there. The remains would be interred at Greenbank Cemetery by Avon Council. Now I knew from things told me that I had a grandfather buried there (under the wall), my mother would say, so I went in on 24th February 1981 to Room 5 as the paper advised one to do.

Really I wanted to find out more and know about those who came before me. A gentleman looked up different things and gave me a plan of the churchyard, part of which Avon had and is in a road widening scheme at some time in the future. Lo and behold I believe two grandparents are in that part and the graves untouched (not sure of one). He told me the Caribbeans had bought the land on the other side of the church. So be it. I believe that in about 1840 times were so very very hard and not many able to buy a last resting place, and those left behind had to go to the Parish to assist them. Also many died so very young. I wish to state that the gentleman in Room 5 Avon House was a very kind person and thank him for his kindness (Mr. Wheeler).

The following story as far as I know to be true as told by my mother, and the family names are Morgan, Coles and Bidder. Also Fuller. I have written to Church House Bristol (City), the address given to me to obtain more evidence if possible and in the following pages write my mother's story for my girls. Also whatever happened all those years ago to our family? Today, me being a Miss Morgan, married George Aldridge. We are very proud of our own family of both names and their children, who being descendants of the past persons, somehow know we have been helped in spirit from the shadows. As it is quoted their children shall rise up and call them blessed. Our girls names both married are Anderson (Joy) and Bennett (Barbara). Being 75 years of age and before I forget I will tell you of the past as told by my mother in the following pages.

My mother's name was Elizabeth (Coles). When she was young she was sent to earn her lessons at Castle Green Day School for which she would pay one penny. My father and his brother Harry went to Redcross School in Redcross Street. The headmaster was a Mr. Read.

My mother could not even write her own name on leaving school, only to put a cross "x". But my father was very gifted and a good singer and in the summer he would walk with his brother Harry holding horses outside inns to earn some money and make his way and that to Weston-Super-Mare and would sing with Charlie Goodman and his merry folk on the sands near the pier. But the time came that both brothers had to go off to work to help the family so both of them had a job with Pullin, Thomas & Slade, later to become Webbs (Pork Butchers) later, in West Street, almost opposite Trinity Church.

They had to start work at 5 o'clock in the morning and drive a horse and cart, and deliver meat to the big houses around Clifton Downs but they would finish work about 3 o'clock in the afternoon. There were 3 more brothers and 3 sisters, seven in the family and they lived in Bright Street off Morley Street, Lawrence Hill (near the station). Chandlers the Chemist was on the corner and my Gran's house in Bright Street went uphill, first turning on the left.

Now they were very poor and all I know of my grandfather was he had a temper. One Sunday when my parents were courting they arrived home about supper time to find Gran had received a beating and that-so-my father beat him and he went upstairs to nurse his wounds. But later he came down and beat father on the head with a stick and he had to go and have stitches in his head.

Never any more was told about the old man but I have an idea he left home or went up country, his age was about 37 or 38. There are no records of a grave or funeral but when I find a bit more out will say. Somehow I have a feeling he was buried by the Parish somewhere because my Gran had his youngest daughter marry and come to live with her (1902). His name was Foley but he was not Irish (Catholic). We just called him Uncle Dan.

Elizabeth Morgan (nee Coles), 1875-1963

There came the time they had to get a little house as children were coming along so they went to Twinnell Road, Easton. Then Dad's brother who lived in Wellesley Street died, his name was George. My Gran became very sad and depressed, although all the family of 6 remaining helped Gran with amounts of money, whatever they could afford. My parents took over the "Rising Sun" Redfield, Uncle Tom the "Weaver's Arms" Barton Hill, and Uncle Harry the "Talbot" at the bottom of Croydon Street and Easton Road. Another sister Alice married Albert Stephens and kept the "Lord Raglan" on Stapleton Road. Florence, Jack and Clara and the others seemed not to get ahead. Before mother and father took the "Rising Sun" they had a little grocery shop in Bellevue Road and Dad still worked. So they began to save money.

Now my Gran became ill and confused and gave up her little house in Bright Street to live with Aunt Florrie. She was 68 years of age then, and one Saturday she sadly made her way to Penny Terrace* Bridge off Avon Vale Road and walked into the water with her cape over her head leaving her boots on the bank. The family searched for 2 days and she was found in the Floating Harbour on the Monday morning. I was about 6 years old and I was taken to see her in her coffin and her poor face was all cut about. I never forgot. All the family were so unhappy but she was buried in Avonview Cemetery with her son in a spot along the bottom path, 3 graves in near Strawberry Lane. She was a Miss Williams when single, had a brother Isaac and a sister Harriet, Great Uncle and Great Aunt to me. They all had a very hard life.

*Probably Pinney Terrace Bridge at the bottom of Marsh Lane.

Uncle Ike would help anywhere to do with animals or horses. He could always tell a story from the past and give many a good laugh. One day when asked I remember he brought a live fowl to my mother and took to the back yard, hung it up and cut its head off. The fowl ran around the yard without it, it was horrible, something I never forgot.

As I have noted before in my personal story, Aunt Harriet married an old man with a beard* late in life and died aged about 70, Uncle Ike about 80 or so. We all grew up, got married and lived in different houses around the "Rising Sun".

*This would be John Cureton, who she married on 5th July 1903. She had previously married Walter Woodland in 1878 but sadly he passed away that same year.

Now about my mother, she must have had a very hard life. Her father used to have a horse and cart and go selling china round villages outside Bristol. They lived in Ellbroad Court, almost opposite St. Jude's Church. There were three children, Harry (eldest), mother, and Aunt Mary Anne (also her mother's name). She was a Miss Bidder. It seems she was very fond of a drink, when her husband was away selling his wares she would go to the pub. She was there one day when my Grandfather came home. Uncle Harry went to fetch her home and trouble ensued and Grandad put his arm through a pane of glass and lost part of it up to his elbow. He never really recovered and died about 32 or 33 years of age. Mother said he was in his coffin in the living room till buried at Holy Trinity Church by the Parish and she told me a tramp broke in and slept in the room where her father was in his coffin and remains of matches etc. which had been lit were on the floor, found in the morning. Mother was so upset, she was about 13 years of age and always said her father was buried under the wall. I have found through enquiries that 4 graves are under the wall near Clarence Road. They had no names so I presume they were for people buried by the Poor Law.

The Cotton Factory, Barton Hill.

As St. Nicholas Roman Catholic Church was near Ellbroad Court, Ellbroad Street, somehow my Grandmother met up with a little old Irish Man and they married. Two sons were born, Jack and Maurice. The old man Hennessy was very cruel to mother, Harry and Aunt Mary Anne tried hard to make them go to his church, so Mother's Aunt Phoebe Bidder (Husband's name Fuller) took them into her house off Avon Vale Road, opposite the Cooperage where barrels were made.

Mother got a job in the local cotton factory and wove cotton. This was after she took her brother and sister to school. Then her aunt would make wine and mother would sell it for her in the factory. Then she would return home and do her aunt's work as she was a frail lady. She died when I was 11. Mother loved her very much and was with her till the end.

My mother's own mother died 10 years before aged 42, and lies in Avonview Cemetery. Mother named her Coles on the tombstone as she never thought the Irishman had married her, but in later life I indeed found he had*.

*No evidence to this effect has been discovered – however the 1891 Census does shows her as married but this is probably incorrect.

My father bought a brick-lined grave at Avonview Cemetery for 25/- so there rests Mother and Father, Uncle Harry, my Gran and a brother's child a few weeks old and Aunt Mary Anne. God bless their souls.

Mother's half-brothers were brought up by a woman called Bridget but mother was always friendly with Uncle Jack but Maurice was more like his father in looks. Sad to say the old Irishman took over the horses and cart and china round when Mother's Father died and my mother hated it when he would leave it outside the "Rising Sun". I never remember her speaking to him.

So this sad story is ended. I have put together as much as my memory can help me.

CHAPTER 16.
WORLD WAR II AND BEYOND.

Ivy's recollections of World War II and the Blitz years are astoundingly accurate and detailed, and it is likely that some of stories she remembered have never been published before. Sadly, many of her stories were told to us over the years but were never recorded on paper.

However, recently-found documents have revealed that she trained as an Air Raid Warden back in 1938, and received a certificate confirming this which is reproduced below:

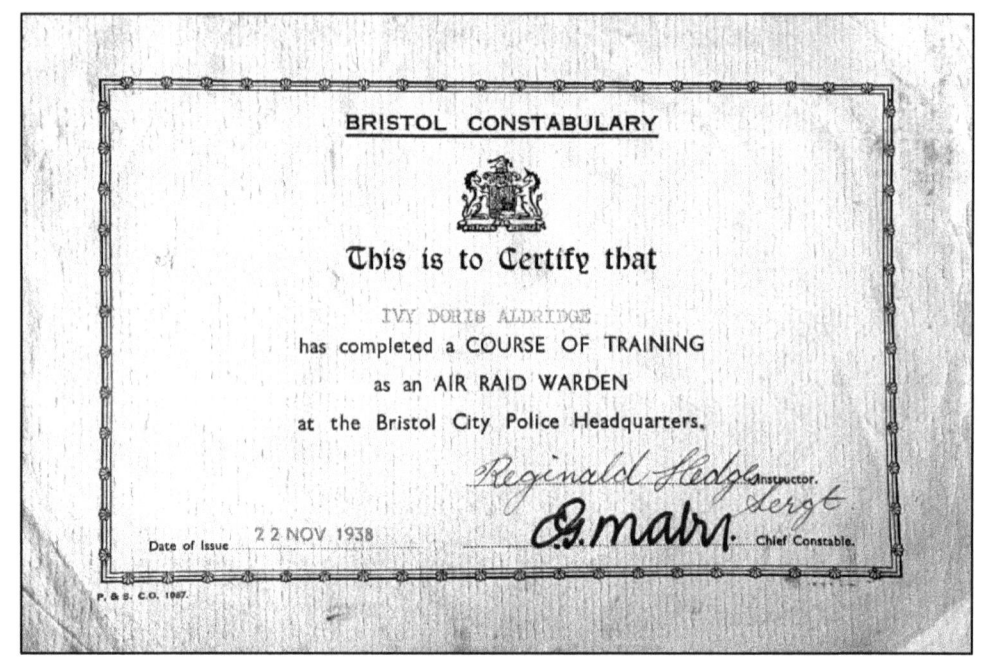

Ivy's Certificate of Training as an Air Raid Warden, 22nd November 1938.

Ivy's First Aid Course certificate from 27th June 1939.

B R I S T O L   C O N S T A B U L A R Y.

A.R.P. Department,
Police Headquarters,
Bridewell Street,
BRISTOL, 1.

28th April, 1939.

Dear Sir or Madam,

    I enclose herewith your Information Form which contains details relative to the Air Raid Wardens' Organisation in your Division. You are asked to keep this form carefully as additional information will be supplied to you from time to time, and your Information Form should be completed accordingly.

    I should like to impress upon you the necessity of always referring to your Group Letter and Sector Letter in any communication you may have with this Office, your Head Wardens or Divisional Wardens. There is also attached to your Information Form a slip giving the details of your Sector, and you will note that you are asked to cover everything which is within the boundary referred to on the slip, including any new roads which may be built upon. Maps will be available at your Divisional Headquarters in the near future, and the revised training, which will begin during the week commencing the 8th May, 1939, will contain a lecture on the Divisional Maps.

    With regard to your additional training, I should like to emphasise the necessity of making yourself familiar with the information which is given in A.R.P. Handbook No.8 "The Duties of Air Raid Wardens", as much of your training will be based upon this book. Arrangements are being made for the training to be carried out by Groups in the nearest available school to each particular Group, and I hope you will make a special effort to attend the lectures.

    On the back of the Information Form you will find a list of Wardens who are allotted to your sector, and it is hoped that you will make yourself known to each other, and make contact with your Head Wardens as early as possible.

    The "Western Daily Press", "Evening Post" and "Evening World" kindly publish information relating to Air Raid Wardens in a special column of their respective newspapers weekly, and it will be of assistance to you and the Organisation generally if you will make a practice of reading these notes regularly every Monday.

    The distribution of respirators is nearing completion, and it will be necessary for you, when visiting houses within your sector, to satisfy yourself that each person is correctly fitted, and the safety pins adjusted.

    The appointment of Senior Wardens is receiving consideration, and the necessary information will be conveyed to you in due course.

Yours faithfully,

Chief Constable.

Letter from the Chief Constable of Bristol with details of the training of Air Raid Wardens dated 28th April 1938.

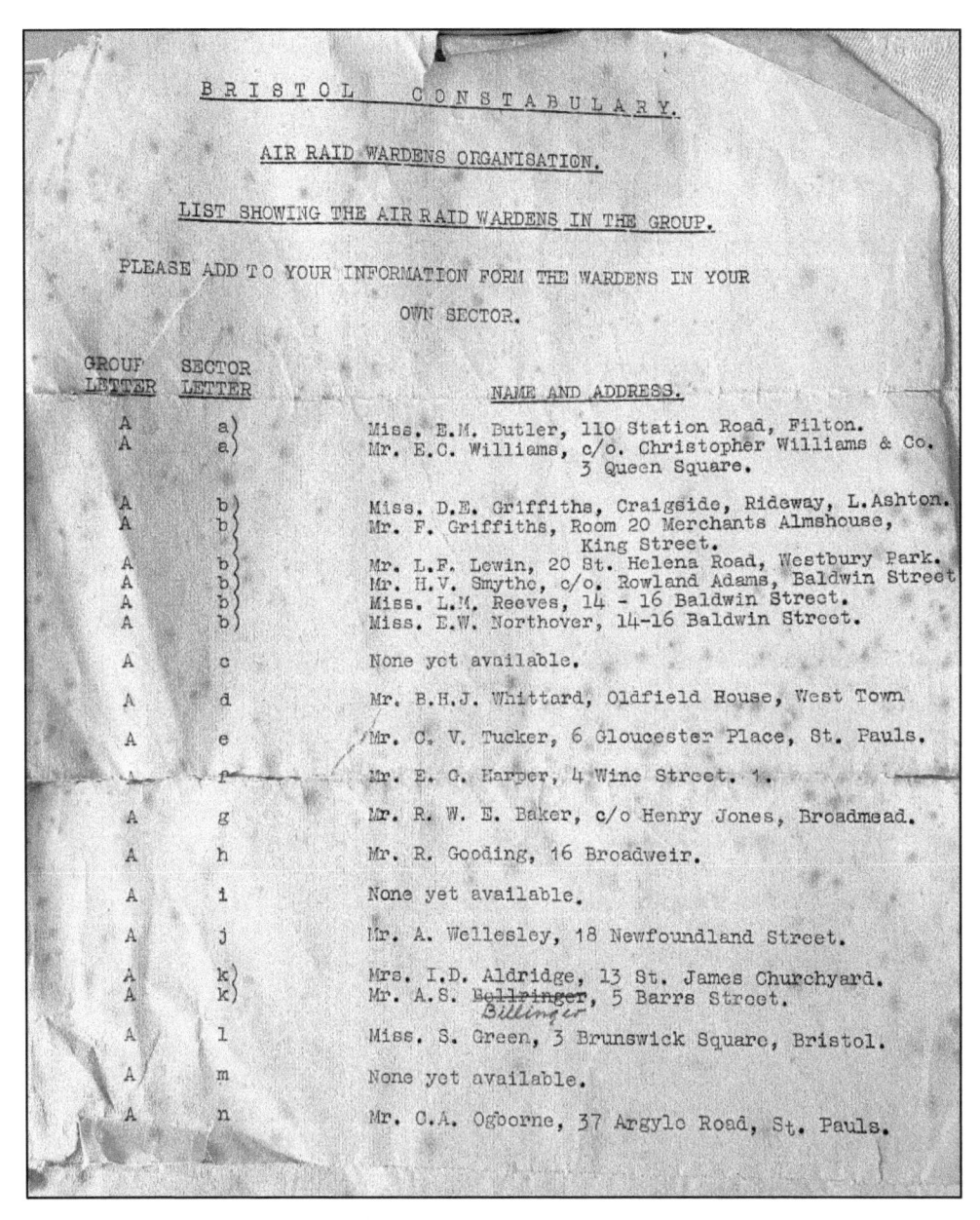

```
                    B R I S T O L    C O N S T A B U L A R Y.

                         AIR RAID WARDENS ORGANISATION.

                  LIST SHOWING THE AIR RAID WARDENS IN THE GROUP.

                  PLEASE ADD TO YOUR INFORMATION FORM THE WARDENS IN YOUR
                                      OWN SECTOR.

         GROUP      SECTOR
         LETTER     LETTER                    NAME AND ADDRESS.

            A         a)      Miss. E.M. Butler, 110 Station Road, Filton.
            A         a)      Mr. E.C. Williams, c/o. Christopher Williams & Co.
                                      3 Queen Square.

            A         b)      Miss. D.E. Griffiths, Craigside, Rideway, L.Ashton.
            A         b)      Mr. F. Griffiths, Room 20 Merchants Almshouse,
                                      King Street.
            A         b)      Mr. L.F. Lewin, 20 St. Helena Road, Westbury Park.
            A         b)      Mr. H.V. Smythe, c/o. Rowland Adams, Baldwin Street
            A         b)      Miss. L.M. Reeves, 14 - 16 Baldwin Street.
            A         b)      Miss. E.W. Northover, 14-16 Baldwin Street.

            A         c       None yet available.

            A         d       Mr. B.H.J. Whittard, Oldfield House, West Town

            A         e       Mr. C.V. Tucker, 6 Gloucester Place, St. Pauls.

            A         f       Mr. E.G. Harper, 4 Wine Street. 1.

            A         g       Mr. R.W.E. Baker, c/o Henry Jones, Broadmead.

            A         h       Mr. R. Gooding, 16 Broadweir.

            A         i       None yet available.

            A         j       Mr. A. Wellesley, 18 Newfoundland Street.

            A         k)      Mrs. I.D. Aldridge, 13 St. James Churchyard.
            A         k)      Mr. A.S. Bellringer, 5 Barrs Street.
                                       Billinger

            A         l       Miss. S. Green, 3 Brunswick Square, Bristol.

            A         m       None yet available.

            A         n       Mr. C.A. Ogborne, 37 Argyle Road, St. Pauls.
```

List of Air Raid Wardens in the Local Group, 1938. Ivy shown as living a 13 St. James Churchyard, the 'Carpenter's Arms' public house.

The Central Bristol area was defined as: Everything enclosed within the following boundary line- from York Street, left hand side Cumberland Street, left hand side North Street and Bond Street to the Haymarket, left hand side of Haymarket, Horsefair, Milk Street and York Street, to Cumberland Street.

Typically, she starts her memories with a paragraph of her memories of the Carpenter's Arms at 13 St. James' Churchyard:

Having evacuated Dunkirk we had soldiers all around us. Also the Lancashire Fusiliers were sent to our town. I had brought a wind-up gramophone for £2 second-hand and bought a few records. *'Bless 'em All'*, *'Roll Out the Barrel'*, *'Lily Marlene'* and *'Hang Out the Washing on the Seigfried Line'* etc. My word, our little pub echoed over and over again with the singing. Two of the fellows were killed in Salerno, Italy, later in the war.

R.I.P.

More details of the Air Raid Wardens in the Central Bristol Area.

Sunday Blitz, 24th November 1940.

I was sat upstairs in my front bedroom window about 3.30 p.m. or near when the A.F.S. Service etc. slowly wended its way from Stokes Croft into the Horsefair, past St. James' Church and St. James' Churchyard where I and my family lived at No. 13 and then on to the Bridewell etc. My next-door neighbour was with me, Mrs. O'Leary, and she said "whatever is going to happen?"

You see, it was Sunday and the children would be returning from Sunday School at St. James-the-Less across the Parade just around 4 o'clock.

Now the previous week Coventry was burned and bombed by the enemy and seeing this lot of grey vehicles put a thought into my head for a brief moment. Oh no, not Bristol! My friend was alarmed but I told her I would go and prepare tea. My two girls were later returning from Sunday School than usual, and on their arrival at 4.45 we had tea and got around to talking about Christmas. Just then my husband went to the front door and looked out – and to his horror fairy lights of flares were coming from the sky and he called me. All I remember was a young couple just entering the park leading to the Haymarket Public House and at the bottom of Union Street a girl was carrying a bunch of flowers.

I went into my friend's house next door and brought her into our house as she lived alone. Then 'clang, clang', ambulances and fire engines were all around us and fires raging with St. James' Presbyterian Church all alight. It was as though a service was being held as all the windows were as though lit up for the service. We packed a few possessions into a bag, grabbed the canary and all of us wended our way down to the Lower Arcade. You see, the Top (Upper) Arcade was all ablaze and we had friends who had a cellar in the lower one. People came after us from all places and I well remember the Baptist Church with all the people singing hymns although all around was burning.

From H.M. Stationery Warehouse to the old Fry's offices, burnt paper was blowing over our heads like feathers. I can still taste and smell the bits as they fell. I looked back at the Arcade and it had to burn itself out as there was no water being played on it till later. It was obtained from the River Frome but too late indeed.

Our friends whose shop was second in the Lower Arcade admitted us to the cellar with others who lived around and one man gave me his wife's jewellery to take care of as she had gone to visit a friend that evening. I was honoured to do this service for him. As regards the 'call of nature' we had one potty and we went to the end of the cellar to empty the contents one by one after use.

We did not feel the cold as the heat from the inferno was all around us and this Hitler 'The Antichrist' vented all he could through these aeroplanes upon the residents of our no mean City. Who were these men pouring these loads of destruction upon us men, women and children? As our Saviour said "Forgive them, for they know not what they do".

I often wonder if they had families, or they themselves were returning to the place from which they came had any thought to say "why, why, why they had to set out by order to destroy with loads of bombs and flares and Molotov Cocktails?" As time went by I learned to put them out with the lid of an ashbin although sometimes my hair and eyebrows were singed.

Now we had two 'all clears' that night of the 24th November and after the first my husband and I went back to our house but the Home Guard were around and as went in, the people were looting the shops who had windows blown in. Shame upon these people. We had a small pram and I gathered up a few blankets and two bottles of whisky and a large home-made Christmas Pudding and placed on top of the heap. As you can guess the basin and pudding rolled off into the gutter and a gentleman passing heard me say we have one Christmas Pudding – and he said "Madam, I admire you for your courage" and raised his hat.

On our return to the cellar, the whisky was handed round – we were all more relaxed although sad at heart.

Suddenly my brother Bert from Redfield, a good way away, arrived. Someone had told him where we were and he cried with relief, his face as black as soot. He said from Lawrence Hill hose and firemen were engaged in putting out flames, and A.R.P. men were all around too (brave men). He was soon away stepping over the hoses to inform our families we had survived.

As dawn broke, we all knew the last siren meant we could return to our homes and this we did. Mrs. O'Leary, aged about 79, said she would go to her bed but alas for George and myself another siren sounded. I am glad now we called there as it was a heavy raid and mother was all alone. We all got under the stairs with a small light and had a sing-song but of course we could not close the door. In between, an air raid warden would call at different houses he knew to reassure us. Before 12 o'clock all was over, I had a premonition that mother's house would go, so I made her promise to go to the St. Matthews Church shelters at the top of Dove Lane. She assured me she would next time.

The raids went on at different times but on the Good Friday at Easter the sirens went later than usual and we spent that night in an air raid shelter in St. James' Park. Now we were told next morning that mother's house had a direct hit and went up like a pack of cards, killing many people all the way up Victoria Avenue. So my premonition was to be fulfilled and my mother, who by the way had spent the night in St. George's Park air raid shelter with my sister and her husband and friends, was indeed safe and all she had was the clothes she wore. Later on, she came to live with us, as we had moved out of the city and my husband went away on war service, and she lived to 88 years so God had truly blessed her.

The first air raid on Bristol was on a Sunday. All we heard was 'clang, clang', bells ringing and ambulances. We took shelter in our cellar until the 'all clear'. The next morning along the Parade (St. James' Parade as it was called), we found at the end a bomb had dropped in the lane between Champion Davis (Sweet Factory) and Bristol Eye Hospital where an ice cream shop had a direct hit killing the family named De Santos. They had to dig for the persons concerned. Maybe this was a trial run for the enemy.

Much of the information was verified by my late mother, who recalled the fire in the Upper Arcade, causing the back wall of the 'Carpenters Arms' to glow orange with the heat and impossible to touch.

In 1943, to avoid further possible air raids, the family moved to the outskirts of Bristol to a new house at 32 Coronation Road, Downend, and in 1949 they moved again to 23 Maywood Crescent, Fishponds, Bristol. The National Identity Cards of Ivy and George recalled these moves, and it is interesting to note George's address changes which included residences in Chippenham and Portsmouth. These were due to his important work for the war effort, details of which he was of course forbidden to disclose.

However, from information gleaned from family members, it was clear that his work involved building the concrete sections for the Mulberry Harbours used during the D-Day landings. Many of the sections found their way to Burnham-on-Sea in Somerset after the war, where they are still used for sea defences and to protect the sand dunes against the tide.

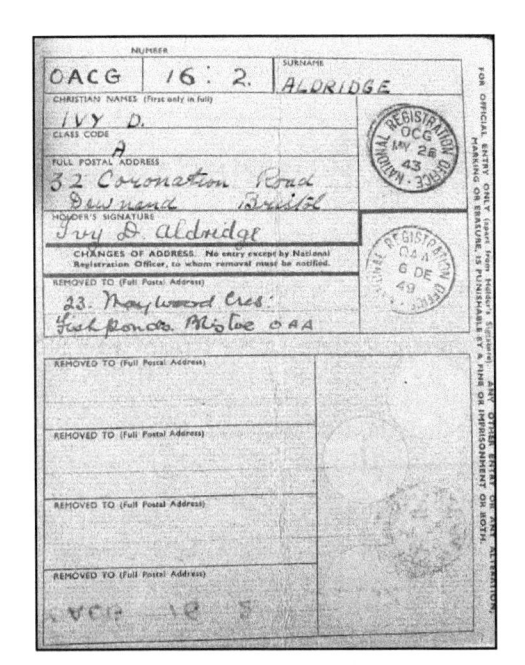

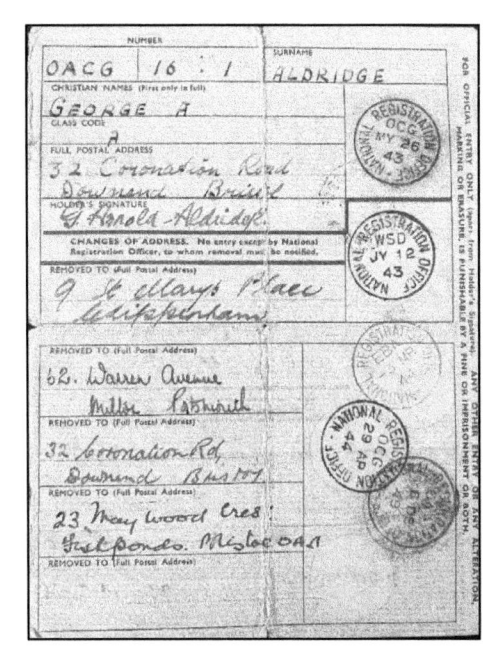

Ivy's and George's National Identity Cards, showing George's moves to Chippenham and Portsmouth.

However, she continued to recall her life in the area during the war, and along with her husband George wrote many times to the *'Bristol Evening Post'* to remember those times.

CHAPTER 17.
THE FOOTBALL CAREER OF FREDERICK 'JERRY' MORGAN.

Frederick, better known as 'Jerry', played for various local clubs in the Bristol area before embarking on a successful Football League career.

His first club was a local side in Bristol, Horfield United; thence Fishponds City followed by a couple of appearances for Bristol City before the outbreak of World War 1.

He played for the latter club in the Football League Division 2 during the 1912-13 season, away at Leeds City on 7th December 1912, and home against Grimsby the following week. He never played again for the club, joining the Royal Navy Volunteer Reserve in September 1916.

As the conflict came to a close, he played in a few friendly matches for various clubs. One friendly match where he turned out for Fishponds City against Bristol City, played on 26th January 1918, saw Jerry score the only goal in a 1-0 victory. Press reports note that "Morgan walked the ball in".

He then played for a short time for Caerphilly, before returning to the West Country to play for Bath City.

His career there was short; he joined the club from Caerphilly in 1919, in a swap deal for Tremlett, to join his brother Jim who also played for the club. After scoring a remarkable 12 goals in 13 appearances, he moved to Bristol Rovers in early 1920.

He made his debut for Bristol Rovers in the last fixture of the 1919-20 season, when the club were still in the Southern League. This match, away at Gillingham, resulted in a 2-2 draw, with the club finishing in 17th place.

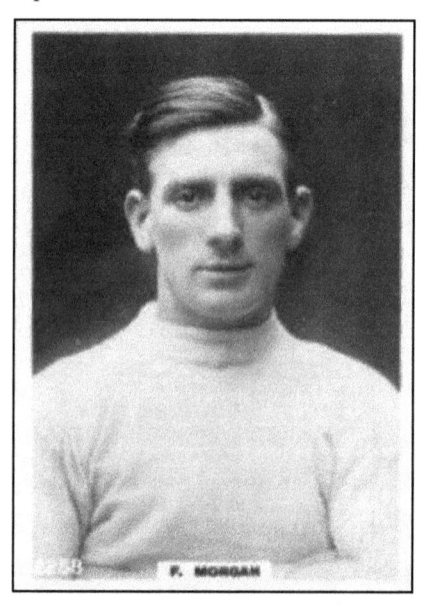

Collectors' card showing Frederick 'Jerry' Morgan.

However, the club were accepted into the Football League Division 3(S) the following season 1920-1921, and finished a respectable 10th. Jerry made 21 appearances, scoring 3 goals. His first for the club came in a home 2-1 defeat to Southampton on 27th November 1920. He next scored in a 3-2 victory over Reading on December 11th 1920, and his final league goal of the season came in a 2-2 away draw with Merthyr on 16th April 1921.

He did, however, score a hat-trick in a devastating 9-0 victory at home over Worksop Town in the F.A. Cup on December 18th 1920. This was only the second hat-trick scored by a Bristol Rovers player since the club joined the Football League in the 1920/21 season.

He had a far more successful season in 1921-1922, featuring in 32 of the 42 league fixtures, scoring 8 times; against Charlton (A) on September 10th 1921, Merthyr (A) on 29th October 1921, twice against Norwich (H) on November 12th 1921, another brace against Aberdare (H) on January 14th 1921, Newport (A) on January 29th 1922, and finally one against Exeter (A) on April 1st 1922. The team finished in 14th position.

The earliest photograph found of Jerry Morgan and the Bristol Rovers team. This one dates from 1921/22.

Team (L-R): Joe Walter, Frederick 'Jerry' Morgan, Bill Payne, Steve Sims, Joe 'Jimmy' Kissock, Jesse Whatley, Sid Leigh, Jack Ball, Billy Palmer, Tom Winspear, David Steele.

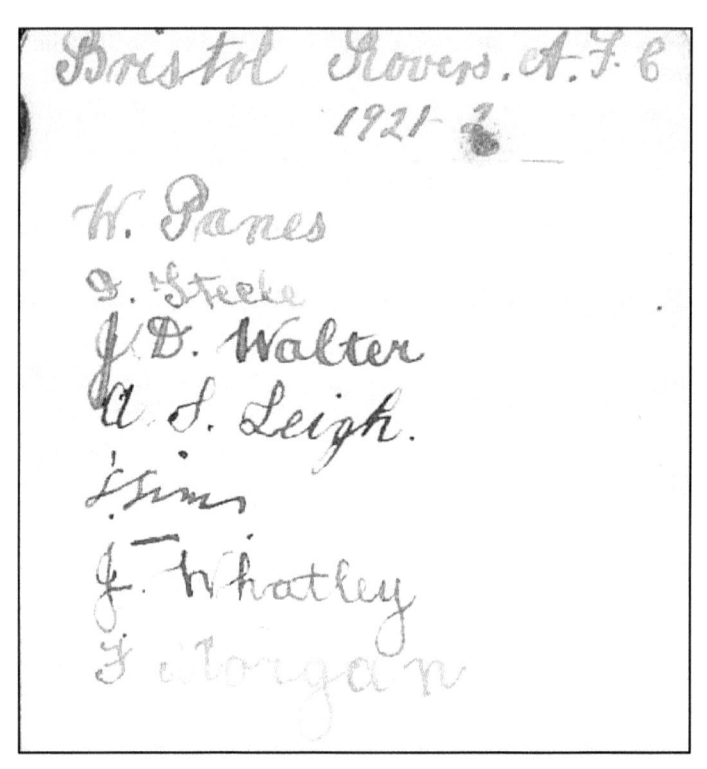

An autograph sheet from 1921 showing Jerry Morgan's autograph at the bottom.

The 1922-1923 saw Jerry again having a successful season, with 34 appearances and 6 league goals, as the side comfortably finished in 13th position.

His goals came against Newport (H) on 28th August 1922, Luton (H) on 10th February 1923, Merthyr (A) on April 3rd 1923, finishing with a hat-trick against Norwich (H) on 23rd April 1923.

He also played a few times for the Rovers' reserve team, and one match in particular against Bristol St. George on September 25th 1922 is worth recalling, in which Jerry scored two goals in quick succession, "completely monopolising the play in a 4-2 victory."

Another scanned photograph from 1921/22.

Back Row (L-R): Dennis Howes, Sam Furness, Joe Kissock, Billy Palmer, Steve Sims.
3rd Row: Andrew Wilson (manager), Jack Thomson, Tom Winspear, Jesse Whatley, Joe Hall, Jack Ball, Jack Stockley, G. Pay.
2nd Row: W. News, David Steele, Joe Walter, Sid Leigh, Harry Boxley, Edward Lee Harvey, Jimmy Liddle.
Front Row: Unknown, Jerry Morgan, Unknown, Unknown.

He did miss a few matches in early December 1922 due to injury during that season, as the *'Western Daily Press'* reported:

"Lunn takes Jerry Morgan's place at inside left. Morgan's luck is dead out at present, for, in addition to getting that nasty cut under the eye at Reading last week, he has now contracted a sore throat."

His appearances during the 1923-1924 season were restricted, and it wasn't until 1st March 1924 that he made his first appearance for the first team that season in a 3-1 home victory over Charlton Athletic.

He only made 5 more appearance that season, scoring twice in a 3-1 home victory over Norwich on 15th March 1924.

The side finished in 9th position in Division 3(S).

Another local press picture of the 1921/22 Bristol Rovers first team squad.

Trainer and Players (in white shirts):

Middle Row (L-R): Les Endicott (Trainer), Dennis Howes, Walter Bird, Jesse Whatley, Sam Furness, Harry Boxley.
Front Row (L-R): Billy Panes, Les Chance, Jerry Morgan, Joe Hall, Joe Norton, Harold Bell.

However, he did score a couple in an F.A. Cup fixture against Yeovil & Petters on November 20th 1924, and also scored against Bristol City in a Gloucestershire Cup Final replay at home on 29th April 1925 in a 2-0 victory. The local press reported the Yeovil fixture in somewhat scathing terms:

"On 29 November 1924, Bristol Rovers played Yeovil and Petters United in the F.A. Cup, who were playing for the first time in the first round proper. A record crowd of around 6,500 including many from Bristol, who naturally made themselves heard. A pitch that was sodden after days of heavy rain made decent play difficult, Rovers feeling the ire of the crowd after hard tackles that the referee allowed to go unpunished. Yeovil took the lead after thirty minutes through man of the match Gardiner, only for Rovers to equalise just a minute later, through Ernie Whatmore.

Again Yeovil took the game to Rovers and once more Yeovil took the lead after fifty minutes with hero Johnny Hayward scoring after a goalmouth scramble. Not long after it was 2-2, with Wilco Phillips scoring.

Pandemonium reigned – bowlers, sticks, caps and programmes were thrown into the air!

After a strong tackle Yeovil's Harry Edwards was taken off, not to return. The 11 v. 10 soon became 11 v. 9 as again an unpunished tackle saw Watts removed from the field. Rovers took full advantage, scoring twice more through Jerry Morgan, with Yeovil left with the 'what might have been' feeling.

However, even the Bristol press were writing that the best footballing team lost, and the tactics of Rovers were against the good name of Bristol football. Also the Bristol press were keen to report the unique Huish pitch: "The peculiarities of the pitch at Huish, it has a slope from one far corner flag to the lower one. It was a handicap to Rovers as it is to all visiting teams and in this the Somerset side have an advantage of their knowledge of its idiosyncrasies."

A clearer photograph of the 1922 Bristol Rovers squad.
Back row (L-R): Kenneth Boyes, John 'Jack' Pattison, Arthur Wainwright, Ernie Sambridge, Harold Armitage, George Webb, Leslie Murphy.
Second Row: J. Mason (trainer), Frederick Lunn, John 'Jack' Taylor, Jesse Whatley, S. Smith, John Parker, Andrew Wilson (manager)
Sitting: Samuel Furniss, James 'Tommy' Howarth, Harold 'Harry' O'Neill, Walter 'Wattie' Currie, John 'Jack' Rutherford, James 'Jimmy' Haydon, James Liddell, Thomas 'Tancy' Lea.
Seated: George Chance, Frederick 'Jerry' Morgan.

This Bristol Rovers team photograph is from the 1922/23 season.

Back Row: Jack Taylor, James Liddell, Harold Boxley, Sidney Leigh, Woodward, Jesse Whatley, Harold O'Neill, Kenneth Boyes, Harold Armitage, Jack Parker.
Middle Row: Samuel Furniss, Walter Currie, Ernie Sambridge, Sydney Smith, Frederick Lunn, Jimmy Haydon, Wally Hammond.
Front Row: George Chance, Jerry Morgan, H. B. Rose, Arthur Wainwright, Tancy Lea.

The Bristol Rovers first team, 1923-24 season. Jerry Morgan in the middle row, third from the right.

1924-1925 was his last season for the club, although he did play 22 times in league fixtures and scored 6 goals; once against Bournemouth (H) on 20th December 1924, twice against

Queens Park Rangers (H) on 18th March 1924, followed by a couple more the following week in a 3-0 home victory over Norwich. His final goal for the club came in his last-ever appearance, scoring a penalty in the last match of the season away at Reading, a match which Bristol Rovers lost 4-1. The side finished a poor 17th in that campaign.

After leaving Bristol Rovers, he continued his football career with local teams in Bristol such as Brislington Wednesday, Showmens' Guild, Bristol City Wednesday, and Bristol South Wednesday team. It also appears that he turned out for the Brecknell, Munro & Rogers team alongside his brothers George and Harry.

He later appeared for Taunton Town in 1927, and the local press were keen to applaud his attributes, as one report shows:

"Jerry Morgan was Taunton's most progressive forward, and his footwork was quite as good as when he wore Rovers' colours."

When Taunton played a Bristol Rovers side later in 1927, it was noted that: "Jerry Morgan gave a good display against his former colleagues, but they did not permit him to get very near their goal."

He followed this up in January 1928 in a match against Bristol City reserves which Taunton won 4-1:

"Jerry Morgan was outstanding at inside-left. The former Bristol Rovers forward controlled the slippery ball with wonderful artistry, and had the satisfaction of completing his hat-trick, while he also had much to do with the other goal scored by Wheeler."

And in early 1928, one report continued in a similar vein:

"Jerry Morgan, whose deft touches and thoughtful passing makes his football a real pleasure for the spectators, has filled the inside-left position with success. He is the soul of the attack and combines well. Although he has obtained many good goals, his shooting generally lacks direction. He is another favourite of the crowd, and has served the side well."

He made another appearance for Taunton against Bristol Rovers Reserves in a Western League match in Bristol on 7th April 1928. In an exciting 2-2 draw in front of 3,000 spectators, he scored a penalty with a 'lame' shot. The Taunton press noted that "Morgan and Wheeler came near the mark with splendid efforts" and "both Morgan and Wheeler were guilty of missing gilt-edged chances."

He later made an appearance for a Great Western Railway team in an exhibition match against Taunton in May 1928 at Priory Park, which Taunton won 4-2. It was reported that he had been absent from Taunton's side through injury for weeks, and played inside-left for the Railway team. The local press reported that "Morgan has not had sufficient opportunity to return to his true form" which explained his absence from the Taunton team.

It would appear that this could have been his final competitive match, as no trace of his involvement with any further fixtures has been found. He did, however, stay in football by coaching the National Smelting Company team at Avonmouth, where he and his brother Harry worked.

The 'National Smelting Company' (NSC) football team from 1928/29 (Bristol & District League Division 3 Champions) which was coached by Jerry. He is second from the right in the middle row. His brother Harry is holding the ball in the front row.

He was of course a regular player for the famous 'Morgan Family' football team as well as playing for charitable causes. As late as 1938, he was selected for a Redfield XI along with Johnny Morgan, as noted in the local press:

'CHARITY MATCH AT NETHAM'

Redfield v. Ashtonians at Christmas.

On Christmas morning an association football match will played on the Netham Ground, by permission of the I.C.I., in aid of the Handel Cossham Memorial Hospital, Kingswood between Redfield and Old Ashtonians (Mr. Bob Hewison's XI).

Mr. Baston will kick-off at 10.30, and the Redfield XI will be selected from Billy Coggins (Bristol City, Everton), Wintle (Netham), Haydon (Bristol Rovers), E. Bennett (Manchester City), Milford (L.M.S.), Bateman (Avon United), Walters (Bristol Rovers, Huddersfield Town), Jerry Morgan (Bristol Rovers), Whitby (Netham), Johnny Morgan (Bristol City), and Hunt (Netham).

The St. John's Ambulance Band will provide music.

The record attendance for this ground is 4,000. Mr. S. Hodge of 8 Glebe Road, St. George, wishes all tickets to be in by Saturday, December 22nd."

It is entirely possible that he continued to play local football after this date, although details are proving difficult to confirm.

He is often referred to in various historical articles concerning Bristol Rovers, and one incident was recorded from an article published in 1962:

"While chatting to Joe Walter at Eastville recently, he recalled playing for Bristol Rovers against Reading at Elm Park, where the Rovers were leading 3-1 when the match was abandoned after only 7 minutes' play of the second half due to fog.

Playing at outside-right, on the opposite wing to where the dressing room was, Joe was unaware that the referee had ended the game, not having heard the final whistle. He stayed there for several minutes before being told – by Jerry Morgan, I believe – that all the other players were in the dressing room.

Joe, who told me that he could not recall having ever been in such a thick fog, had another reason for remembering that unfinished Southern Section match. He was one of the Rovers scorers.

Centre-forward Sid Leigh, a fast-moving and bustling type of leader, who many Eastville fans still remember, netted the other two goals."

Jerry passed away on 9th May 1953 and is buried at Shirehampton Cemetery, Bristol.

The headstone of Frederick 'Jerry' Morgan.

As part of an initiative organised by Bristol Rovers Supporters' Club, Jerry was posthumously awarded a 'Cap' commemorating his first-team appearances for the club during the Bristol Rovers v. Lincoln City fixture on 2nd September 2023.

He was awarded cap number 21, indicating that he was the 21st player to play for the first team since the club joined the Football League in the 1920/21 season.

Cap awarded to Frederick 'Jerry' Morgan
To commemorate his
Bristol Rovers league debut
v Norwich City
October 30th 1920

Presented by
Bristol Rovers Supporters Club
Sponsored by The Morgan Family

Number 21

Jerry's cap certificate, issued 2nd September 2023.

The Bristol Rovers caps issued to Jerry (number 21) and Jimmy (number 277).

CHAPTER 18.

THE FOOTBALL CAREER OF WILLIAM JAMES 'JIMMY' MORGAN.

Jimmy made 104 appearances for Bristol Rovers between April 1946 and 1952, scoring 24 goals. He later played a few games for Stonehouse F.C. and other local clubs in Somerset, although complete details of his appearances have not been recorded.

Prior to his footballing career he had served in the Royal Marines during the World War 2, and served during the Normandy Landings in 1944. After the war he was apparently offered a contract with one of the professional clubs in Sheffield, but rejected the deal, and opted instead to join his home town team Bristol Rovers.

Bristol Rovers 1945-1946.

Top row (left to right): Neads, Harry Smith, Davis, Bobby Gardiner, Allen, Douglas Baldie, Long, Jennings, Topping, Butterworth, Mann (instructor).
Second row: E. Giles, Meacham, Watkins, O'Brian, Jack Weare, Eric Studley, Frowde, Bridge, Bert Williams (trainer), Jack Cooper (trainer).
Bottom row: Parkinson, Harry Bamford, George Peacock, W. Smith, C. F. Ferrari (secretary), Ray Warren, Brough Fletcher (manager), Vic Lambden, Jimmy Morgan, George Petherbridge, Wilfred Whitfield.
Sitting in front: K. Baker, T. Spicer (Ball boys).

The *'Western Daily Press'* announced the arrival of Jimmy at the club on 12th April 1946, when it noted:

"Latest Rovers' signings on amateur forms are: Joseph Powell, left-half, and James Morgan, right-half, who has just been released from the forces."

He made his debut for Bristol Rovers Colts in March 1946 against Downend ATC Old Boys, and one month later made his debut for the first team in the 1945-1946 season on April 19th (Good Friday) that same year, in a 3-1 victory over Torquay United in a cup fixture. The official report of the match stated:

'LOCAL AMATEUR'S FINE DEBUT'

"Lambden, the centre-forward and an impressive debut by Morgan, were highlights of yesterday's League Three (South) Cup qualifying game at Eastville Stadium, where Bristol Rovers gained a well-deserved success over Torquay United by three goals to one. The Rovers held the upper hand all through and dominated play for long periods, particularly in the second half, when their forwards well led by Lambden, gave an improved display on recent matches Morgan, a local amateur recently released from the Forces, did exceptionally well at inside-left. After a quiet start he settled down to play a sound game, beating his man cleverly and passing with discrimination."

His first league appearance came the following day in a 6-1 victory over Brighton and Hove Albion, scoring two of the goals, and retaining his place for the final matches of the season. The local press were suitably impressed:

'BRIGHTON NO MATCH FOR ROVERS - Forwards Run Riot.'

BRISTOL ROVERS 6 BRIGHTON 1

"Bristol Rovers gave one of their best displays of the season when they wound up their League Three South Cup home programme with a convincing win over Brighton and Hove Albion by six goals to one at Eastville on Saturday.

Brighton were no match for Rovers, who, stronger in all departments, played fast, open and attractive football.

The inclusion of Baldie, inside-right and Morgan, inside-left, brought new life into the attack, and transformed it into a well-balanced line.

Morgan gave another impressive display and when joined by Petherbridge, who changed places with Russell, later in the game, treated the 9,347 spectators to some clever left-wing play.

Baldie and Petherbridge formed a good right wing, however, changing positions with marked effect and Lambden, a lively leader, received much more support.

Bamford and Whitfield were two constructive wing halves, the latter being also an outstanding defender. Smith. Warren and Watkin formed a rock-like defence and Weare, in goal, had a holiday.

'GOOD MARKSMANSHIP'

Weak though the opposition was, the Rovers' display was most impressive and augurs well for next season. They were yards faster on the ball and their forwards revealed excellent marksmanship.

Brighton, with Davie, their centre-forward, limping for the major portion of the game, were most disjointed in attack, and their defence made several unpardonable errors, though Trainor, centre-half, and J. Wheat, left-half, battled well against overwhelming odds.

Brighton opened well, but soon faded out and after 13 minutes Baldie sold a perfect dummy allowing a pass by Bamford to run to Petherbridge, Lambden tapping the winger's centre past Baldwin.

Ten minutes later a defensive error gave Morgan an easy chance to put the Rovers two up, and just before the interval Warren converted a penalty and Lambden, receiving a well-placed down-the-middle pass from Baldie, gave the Rovers an interval lead of four clear goals.

Morgan headed a picture goal 10 minutes after the restart from a Petherbridge centre, and Brighton's solitary goal followed soon after, Stephens scoring from a penalty. Baldie completed the scoring mid-way through the half."

August 24th 1946 saw an unusual game at Eastville, when a practice match was played between the 'Probables' and the 'Possibles', which would decide the line-up for the first league match of the 1946/47 season the following Saturday. Jimmy played for the 'Probables', and it was reported that he was a 'clever inside-forward'.

The new season saw Jimmy making 15 appearances and scoring 5 goals including a brace against Leyton Orient in a 6-1 victory at Eastville on Easter Monday 7th April 1947. At the time there was another Morgan who played briefly for the club, one Wyndham Morgan, but he appears not to be related to Jimmy or the wider Morgan family.

Bristol Rovers, 1946/1947. Featured players are:
Back Row: Jackie Pitt, Jack Weare, Harry Bamford, Wally McArthur, Ray Warren, Barrie Watkins.
Front Row (L-R): Ken Wookey, Len Hodges, Fred Leamon, Jimmy Morgan, Lance Carr.

One of Jimmy's best seasons came the following season in 1947-1948 when he scored 7 goals in 27 appearances in a very poor year for the club, escaping relegation by virtue of a superior goal average. In the F. A. Cup fixture against New Brighton on December 13th 1947 he scored twice in a 4-0 victory at Eastville. However, the club only won 13 of the 42 matches in League Division 3(S), finishing with a total of only 34 points.

Despite the poor season, the New Year's Day fixture against Notts County would appear to have been one of Jimmy's best performances in a Rovers shirt. The *'Bristol Evening Post'* praised the whole side for a dogged 3-2 victory after being 2-0 ahead at half time: "The fireworks came in the second half when the County 'went mad'.

They stormed the Rovers' goal, Johnston and Hold scoring within three minutes but within 60 seconds Jimmy Morgan had netted the winning goal for the Rovers.

I made Morgan, a tremendously hard worker, the most prominent of the Rovers' forwards. Neither Petherbridge nor Watling got enough work to do but we must not forget the terrible state of the ground. A great win."

Matches against Bristol City are always feisty encounters, and to score against the 'other lot' brings instant legendary status, despite the final result. Jimmy achieved this on February 14th 1948 in a 5-2 defeat at Ashton Gate: "The Rovers' other goal came in the 75th minute when with a terrific drive from 25 yards, Jimmy Morgan just left Clack standing."

It was in the last match of the season away at Ipswich Town that Bristol Rovers had to win to avoid re-election to the football league. The *'Bristol Evening Post'* reported the match with typical enthusiasm:

"Rovers fielded an unchanged defence but in their attack George Petherbridge resumed in place of 'Josser' Watling while Jimmy Morgan was preferred to Len Hodges at inside-left. Petherbridge scored two of the Rovers' four goals, the others coming from Brian Bush and Jimmy Morgan. The Eastville side won 4-0 to complete a magnificent double over Ipswich and put paid to the chances of the East Anglian players getting talent money as they finished in fourth position.

The Rovers escaped having to apply for re-election by a slightly superior average over Norwich City and Brighton and Hove who occupied the two bottom positions. All these clubs finished with the same number of points (34).

Here is the Rovers line-up for that vital match at Ipswich: Harold Lilley, Harry Bamford, Geoff Fox, Jackie Pitt, Ray Warren, Wally McArthur, Brian Bush, Barrie Watkins, Vic Lambden, Jimmy Morgan, George Petherbridge."

He made irregular appearances for the club over the next six seasons, and was kept out of the team by legendary players Bill Roost and (latterly) Geoff Bradford.

The 1947-1948 Bristol Rovers team.

Back Row (L-R): Jackie Pitt, Ray Warren, Jack Weare, Harry Bamford, Barrie Watkins, Wally McArthur.
Front Row (L-R): Ken Wookey, Len Hodges, Vic Lambden, Jimmy Morgan, George Petherbridge.

On Saturday August 7th, 1948, Jimmy was part of the strong Bristol Rovers team who visited the Netherlands, and played two pre-season fixtures. The first, at N.E.C. Nijmegen, resulted in a 1-0 defeat, whilst the second, against Racing Club Haarlem, saw the Rovers win 4-2.

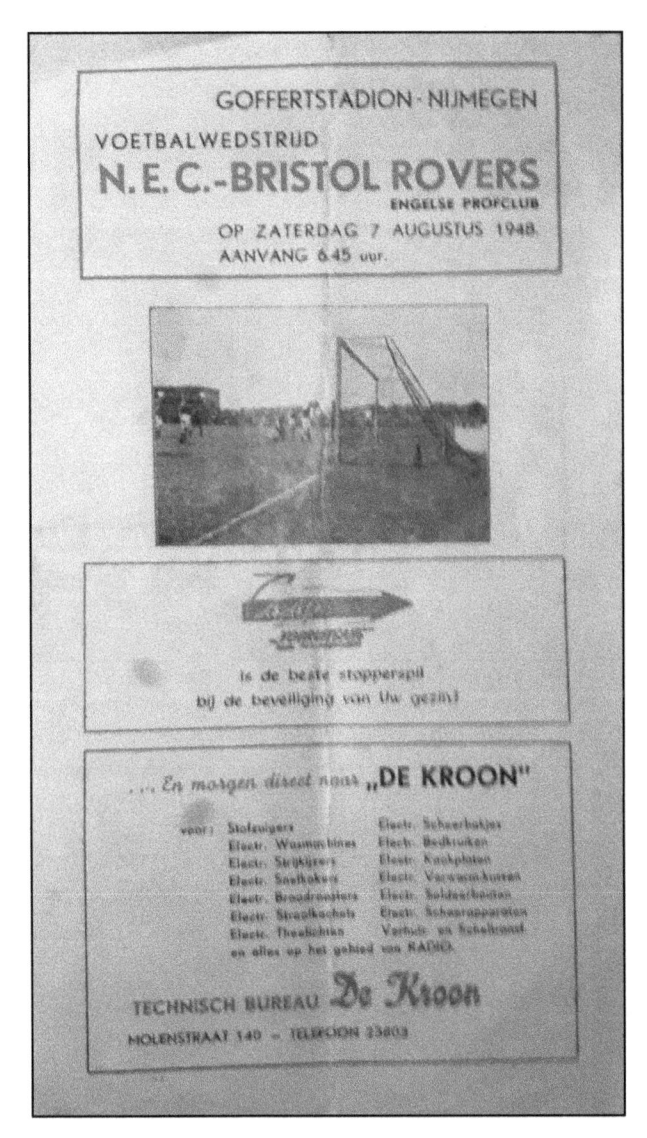

Programme cover for the fixture.

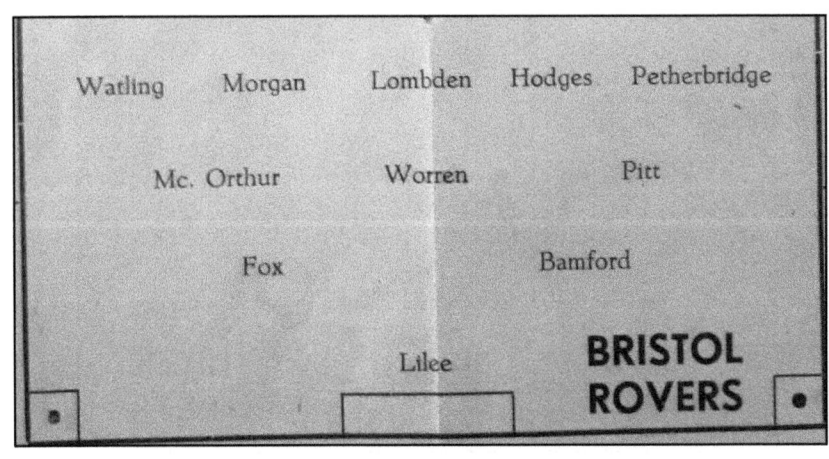

The Bristol Rovers team who played N.E.C. Nijmegen in August 1948. Some interesting variations of certain players' names!

The Bristol Rovers and N.E.C. Nijmegen teams prior to the match. Jimmy Morgan 5th from the right in the back row.

The Bristol Rovers squad at the Jonkerbos War Memorial. Jimmy at the extreme right.

A friendly get-together in the Netherlands, 1948. Jimmy can be seen to the left of the table.

The squad pose for the camera during their Netherlands visit, 1948. Jimmy can be seen to the left of the door in the background.

The 1948-1949 season was slightly improved over the previous campaign, despite a 6-1 drubbing home defeat against Ipswich in the opening fixture, the club eventually finishing

16th in Division 3(S). Jimmy made 37 appearances and scored 7 goals including a couple against Bournemouth at Eastville on August 30th.

Another formal picture of the team squad in the Netherlands, 1948.

The squad enjoying a boat trip in the Netherlands, 1948. Jimmy clearly visible 4th from the right.

It was reported that in a fixture against Torquay on 22nd January 1949, "Inside-forwards Hodges and Morgan worked industriously and well, though Morgan just spoiled one or two splendid runs by holding on too long."

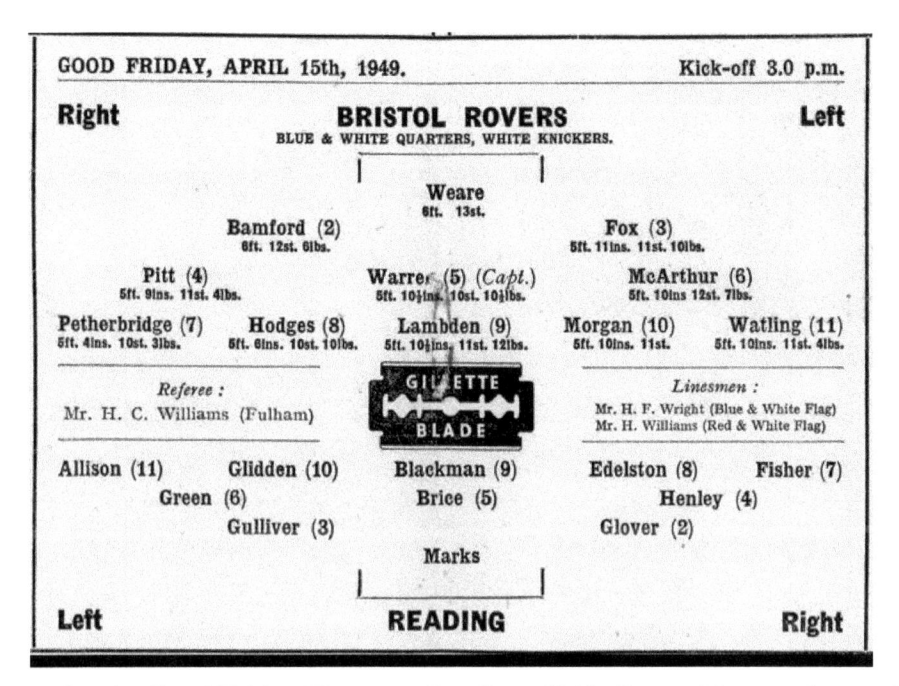

```
GOOD FRIDAY, APRIL 15th, 1949.                    Kick-off 3.0 p.m.

Right                    BRISTOL ROVERS                        Left
                  BLUE & WHITE QUARTERS, WHITE KNICKERS.

                              Weare
                             6ft. 13st.

              Bamford (2)                      Fox (3)
              6ft. 12st. 6lbs.                 5ft. 11ins. 11st. 10lbs.

        Pitt (4)            Warren (5) (Capt.)        McArthur (6)
        5ft. 9ins. 11st. 4lbs.   5ft. 10½ins. 10st. 10½lbs.   5ft. 10ins 12st. 7lbs.

  Petherbridge (7)   Hodges (8)   Lambden (9)   Morgan (10)   Watling (11)
  5ft. 4ins. 10st. 3lbs.  5ft. 6ins. 10st. 10lbs.  5ft. 10½ins. 11st. 12lbs.  5ft. 10ins. 11st.  5ft. 10ins. 11st. 4lbs.

        Referee:                                 Linesmen:
   Mr. H. C. Williams (Fulham)            Mr. H. F. Wright (Blue & White Flag)
                                          Mr. H. Williams (Red & White Flag)

   Allison (11)   Glidden (10)   Blackman (9)   Edelston (8)   Fisher (7)
            Green (6)            Brice (5)         Henley (4)
                   Gulliver (3)                  Glover (2)

                              Marks

Left                       READING                           Right
```

The teams for the Good Friday Fixture v. Reading, 1949. Jimmy Morgan featured at No. 10.

The 1948/49 Bristol Rovers team.
Back Row (L-R): George Petherbridge, Jackie Pitt, Jack Weare, Geoff Fox, Vic Lambden, Wally McArthur, Brough Fletcher (Manager).
Front Row (L-R): Harry Bamford, Len Hodges, Ray Warren, Jimmy Morgan, 'Josser' Watling.

Jimmy endeared himself again to the Rovers fans when he once again scored against Bristol City in the Gloucestershire Cup Final on May 14th 1949 in front of over 15,000 spectators at Eastville in a 2-0 victory.

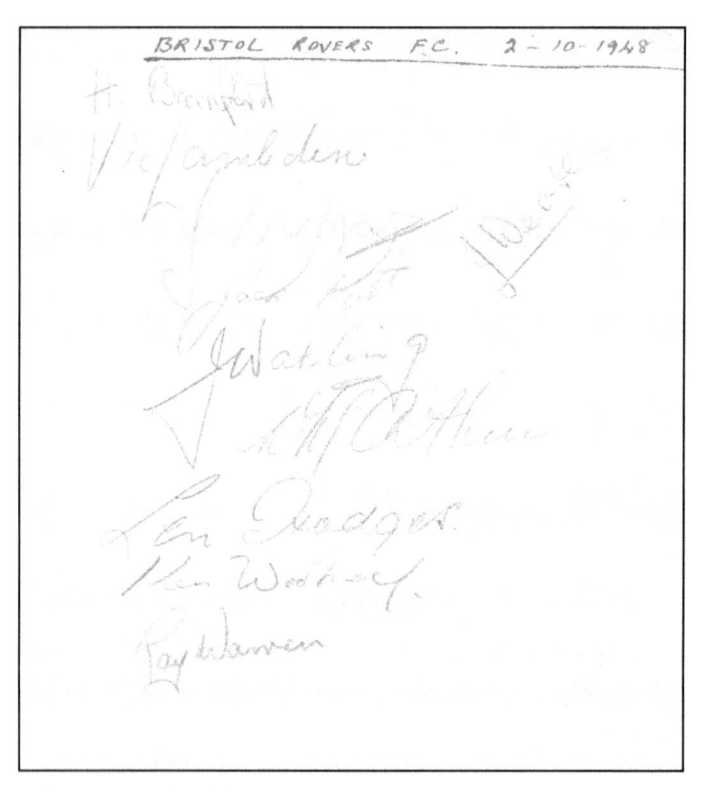

Bristol Rovers FC autographs, 1948. Jimmy Morgan with some illustrious team-mates.

Jimmy Morgan – by 'Pak'.

***Bristol Rovers head to an away fixture. Jimmy second from the right.**

The 1949-1950 season saw Jimmy play only 12 matches for the first team, scoring just one goal in a 2-0 victory over Bournemouth at Dean Court on 21st January 1950. The club had a far better season however, finishing 9th in Division 3(S).

In a reserve fixture against Bournemouth on 22nd February 1950, Jimmy was injured and had to leave the field (no substitutes allowed then). The *'Bristol Evening Post'* carried a report on the match the following day:

"It was a bad day for Bristol Rovers Reserves and inside-forward Jimmy Morgan in particular, when they played Bournemouth and Boscombe Athletic Reserves in a Combination Cup game at Eastville yesterday. Morgan was brought in at the last minute in the inside-right position in place of James, who failed to pass a fitness test.

After 15 minutes he severely injured his left ankle in a tackle and spent the rest of the half hobbling around on the wing. In the second half he came out with his foot strapped up and carried on as best could for 10 minutes before, very wisely, deciding to give up. After the game Morgan was taken to hospital for an X-ray."

Jimmy 'immortalised' in cartoon form from the Port Vale match from 1949 – artist known as 'Pak'

Bristol Rovers, 1949-1950. Jimmy Morgan is in the back row, 10th from the left.

The 1950-1951 season showed a great improvement for the team, which finished the season in 6th place.

However, it was clear that his days at the club were numbered, with Geoff Bradford and Bill Roost coming into form, and selection of the first team no longer guaranteed.

No doubt because of the emergence of these new players, club manager Bert Tann decided to change Jimmy's role from an inside-forward to a wing-half. The *'Bristol Observer'* of 30th September 1950 reported:

"The move has been successful and Morgan has had one of his best games in this position at Shepherd's Bush this weekend, where Rovers' reserves shared two goals with Queen's Park Rangers.

Morgan comes from a well-known local family of footballers, and his father George was a Gloucestershire County player.

Jimmy made his debut for Rovers in April 1946, and scored two goals in his first game. During his service career he played for the Royal Marines."

He only featured in 5 first-team fixtures in that campaign, although he did score two goals; one in a 2-1 away victory at Swindon on 16th December 1950, and the other in a 2-1 win over Walsall at Fellows Park on February 15th 1951.

He continued to play regularly for the reserve team throughout the season, playing consistently enough to be considered for first-team selection when required, sometimes travelling with the senior team to cover for possible injuries.

One report, from April 1951, featuring the 2-1 home defeat against Aldershot Reserves, referred to Jimmy as an 'outstanding player'.

10th February 1951 saw the team involved in a money-spinning F.A. Cup tie at home to Hull City. The *'Bristol Evening World'* reported the preparations for this fixture on 6th February 1951, which gives a fascinating insight into how the club prepared for 'big' matches:

Bristol Rovers FC, 1950-51 Season.

Back Row (L-R): Jackie Pitt, Les Edwards, Harry Bamford, Bert Hoyle, Geoff Fox, Peter Sampson, Bert Williams (trainer).
Front Row (L-R): Bryan Bush, Geoff Bradford, Vic Lambden, Ray Warren, Jimmy Morgan, 'Josser' Watling.

'MORGAN, BUSH, JOIN PARTY – THE ROVERS LEAVE FOR SOUTHEND TRAINING.'

It's in the bag - Bristol Rovers' party went off to Southend for Cup training today. Men in this picture, left to right, are: Jimmy Morgan, Harry Bamford, Bert Williams (trainer), Geoff Fox, Ray Warren (in Trilby), Jack Pitt, Bill Roost, George Petherbridge, John Watling, and manager Bert Tann.

"Early today Bristol Rovers team stole away from Bristol and the Cup fever at Eastville to spend the remaining days before their Fifth Round game against Hull City in the quiet of Southend-on-Sea. There were no Rovers' fans at the Stadium at 8.30 a.m. when manager Mr. Bert Tann spirited them off in their private luxury coach.

For half an hour before they left, Petherbridge was in the dressing-room having treatment for his pulled thigh muscle.

Bryan Bush and Jimmy Morgan accompanied the Rovers' established team.

This is the Rovers' out-of-town progamme:

Today: Lunch at Ilford, reach Southend at four o'clock, and visit a local cinema in the evening.

Wednesday: Training at Southend's ground, brine baths at the invitation of Southend Corporation, and probably a quiet evening at their hotel playing snooker and table tennis.

Thursday: Same training routine, but no brine baths. They will then catch a coach to London and will go to the Victor's Palace to see the Crazy Gang in "Knights of Madness".

Friday: Walks along the pier in the morning. In the afternoon they will leave for Newbury, where they will spend the night.

Saturday: Coach journey back to Bristol, having lunch at Bath or Chippenham, and arriving at Eastville just over an hour before the kick-off.

Bristol Rovers Supporters' Club have decided to distribute their allocation of 1,500 Cup tickets at a special meeting at All Hallows Church Hall, All Hallows Road, Easton, tomorrow evening at 7.45. They will be sold only to members of the Supporters' Club and each member will be entitled to one ticket.

Mr. Eric Godfrey, chairman of the Supporters' Club said: "Members who had not paid their subscriptions for the current season by last evening will not be eligible for a ticket. Members must produce their current membership card and are requested to have the correct money"."

Sadly, Jimmy was not selected for this fixture, which resulted in a 3-0 victory for the Rovers. This set up the famous quarter-final fixture against the mighty Newcastle United.

Following the success of the trip to Southend-on-Sea for the Hull fixture, the training journey was repeated prior to the Newcastle match; Jimmy was given the option of travelling with the squad but declined on this occasion.

In the event, Rovers drew the match at Newcastle 0-0 in front of a crowd of 63,000, but lost the replay at Eastville 1-3 with 30,074 in attendance, Jimmy not being involved in either game.

In April 1951 Jimmy scored a couple of goals in a 4-1 victory over Warminster Town to secure the Warminster Cup for the team.

May 1951 saw Jimmy, along with other first-team players, involved in groundwork at Eastville Stadium, as the *'Bristol Evening Post'* reported:

"Bristol Rovers players are assisting in raising the pitch some 15 inches. Five senior members of the first team – Ray Warren, George Petherbridge, 'Josser' Watling, Geoff Bradford and Bill Roost – were all busy today.

In company with Jimmy Morgan and Leslie Edwards, they were in their shirt sleeves, using shovels, picks, pushing wheelbarrows, and doing other jobs. The players have been putting as much effort and energy into their new work as in their achievements on the field during the past arduous season."

He continued to play for the first team throughout the 1951-1952 season, although his place in the side was threatened by the continued emergence of Geoff Bradford, soon to become a Bristol Rovers legend. Jimmy had a nightmare of a match on 3rd November 1951 at Bournemouth, the team losing 2-1 and "after the interval Jimmy Morgan failed with the easiest of scoring chances. A goal at that time may well have brought bonus money for the Rovers' players".

On Christmas Day of that year it was reported that "Jimmy Morgan, who deputised for the injured Watling at outside-left, gave a pleasing display" in a 4-1 victory over Port Vale, a fixture in which the aforementioned Geoff Bradford scored 2 goals.

He finished that season with 8 appearances and 2 goals, one away at Port Vale in a 1-1 draw on Boxing Day 1951, and the other in a 3-0 away win over Watford on January 3rd 1952. His final game for the club came in a 2-1 home defeat against Plymouth on 26th January 1952, in front of a huge crowd of 29,003.

He was released by Bristol Rovers at the end of that season with the team finishing in an encouraging 7th place, having played only 8 times during that campaign. Overall, he played 104 times for the club and scored 24 goals. On his release he joined Stonehouse in May 1952. His departure was announced in the local press on 3rd May 1952:

"Bristol Rovers have placed 10 players on the free transfer list. Jimmy Morgan is the best-known of the Rovers' players for transfer. He made eight first-team appearances last season."

The *'Bristol Evening Post'* reported on 18th July 1953 that Jimmy (amongst others) received a benefit payment from Bristol Rovers:

"Since the war, Bristol Rovers have granted 14 benefits to their players, including two to their skipper, Ray Warren. The others concerned are Vic Lambden, Harry Bamford, George Petherbridge, Jackie Pitt, Geoff Fox, Bryan Bush, Barry Watkins, Jimmy Morgan, 'Josser' Watling, Bert Winters, Wally McArthur, and Maurice Lockier.

My estimate of the cost to the Rovers of these benefits is over £8,000. It is, indeed, a remarkable record for a club in the Third Division. Very, very few clubs in the Football League and certainly none in either section of Division III, have paid out so much money in benefits in post-war football.

With the exception of Jimmy Morgan and Maurice Lockier, who have re-signed for Stonehouse and Bath City respectively for next season, all the players mentioned are still with the Eastville Club."

During his Stonehouse days, he played alongside former Bristol City forward Sid Williams, scoring in a 3-2 Western League Victory over Weymouth in October 1952. He also assisted Williams in a 1-1 draw away at Street in January 1953, and very nearly won the game for the visitors but screwed the ball inches wide with the Street defence in a flap.

The Bristol Rovers team visiting a colleague – Jimmy Morgan 3rd from the left.

Bristol Rovers F.C. at the Tote End Bar. Jimmy Morgan can be seen in the centre of the photograph in the second row.

The Bristol Rovers team gather before an away fixture, 1952, just before Jimmy Morgan left the club. He can be seen in the front row, extreme left.

He also briefly also played for Chippenham Town, and in August 1955 it was reported that he had signed for Wells City, but he subsequently signed for Glastonbury the following month:

"Glastonbury manager Ray Parsons, the former Glastonbury and Chippenham Town left-back, can be congratulated on securing the signature of Jimmy Morgan, the ex-Bristol Rovers and Chippenham Town inside-forward. Morgan should be just the player to bring the best out of the speedy Nash twins."

His debut was recorded locally:

"This (Thursday) evening, Glastonbury will visit neighbours Wells City in the first 'leg' of the Western League Professional Cup (kick-off 6.30 p.m.). Ernie Jones, who captained Glastonbury in their two opening matches has been released from his contract in order to carry on as player-manager of the City Club. He plays at centre forward this evening and his place in the Glastonbury side will be filled by Jimmy Morgan, the former Bristol Rovers and Chippenham Town player."

Glastonbury won 5-3, Jimmy scoring two of the goals.

He made his final F.A. Cup appearance on 24th September 1955 when Glastonbury were defeated by Street 3-1, missing a penalty in the process.

He was certainly still playing for Glastonbury in December 1955 as he was mentioned in a report concerning their match against Portland United, which they lost 6-3. Jimmy played at left-half that day due to a late injury, and it was stated that: "Morgan gave a good display in the half-line and was one of the few Glastonbury players to emerge with credit in the second half".

It would appear that Jimmy retired from football sometime in 1956, although he did play the occasional charity match for the Morgan Family team right up to the mid-1960s, captaining the side when required.

Jimmy Morgan's grave, Avonview Cemetery, Bristol.

As part of an initiative organised by Bristol Rovers Supporters' Club, Jimmy was posthumously awarded a 'Cap' commemorating his first-team appearances for the club during the Bristol Rovers v. Lincoln City fixture on 2nd September 2023.

He was awarded cap number 277, indicating that he was the 277th player to play for the first team since the club joined the Football League in the 1920/21 season.

Cap awarded to Jimmy Morgan
To commemorate his
Bristol Rovers league debut
V Northampton Town
November 23rd 1946

Presented by
Bristol Rovers Supporters Club
Sponsored by The Morgan Family

Number 277

Jimmy's cap certificate, issued on 2nd September 2023.

CHAPTER 19.
THE MORGAN FAMILY FOOTBALL TEAM.

As we have already discovered, sport was an important part of the life of the Morgan family. Swimming, water polo, and pigeon racing were high up on the interests of both family and friends. However, football was a passion within the family, with many members playing for local teams in the Bristol area, and a few even playing professionally at a high level.

There was of course the joke that 'the family could play a team made up totally of family members' - a joke which turned into fact in just after World War 1, when a team of Morgan family members was organised to play a charity match.

Landlord of the 'Rising Sun' public house, James Morgan, is credited with forming the family team, using his pub as the *de facto* headquarters of the team.

A fascinating restored photograph of the inaugural Morgan Family team, taken on 3rd March 1919.

Back Row (L-R): James Morgan, Unknown, Unknown, Jack Morgan, Unknown, Unknown, Unknown, Fred Morgan, Reuben Morgan.
Centre Row (L-R): Nicky Morgan, Tom Morgan, Bill Morgan.
Front Row (L-R): Harry Morgan, Frederick 'Jerry' Morgan, Johnny Morgan, George Morgan, Unknown.

This proved so successful that the family were asked to play numerous charity matches over the next five decades, raising valuable amounts of money for charity.

There was great local interest of course, and extracts from press reports indicate how popular these matches were.

The earliest mention of the Morgan family team comes from a report dated 1st April 1919, concerning the Bristol Theatrical Thanksgiving Committee, where it was stated that "a Morgan Family v. Comrades of the Great War football match organised by "Half Back" raised £25 10s 1d." This would no doubt be the match relevant to the above photograph.

Another match was reported in April 1926, when a 'Morgan's XI' played a charity match against A. Stephens' XI at St. Philips in Bristol. The report stated:

'CHARITY FOOTBALL AT ST. PHILIP'S'

Morgan's XI. v. A. Stephen's XI.

Played at St. Philip's Ground, in aid of the Lord Mayor's Hospital Fund and St. Philip's old people. About 600 spectators were present, Morgan's XI kicked off and within ten minutes were a goal up through J. Morgan. Ten minutes from half-time they increased their lead through Skuse. Half-time: J. Morgan's XI, 2; A Stephen's XI, 0.

Stephen's XI started the second half in great style, but their forwards missed numerous chances of scoring in front of goal. Midway through this half, Sheppard shot for goal, and Nethercott, in attempting to clear, put into his own net. Johnny Morgan, the old Bristol City player, showed he is no spent force, his goal was easily the best of the match. Towards the end, each goal had narrow escapes, but Morgan's XI ran out deserved winners by 2-1.

It is not clear from the article that this was an actual *'bona fide'* Morgan family team, or just a team selected by or managed by Johnny Morgan from his friends or work colleagues, as Messrs. Skuse and Nethercott were mentioned in the match report. However, there was certainly a Morgan family involvement which merits inclusion.

The Morgan Family Football Team, 1935

L-R: Tom Morgan, George Morgan Jr., Arthur Morgan, George James 'Nicky' Morgan, George Morgan Sr., Gilbert Morgan, Harry Morgan, Frederick 'Jerry' Morgan, John Morgan, Reuben Morgan, William 'Billy' Mansfield, Frederick Morgan.

It was reported on 11th January 1935 that the Morgan family team would be playing a Wren family team on Easter Monday (April 22nd) of that year.

"Eleven Morgans and Eleven Wrens will meet in a football match in Bristol on Easter Monday morning. The match has been arranged by Mr. W. Morgan, of the Redfield Club, who organised the charity match on Christmas Morning between Redfield and the Old Ashtonians. After that game he issued a challenge that a team of Morgans would meet any other family team in the West of England.

Mr. Jack Wren, a former Bristol City player, has accepted the challenge, and a team of Wrens will take the field.

The proceeds of the Redfield-Old Ashtonians game will be handed over to the Cossham Hospital."

The match was played at the Chequers Ground in Kingswood and finished in a 0-0 draw. Captain Prince-Cox, manager of Bristol Rovers, refereed the game, in which the Cossham Trophy was contested. The teams agreed to replay the fixture the following month.

On 13th May 1935, the Morgans played the replay at Eastville Stadium (the home of Bristol Rovers). The local press reported the match in typically evocative fashion:

'MORGANS v. THE WRENS'

Family Football at Eastville.

Captain Prince-Cox, the manager of Bristol Rovers' Association Football Club, will present the Cossham trophy at the conclusion of the Association Football match at the Rovers' Ground at Eastville today, between the Morgan Family and the Wren Family.

The proceeds will go to the hospital.

The teams will be:

MORGANS: Fred Morgan; Willie Morgan; Johnny Morgan; Gilbert Morgan; Harry Morgan; Reuben Morgan; George Morgan; Frederick 'Jerry' Morgan; George Morgan; Arthur Morgan; Willie Morgan.

Reserve: Tom Morgan.

WRENS: Fred Wren; Jesse Wren; Albert Wren; Tom Wren; Jack Wren; Tom J. Wren; Stan Wren; Fred Wren; Sam Wren; Ted Wren; Joe Wren.

Reserves: Ted A. Wren; Tom Wren; Bert Wren; George Wren; Ern Wren; Sam Wren; Jack Wren; Fred Wren; Will Wren; Chris Wren.

Jack Wren is the old Bristol City player, and 'Jerry' Morgan a Rovers inside-right. Johnny Morgan played for Bristol City and went to Caerphilly, to come back again and have a trial with the Rovers. Tom Morgan was the first player to break the net with a shot. He did it at Grimsby once with a penalty. They used to call him the Penalty King.

In addition to the four professionals, three of the Morgans named played football for the county, whilst one was a county water-polo player*."

* *The county water-polo player was Fred Morgan, who was a regular at the Barton Hill Swimming Baths for many years.*

The Morgan family won the fixture 2-0, but sadly details of the goal scorers have not been located.

An article in the *'Sunday Mirror'* dated 6th October 1935 quoted a letter from Gilbert Morgan, which also gave details of the two matches against the Wrens:

'MORGAN'S SOCCER XI WANT MATCH'

"It is an old and well-worn joke about the family man who had so many children he could turn out a football team. I have received a letter from Gilbert T. Morgan, of Bristol, who can turn out a family team of Morgans.

Gilbert Morgan says: "We played the Wren's family last Easter Monday at the Chequers Ground, Kingswood, Bristol, and we made a draw of it, 0-0. Jack Wren, the former Bristol City centre half, captained the side, the Morgan's being captained by Jerry Morgan, the former Bristol Rovers' inside right. "We played again on the Bristol Rovers' ground for the Cossham Hospital Trophy. The Morgans won the cup by two clear goals. "If anyone fancies their chance, we should be only too pleased to do some good for the hospitals. I wish someone would promote such a game in London as l am sure the spectators would be surprised at the football."

THE "MORGAN FAMILY"

GOAL
"TOM"
(Ex Bristol City)

RIGHT BACK   **LEFT BACK**
"WILLIAM"   "DAVE"
(Frome Town)   (1st. Div. Bristol League)

RIGHT HALF BACK   **CENTRE HALF**   **LEFT HALF BACK**
"GEORGE"   "HARRY"   "JOHNNY"
(Brecknell Munro & Rogers) (Gloucestershire County) Ex Bristol City
                                                       " Caerphilly
                                                       " Bristol Rovers

OUTSIDE R.   **INSIDE R.**   **CENTRE FORWARD**   **INSIDE L.**   **OUTSIDE L.**
"DOUGLAS"   "FREDDY"   "RUEBEN"   "ARTHUR"   "GORDON"
(1st. Div. Downs L.) (Ex Bristol R.) (Downs League) (Lombardians) (Unattached)

RESERVES "BOB" (University Settlement)
"GILBERT" (Wellington Arms Hotel)

O

REFEREE "BILLY" WEDLOCK   **TOUCH JUDGES** "SAM" TUCKER
Ex England XI.   (England XV.) by request.
("The Wizard")   "STIFF" SIMS
                                                      ("The Ever Popular")

(Guild's College of England XI Trials Liverpool & 1st. Div. B.L.; 1st Div Bristol L.; 1st. Div. Bristol.)
(Engineering London; Capt. Glos. C. A.F.C.)

OUTSIDE R.   **INSIDE R.**   **CENTRE FORWARD**   **INSIDE L.**   **OUTSIDE L.**
"FRANK"   "STEVE"   "NOEL"   "OZZY"   "KEN"
(St. Paul's Coll.) (Glos. Country & 1st. Div. Bristol L.) (King's College, Taunton)

RIGHT HALF BACK   **CENTRE HALF**   **LEFT HALF BACK**
"TOM"   "HERBERT"   "PETER"
(1st. Div. Bristol League)   (All Saints O.B's)

RIGHT BACK   **LEFT BACK**
"NORMAN"   "ELWYN"
(R.M.S. "Empress of Britain" A.F.C.)

GOAL
"JOHN"

BRISTOL, Sons of Mr. HARRY BROWN.
THE FAMOUS "BROWN BROTHERS"

Inside of the programme for the Morgans v. Browns football match.

Another charity match took place at Ashton Gate, the home of Bristol City F.C. on Wednesday 8th December 1937, where it was reported that:

'FAMILY SOCCER MATCH'

£100 Raised for Lord Mayor's Fund.

"The splendid sum of £100 has been raised for the Lord Mayor's Christmas Dinner Fund by the Morgan and Brown families, of Bristol, who played a football match at Ashton Gate yesterday in aid of this deserving cause. The match resulted in victory for the Brown Brothers XI over the Morgan Family by five goals to three, all the goals being scored in the second half. The scorers were Steve Brown (3), Noel Brown (2), Freddie, Reuben and Arthur Morgan. The referee was Billy Wedlock, and the linesmen Sam Tucker and Steve Sims.

After the match, both teams, with the officials and a few friends, were entertained to at the Prince's Restaurant by Mr. Harry Brown, who announced on behalf of the Morgan and Brown families that a round sum of £100 would be handed to the Lord Mayor's Christmas Fund. That was a wonderful result and had only been made possible by the enthusiastic co-operation of all concerned.

He expressed thanks to the Sheriff for according civic patronage to the match by his presence and kicking off, to Mr. George Jenkins and his co-directors of Bristol City F.C. for the use of their ground free of expense, and to Mr. Fred Ashmead and the directors of Bristol Rovers for offering ground should the City ground not have been available through Cup ties, also to the local Press for their services, the referee, linesman, and the Morgan family for so sportingly taking up the challenge of the Browns."

Looking at the Morgan team, all can easily be found within the Morgan family archives. 'Gordon' could be Gordon Hodge (born 1913), son of William Hodge and Alice Perkins; Alice married Thomas Morgan in 1919 following William Hodges' death in France in 1917.

'Dave', however remains a mystery.

Cover of the match day programme.

The Brown Family team photograph from the local press of 1937.

Another photograph of the Brown Brothers football team, 1937.

In the *'Bristol Evening Post'* of 11th April 1951, an appeal for a fixture from the enthusiastic Gilbert Morgan appeared:

'FAMILY SOCCER MATCH FOR BRISTOL?'

"Mr. Gilbert Morgan, of 85, Kingsway, is endeavouring to raise a Morgan family soccer team to play a Bristol or West Country team of family footballers in aid of local charitable institutions. He suggests that it could be played in connection with the Festival of Britain celebrations to be staged in Bristol.

Those interested in the raising of the Morgan family team are asked to meet at the Rising Sun, Redfield, on Saturday 22nd April at 12.15 p.m. It is expected that Bristol Rovers F.C. will allow Jimmy Morgan to play.

The Morgans, who have played the Wren, Brown and Gane* family teams, have raised over £400 for charity."

*No evidence of a fixture against the Gane family has been located.

On 4th October 1951, under the headline of 'Challenge Accepted', the next Morgan family fixture was confirmed:

"Mr. Tom Jones, of the Amusement Park, Severn Beach, and the Hon. Secretary of Heal's Fun City A.F.C. (champions of the Bristol Wednesday League for the past two seasons), has accepted the challenge of the Morgan Family to play a match in aid of the Bristol Blind Children's Fund. Recently, the Fun City team played at Ynysddu where they helped to raise £40 for local old-age pensioners."

A meeting was duly arranged for noon on Sunday 7th October at the Rising Sun public house, Redfield, for both the Morgans and the Heals to discuss the arrangements for this charity match.

A further meeting was arranged for members of the Morgan family for 12 o'clock on Sunday 2nd December of that year at the home of Gilbert Morgan (85 Kingsway, Bristol). This meeting was to allow the Morgan team to be discussed.

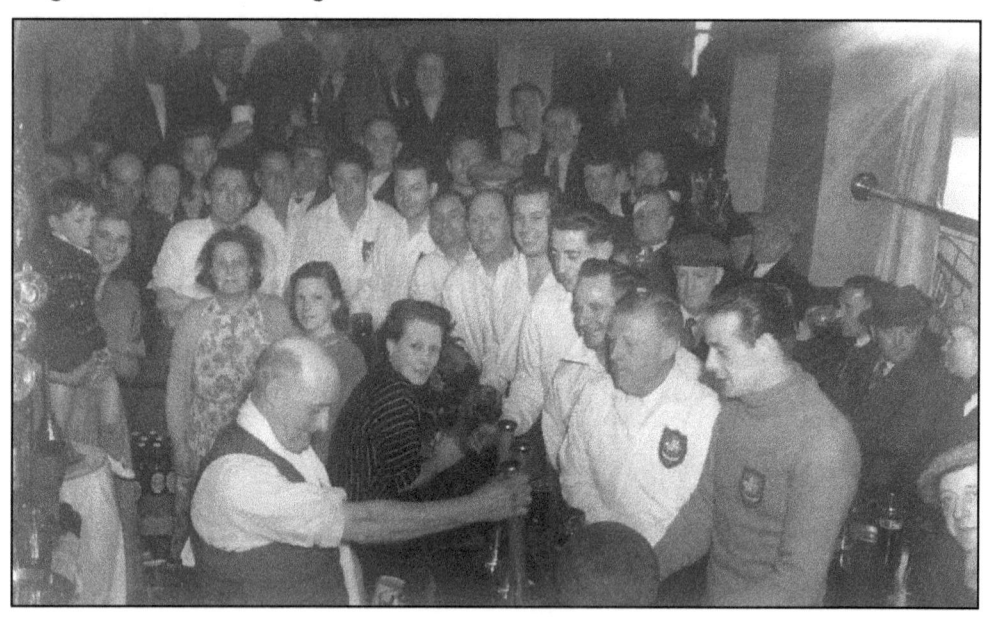

The Morgan family meeting at the Rising Sun on 22nd April 1951.

Wearing shirts donated by Bristol St. George F.C., the players are (right to left): Syd (Bristol City goalkeeper), John, Harry, Harry Jr., Gilbert Snr., Reuben, Arthur, Douglas, George Jr., George Snr, Gilbert Jr.

The landlord at the beer pumps would appear to be Albert (Jim) Webber, and his wife Violet (nee Morgan) can be seen next to him.

The match was duly arranged for Saturday 29th December 1951, and took place at the Douglas Sports Ground in Kingswood. The match was kicked off by one Paula Marshall, who was starring as 'Principal Boy' at the Bristol Hippodrome Pantomime that year. The match was indeed in aid of the Bristol Blind Children's Fund, and kicked off at 10:30 a.m. in front of a good crowd. The local press reported the match in typically evocative detail:

'HEAL'S FUN CITY WIN CHALLENGE MATCH'

"There was no point-hunting fervour or cup-match excitement in today's challenge between Heal's Fun City and the Bristol Morgan's XI at the Douglas Ground Kingswood. The result mattered little. What did count was that about £200 was raised for Bristol's blind children. Two thousand watched stage-star Paula Marshall principal boy at Bristol Hippodrome's Red Riding Hood, kick off. Although the match was a friendly affair to raise funds for blind children, the 22 gave a fine soccer display.

At half-time, when the score was 1-1, someone whispered that Georges' Brewery were giving a barrel of beer to the winning side.

The tempo was fast and 10 minutes from time the Heal's snatched the winning goal - and the beer barrel.

Paula Marshall, who was accompanied by comedian Billy Danvers, was introduced to both before kick-off.

She was told that the Morgan's were a unique team in soccer, made up entirely of brothers and cousins. The side were formed in 1919 and the average age of the latest XI is 26.

The Fun City started in 1935, solely to raise money for needy causes. They joined the Bristol Wednesday League and since 1936 they have won either the league or cup each year.

Poster for the Morgan football team match from December 29th 1951.

The Heal's side opened the scoring after 20 minutes when centre-forward J. Heal sent in a hard shot which glanced in off a post. The Morgans hit back and Les Morgan equalised with a penalty. Ten minutes from time Ernest Morgan* tried to prevent the ball going over the line and deflected it into goal."

Probably Ernest Godsell, son of Violet Morgan and Thomas Godsell.

The reported probable teams were:

Morgan Family XI: Syd (Bristol City), Ben (City Colts), Les (Radstock), Harry (City Colts, captain), Ernest (St. Pancras), George (Douglas), Ernest (Pecketts), Gilbert (Peasedown United), George (Douglas), Fred (Shell-Mex).

Heal's Fun City XI: P. Maggs, B. Cotter, B. Carter, T. Bartlett, B. Woodhams, R. Wedlock, E. Merrick, F. Sherman, J. Heal, J. Payne, R. Bartlett.

However, the Morgans' team on the day differed greatly from the one advertised the previous week, which was:

Syd (Bristol City), Ben (City Colts), Les (Radstock), Fred (Shell-Mex), Harry (City Colts, captain), Jimmy (Bristol Rovers), Douglas (St. Pancras), George (Douglas), Gilbert (Peasedown United), Ernest (Pecketts), Arthur (Hanham Athletic).

One would suspect the latter would have been the more likely.

The team's mascot, Peter Morgan (one of the children of Gilbert) was only 4½ years old. Harry Morgan was made captain for the day in view of his marriage at St. Anne's Church the previous Saturday. Other family members were also involved, Iris Gould (nee Morgan) and her daughter Laura recalled walking around the ground with a charity collection bucket as the match was going on.

The target of £200 was duly raised and use by the charity to defray the costs of a new swimming pool.

Eight thousand programmes were printed for the match, and one hopes that at least one copy remains for posterity.

The well-known film star of the time, Googie Withers, and her husband John McCallum, forwarded a cheque for £10 for the charity, and sent their best wishes for the success of the match.

The *'Bristol Evening World'* carried an article after the match regarding another family sporting team, the Claridges, who were apparently keen to challenge the Morgans to a fixture:

"Christmas time always seems the right seasonal occasion for families of sportsmen to challenge each other and now upon the scene in Bristol step The Claridges.

They are the sons and relatives of the late Pop Claridge. The older school will remember him as a grand utility player for Bristol Rugby Club. He went on to get his county cap for Gloucestershire and there are many who considered he was unlucky not to have been awarded an England cap.

Sport seems to run in the veins of The Claridges and it is at rugger that they make the strongest challenge to any other Bristol family. If there are no takers at that game, they are willing to put out a soccer team or take on opponents at a skittles alley.

The soccer challenge seems like an invitation to the Morgan family who frequently ask teams to play them."

It was subsequently reported that the Morgans accepted the challenge but no details of any fixture can be found.

A letter to the *'Bristol Evening Post'* from Gilbert Morgan was published on 4th August 1962, asking for potential new family members to join the team:

'WHERE ARE ALL THE MORGANS?"

"A few weeks ago, the Green 'Un brought to notice the family soccer teams of the past. The other day I came in contact with George Morgan, father of Jimmy, the former Bristol Rovers' inside-forward.

"What about another family game?" he asked. "Our Jim will lead the attack."

The families have split up so much that I have no idea of their whereabouts. However, if they see this letter they could write to me and let me know if they have a member of the family who could make up the team.

I want to field the strongest side from 12 years of age and over.

If any family soccer team interested in a match for charity – it is quite possible that several family teams are now in existence – then some form of knockout competition could be arranged.

I am aware that a Hanham church youth band require funds for new instruments. I would like such proceeds of a family game to assist in this matter."

Research has indicated that some members of the Morgan team had a somewhat tenuous link to 'our' Morgan family, some being cousins by marriage and others by simply sharing the Morgan surname. A good example of this is goalkeeper Syd Morgan, where the local press records his link to the family as being a cousin to both Johnny and Jimmy Morgan. Unfortunately, detailed investigation by family members has not resulted in finding the family link.

However, it is clear that the overwhelming majority of the team were indeed blood-related, which makes the family one of the very few who could claim to supply the complete 11 needed for a team.

On 2nd November 1963, Gilbert Morgan again made an appeal in the Peter Godsiff page in the *'Bristol Evening Post'* for any Morgan family members interested in representing the family to come forward:

'MORGANS SEEK ANOTHER CHALLENGE FOR CHARITY'

"Bristol's famous family of Morgans have issued another challenge. "We will play against any other team in the area in aid of Cancer Research" declared Gilbert Morgan, one of the many cousins in this footballing family.

He told me this week: "The Morgan family had a roll-call this week and we find we have about 18 players to call on – uncles, cousins, sons and brothers."

"We believe that a Sunday morning match near Christmas would be the best idea, and we hope to secure the loan of the St. George ground at Bell Hill for this purpose."

The Morgans have been playing family matches since 1919 – about one every ten years. The last time, they met Charlie Heal's Fun City at the Douglas Ground in Kingswood and lost 2-1.

Perhaps the best-known match was in 1937 at Ashton Gate when they met the Brown family – led by Ossie Brown, now president of St. Pancras, whom he served as a player. Again, the Morgans lost, this time 5-3, against the all-brothers team of Browns, but £100 was raised for the Old-age Pensioners' Christmas Dinner Fund.

If there are any family teams in Bristol prepared to meet the Morgans' challenge, I shall be pleased to pass on the acceptance.

Among the Morgans well-known in local football are: Jimmy (former Bristol Rovers), Syd (ex-Bristol City, now Salisbury), Mervyn (House of Faith), Peter (ex-Bristol City), Graham (ex-Soundwell), and John (Kingswood). Jimmy, the captain, would select the side."

The article drew an immediate response from Bristol St. George Football Club, whose secretary was keen to point out that; "It was reported that in the Green 'Un on Saturday that the Morgan family were hoping to play their match against the Wrights at the Bristol St. George ground on a Sunday. I should like to point out that no fixtures are allowed on this ground on a Sunday."

Despite this, it seems the appeal did the trick as on 22nd December 1963, the Morgans played a charity fixture against the Wright family, at the County Ground in Bristol, with the match being advertised in a press article displayed overleaf.

Another article appeared in the *'Bristol Evening Post'* on 14th December 1963, which went into great detail:

'CHALLENGE FROM ANOTHER FAMILY"

With the Morgans v. Wrights family football match only eight days away, another challenge has been issued by a Bristol footballing family.

The Heals, a well-known Bristol showman's family, have offered to play the winning side. Their offer has been accepted so there will be added incentive next Sunday morning at the County Ground (10.45).

Courage's Brewery have taken an interest in the match and they are putting up the John Courage Trophy for the winning side. A firkin of beer has also been given by the brewery for the victors.

The Morgan team will be selected tomorrow at Redfield, and the finalised Wright team will also be named next week.

Soccer's clashing clans
WRIGHTS v MORGANS

Here are the Morgans and the Wrights, Bristol feuding Soccer families who meet on Sunday. Top row (left to right): Steve Wright, aged 11, grandson; Alan Wright, ex-Wolves player; Leslie Wright; Paddy Hanlon, son-in-law; John Wright, goalkeeper; Sid Morgan, goalkeeper, ex-Bristol City, now plays for Salisbury Town; Terry Morgan; Tim Morgan, ex-Bristol Rovers; Alan Britt, cousin; Harry Morgan, ex-Bristol City; Ernie Godsell, cousin.

Middle row: Philip Mitchell; Kenneth Wright; Raymond Wright; Norman Wright; Vic Wright; Bill Barker, uncle; Mervyn Morgan; Peter Morgan; George Morgan; Peter White, brother-in-law; Les Harvey, cousin.

FAMILY FEUD WILL DRAW 5,000 FANS

Express Soccer Reporter

TWO families who have influenced Bristol football for generations play each other next Sunday morning to end a pub argument.

The question is: Are the Wrights better than the Morgans?

This is a duel of two feuding footballing families. If your name is not Morgan or Wright or you are not related to them you do not qualify to play in this [...]

Already 3,000 tickets have been sold for the game [...]

Gloucestershire county footballer, Alan Wright, who was in the Downs League team in their success-[...]

Press cuttings regarding the match between the Morgan Family and the Wright Family. Some of the Morgan team may have been 'loosely' related to the family.

The proceeds of the match will be given to the Cancer Research Fund. The next match between the Heal family and the winners of this game will benefit the Famine Relief Fund.

Should the Morgans qualify for this second game, it will be the second time in their history that they have played against the Heals. For, in 1952, they lost 2-1 at the Douglas Ground to Charlie Heal's Fun City side.

John Jones, acting for the Heal family, told me: "Most of us play in the Showmen's Guild XI. We are all related, mostly cousins. We have about 14 useful players to pick from and we are looking forward to the match."

The best-known member of the Heal family is Jimmy Sanders, a former Bristol City wing-half, who played in the Exeter City league side last season, after previously assisting Crystal Palace.

He runs a bingo stall in the summer fun fairs and is now looking round for a Southern League or Western League club.

Final word from the Morgan's chief, Gilbert: "We fell there must be more than three footballing families in the Bristol area, and our challenge to any other families still stands. Maybe we could even run a league."

Despite cold and icy conditions, the match against the Wrights went ahead, with the Morgans winning 4-0.

The press report of the match, published the following day, stated:

"The Morgans and the Wrights went at it hammer and tongs in their match at the County Ground yesterday, with no quarter asked or given. In the end, experience told, and the Morgans, who have been doing this sort of thing since 1919 – they beat Comrades of the Great War 3-1 on that occasion – ran out deserving winners by four goals to nil.

The ground was hard and icy, but the teams refused to allow this to affect the speed of the game. With 'Ginger' Roost, the old Bristol Rovers inside-right as the man with the whistle, they played half an hour each way.

The first cheer for the Morgans came after a quarter of an hour. Pete 'Cannon Ball' Morgan fired in a surprise shot from the right wing which deceived goalkeeper John Wright and the Morgans were in front.

Within three minutes of the second half, John Davidson, a Morgan cousin, playing inside-right, had scored direct from a free-kick.

The young Morgan forwards seemed to have more edge than the Wrights, even though Alan Wright, the former Wolves amateur, was playing a roving game at inside-forward.

One good chance came the Wright's way but inside-left David Mitchell shot straight at goalkeeper Gilbert Morgan. Soon afterwards, Les Harvey, another Morgan cousin, burst down the middle and shot straight past the advancing goalkeeper.

A few minutes from the end, George Morgan, inside-left, clinched the issue with a hard drive from about 20 yards.

After the match, George Morgan, the Morgan's 72-year-old team manager was jubilant. "The best team won", he said. "We're very pleased with them. Now we'll take on any family."

Charlie Wright, who had seven sons in the losing team, said: "It was a fair result. It was a good match considering the conditions."

Over 3,000 tickets were sold for the game, which was in aid of the Cancer Research Fund."

Other local family teams were quick to issue challenges to the Morgans:

"The Morgans, who won the family match against the Wrights, face two more challengers. They meet the West of England Showmen's Guild Heal family soon, and the Pinkers, from Kingswood, have also entered the lists.

Charlie Pinker, their grandfather, was manager of Bath City for many years.

Said Vernon Pinker: "We can turn out a team with at least nine Pinkers."

Photographs of the game show the icy and cold conditions in which it was played, a selection of which are shown below:"

John Davidson on the ball. The cricket scoreboard at the County Ground is visible in the background. The icy conditions can be clearly seen.

John Davidson hoisted aloft by members of the Wright Family team.

John Davidson in conversation with Peter Morgan.

Celebrations as the John Courage Trophy is lifted aloft by Captain Jimmy Morgan.

Captain Jimmy Morgan holds the trophy with the two competing teams.

Another photograph of the Morgans v. Wrights teams. Manager George Morgan in the centre of the picture.

Following the success of this fixture, the match against the West of England Showmen's Guild, for whom members of the Heal family played, was confirmed. It was played on 8th March 1964, and the fixture was advertised locally earlier in the week.

Under the heading of 'Morgans to meet Heals for Charity', the article stated:

"A family football match between the Morgans and the Heals will be played at the Douglas Ground on Sunday at 10.45 a.m. for local charities.

There will be a collection for Kingswood old age pensioners' outing, the Children's Society and the newly-formed Downend Toc H. The collection box for the Children's Society at St. Michael's, Two Mile Hill, was stolen at Christmas, and it is hoped to restore the contents as a result of the game. The Morgan family, who played the Browns in memorable pre-war games, have already beaten the Wright family this season in another charity match.

The Heals and Morgans previously met in 1952*, when the Heals won 2-1."

*Actually on 29th December 1951.

The Heal's were obviously taking the game seriously as they recruited a former professional footballer to their ranks, as reported in the *'Bristol Evening Post'* on March 7th:

'PROFESSIONAL HELP FOR HEAL FAMILY'

"Former Bristol City and Exeter City professional, Jimmy Sanders, will be at centre-half for the Heal Family tomorrow morning when they meet the Morgan Family in a charity match at the Douglas Ground, Kingswood (kick-off 10.45).

Heal's team will be: Jimmy Jennings; Charles Heal; Mike Devonald; John Jones; Jimmy Sanders; Jimmy Heal; Albert Rogers; Billy Clark; Reg Bartlett; Joe Heal; Graham Cleverley."

The match finished in a 1-1 draw, Devonald scoring for the Heals and 'Phillips' equalising for the Morgans. The referee was Bill Roost, the former Bristol Rovers forward.

As an aside, Jimmy Sanders has a wonderful and unique memorial at Arno's Vale Cemetery in Bristol.

The Jim Sanders Memorial, Arno's Vale Cemetery, Bristol.

Following the success of this fixture, another match for the Morgans was arranged against the Pinker family, which took place in Sunday April 19th, 1964. The Morgan team featured many new family members; Graham and John Davidson, who were two of the sons of John (Jack) Davidson and Ethel Morgan; Tony Luther could actually have been Terry Luther, son of Donald Luther and Florence Morgan.

The first announcement of the fixture appeared in the local press in mid-April 1964:

'5,000 ARE EXPECTED FOR FAMILY FINAL'

"A crowd of 5,000 is expected to watch the family final for the John Courage Trophy between the Morgans and the Pinkers at the Douglas Ground, Kingswood, this Sunday, 10.45 a.m.

The match is being organised by the Downend branch of Toc H, and proceeds will go the dependants of the tugboat Kingsgarth* victims.

The finalists are survivors from matches in which the Wrights and the Heals have also taken part. The teams will be:

PINKERS: K. Tomlin; L. Pinker; G. Pinker; R. Pinker; L. Bence; G. Pinker; V. Vowles; T. Tomlin; C. Pinker (Capt.); B. Pinker; A. Pinker.

Reserve: V. Pinker (team manager, D. Strickland)

MORGANS: Graham Davidson; Tony Luther; Terry Morgan; Alan Britt; Jim Morgan (captain); Mervyn Morgan; Paul Harvey; John Davidson; George Morgan; John Morgan; Peter Morgan.

Reserves: Harry, Bert and Philip Morgan.

Referee: G. Titmarsh.

Linesmen: M. A. Cross and D. Brine.

Sir Kenneth Brown will kick off.

Strong support is expected from docks offices at Avonmouth and Shirehampton and boot and shoe factories at Kingswood. Six schools in Kingswood have been given tickets. The 1860 East Bristol Squadron A.T.C. will parade before the game.

Bristol Rovers are supplying kit and John Courage (Bristol) are meeting the printing costs.

A previous match between the Wrights and the Pinkers raised £105, which will provide two television sets for the Children's Hospital."

The tug collided with Port Launceston and sank at Avonmouth Docks. Three of her five crew were reported missing.

The match was also advertised in the *'Bristol Evening Post'* on 26th March 1964, which stated:

'MORGANS V. PINKERS FOR FAMILY TROPHY'

The Morgans will meet the Pinkers for the John Courage family trophy at the Douglas Ground, Kingswood, on Sunday April 19[th,] at 10:45 a.m.

The match is being sponsored by Downend Toc H and will be in aid of the dependents of the crew who lost their lives in the tugboat *'Kingsgarth'*.

Sir Kenneth Brown will kick off at the match.

The Morgan family team have received a donation from Mr. Billy Butlin for new kit in recognition of their efforts for charity."

The Pinkers won the match for the John Courage Trophy 2-1 in front of over 3,000 spectators, the Morgan's goal coming from Peter White, son-in-law of Donald Luther and Florence Morgan, who was not in the original team selection.

The local press reported the match as below:

'PINKERS BEAT MORGANS IN FAMILY FINAL'

The Pinkers became the first holders of the John Courage Trophy when they gained a 2-1 victory over the Morgans in the family final at the Douglas Ground, Kingswood, yesterday.

The game – watched by 2,000 spectators – was organised by the Downend branch of Toc H in aid of the dependants of the tugboat Kingsgarth victims.

The Morgans took an early lead through Peter White, but Colin Pinker equalised and hit the winner in the 57th minute.

Known Morgan Family fixtures:

Date	Opponents	Venue	Result
3rd March 1919	Comrades of the Great War	Unknown	Won 3-1
1926	A.Stephens XI	St. Philips	Won 2-1
22nd April 1935	Wren Family	Chequers, Kingswood	Drew 0-0
13th May 1935	Wren Family	Eastville Stadium	Won 2-0
8th December 1937	Brown Family	Ashton Gate	Lost 3-5
29th December 1951	Heal's Fun City	Douglas Ground, Kingswood	Lost 1-2
22nd December 1963	Wright Family	County Ground, Bristol	Won 4-0
8th March 1964	Heal's Fun City	Douglas Ground, Kingswood	Drew 1-1
19th April 1964	Pinker Family	Douglas Ground, Kingswood	Lost 1-2

Matches against the Claridge Family and the Gane Family, although mentioned as being planned in the local press, do not appear to have taken place.

An interesting postscript to the Morgan family team was that in the early 1980s many related Morgan family members appeared in numerous cricket fixtures for Bedminster Cricket Club, sometimes as many as six in the same team.

John Anderson (son-in-law of Ivy Morgan; Robert Anderson (his son); Kenneth Bennett (another son-in-law of Ivy Morgan); Larry and Ed Bennett (his sons); Jim Webber (son of Violet Morgan); Tim Garland (grandson of Lilian Morgan); Philip Jones (son-in-law of John Anderson); Mark and David Hudson (nephews of John Anderson). Other female family members also helped out with scoring and tea-lady duties.

Many current family members are still actively playing local sport, notably football, where the family tradition continues to this day. The chance of another Morgan Family fixture in the future remains a possibility.

CHAPTER 20.
RELATED FAMILIES AND LOCATIONS.

With such a large family, it is not surprising that other local families have had links to the Morgan family, many being well-known families from the Barton Hill and East Bristol areas. I have researched a selection of significant other families, relevant details of which are recorded in this chapter. For the sake of relevance I have decided to only research the families who married into the Morgan family from the children of William Morgan and Mary Ann Fink.

Details are not meant to be complete or definitive, and only basic details have been included to illustrate the link to the larger Morgan family. However, where interesting or unusual facts have been discovered, these have been added to the basic information. Where there is doubt about the accuracy of information, details have not been included. There is scope for related families to investigate further if necessary.

Tichborne Street in Barton Hill, Bristol, is interesting to recall, as many related families lived there in the early part of the 20th Century. Examination of the 1939 Register has revealed the following families residing in the street:

- 8 Tichborne Street – John and Florence Tranter and family.
- 10 Tichborne Street – Alfred and Amy Cheesley and family.
- 12 Tichborne Street – John and Louisa Morgan and family. Not related to our Morgan family.
- 16 Tichborne Street – John and Sarah Morgan and family.

Tichborne Street, Coronation Day, 1953. Various Morgans, Tranters and Cheesleys can be seen in the photograph.

Of course, other streets in the area were also populated by related families, details of which are included in the relevant family sections.

Dave Cheesley, a descendant of the Tranter family, has provided an excellent overview of Tichborne Street:

"Situated between Beaufort Road and Corbett Street, running parallel with Morley Street, was Tichborne Street. On its south side was a terrace of twelve small flat-fronted houses numbered 2 to 24 (even); on its north side with was intercepted halfway along by Horton Street, followed by a short terrace of three houses numbered 1-5 (odd). On its corners with Beaufort Road, Horton Street, and Corbett Street there were small shop premises, but none of these were actually numbered in Tichborne Street itself.

These small flush pavement houses were two-bedroom with a front room, back room and kitchen downstairs, the toilet being outside with no bathroom. The front doors opened into a passage which led straight through to the back kitchen. The stairs were halfway down the passage between the front and back rooms. Each house had a small yard.

At No.8 lived Jack and Florence Tranter. Jack worked at Lysaght's, as did Jack Cheesley at No.10. Jack Cheesley's wife Amy and Jack Tranter were brother and sister. The Cheesley family had thirteen children, and the Tranters had six; at one time all lived at No.10.

At No.12 lived John and Louisa (Lou) Morgan (unrelated to our Morgan family), and at No.16 lived another John Morgan and his wife Sarah. John Morgan was a docker and his wife was the sister of Amy Cheesley at No.10.

All the houses in the street were sold to the Council under a Compulsory Purchase Order during 1956 and 1957, and were subsequently demolished to make way for development of the area. No trace of the street remains."

Many local churches appear in the history of the Morgan and associated families, notably St. Philip & Jacob Church, at which many family members were baptised or married. The history of the church can be traced back to 900 A.D., and it is still an active church to this day, popularly known as 'Pip'n'Jay' to locals.

St. Philip & Jacob Church, Bristol.

Another church well used by the Morgan family and beyond was Holy Trinity Church, St. Philips. The buildings are still standing but the church is now used as a community centre.

Holy Trinity Church, St. Philips, with overhead tram wires prominently on view.

St Luke's Church, in Barton Hill, Bristol, is another church well-used by family members over the years. Again it is still standing and used to this day.

St. Luke's Church, Barton Hill.

St. Matthew's Church, Moorfields (often known as Moorfields St. Matthew) is another church well-utilised by members of the Morgan family. Located between Redfield and Lawrence Hill, it was used for numerous baptisms and weddings for many years. The church was closed in 1999 and has been converted for use to offices and apartments.

St. Matthew's Church, Moorfields, Bristol.

St. Lawrence Church, Lawrence Hill, Bristol, regularly features in Morgan family history. He church closed in 1954 and was demolished in 1956.

St. Lawrence Church, Lawrence Hill, Bristol c. 1953.

St, Jude's Church, close to Old Market at Lawford's Gate, was located in one of the poorest areas of Bristol. The church buildings are still there, although converted into other uses following the closure of the church in 1982 and subsequently falling into disrepair after being sold in 1987.

St Jude's Church, Bristol.

St. Nicholas of Tolentino Roman Catholic Church is located close to St. Jude's Church at Lawford's Gate, Bristol. This is still an active church with a thriving local community, and was used by the Foley family (one of whom married into the Morgan family) who originally came from Ireland.

St. Nicholas of Tolentino Church, Lawford's Gate, Bristol.

The Bullock family.

The surname of Bullock appears twice in our Morgan family:

- **Alice Bullock** (born 25th November 1867, Bristol); married William John Morgan.
- **Matilda Frances Bullock** (born 30th July 1902, Bristol); married Frederick 'Jerry' Morgan.

Alice was one of the children of William Bullock (born 5th October 1844; died 29th January 1907, aged 62) and Emma Innes (born 1845), who married on 5th April 1853 at St. Jude's Church, Bristol. They had 8 children, including Alice, all of whom were born in Bristol:

William and Emma lived at various addresses in the East Bristol area:

- 1871 Census: 1 Wellington Terrace, St. Philips, Bristol.
- 1881 Census: 1 Wellington Terrace, St. Philips, Bristol.
- 1891 Census: 1 Croydon Street, Bristol.
- 1901 Census: 1 Roach's Buildings, Croydon Street, Bristol.

William was buried at Greenbank Cemetery, Bristol.

WILLIAM AND EMMA'S CHILDREN:

1.   **William James Bullock** (born 1863, Bristol; died 1919, Bristol, aged 56).

William married Sarah Esther Hillyer (born 16th January 1868, Bristol; died 22nd March 1940, Bristol, aged 72) on 22nd April 1888 at St. Silas Church, Bristol. William and Sarah were both buried at Avonview Cemetery, Bristol.

No burial date has been found for William, but Sarah was buried on 29th March 1940.

They had five children:

- **William Bullock** (born 25th September 1892, Bristol; died 23rd October 1969, Aylesbury, aged 77).

William was baptised at St. Philip & Jacob Church, Bristol, on 16th October 1892. The family address at the time was recorded as Easton Road, Bristol, and his father's occupation a Labourer.

He married Catherine James (born 7th December 1891, Bristol; died 1st November 1918, Bristol, aged 26) on 3rd August 1912, at St. Clements Church, Bristol. They had one child. Catherine was buried at Greenbank Cemetery, Bristol.

Following Catherine's death caused by the Spanish Flu pandemic, William married Violet Maud Pollinger (born 15th March 1899, Southwark, London; died 25th April 1978, Lambeth, London, aged 79). They had six children.

William served in the Royal Field Artillery during WW1 and was wounded in action serving with the famed 160th (Wearside) Brigade Royal Field Artillery during WW1. A shell blew him into a ditch or crater, and a dead horse fell on him.

William Bullock as a Beefeater at the Tower of London.

In May 1939, William enrolled in the Yeomen of the Guard (Tower of London), and retired in September 1939 at his own request.

The 1939 Register shows William and his family living at 48 Brigstock House, Lambeth, London, where William was recorded working as a Solicitor's Clerk.

- **Emma Bullock** (born 13th August 1894, Bristol; died 13th June 1967, Manchester, aged 72).

Emma was baptised at St. Philip & Jacob Church, Bristol, on 2nd September 1894. The family address at the time was recorded as 'Marsh' or St. Philips Marsh, Bristol, and her father's occupation a Labourer.

Emma Bullock (1894-1967).

She married Frank Redwood Faux (born 1891, Bristol, died 15th October 1960, Manor Park Hospital, Bristol, aged 69) on 21st August 1920, at Christ Church, Clifton Bristol. They had two children.

The 1939 Register shows the family living at 19 Cobden Street, Bristol, where Frank's occupation was recorded as being a General Labourer. Also living with the family were Emma's mother Sarah and other family members.

Frank and Emma were both buried at Avonview Cemetery, Bristol.

- **Ellen (Nelly) Bullock** (born 23rd June 1897, Bristol; died 1973, Weston-super-Mare, aged 75).

Ellen was baptised at St. Lawrence Church, Bristol, on 13th July 1897. The family address at the time was recorded as 5 Fleet Street, Bristol, and her father's occupation a Labourer.

She married James Britt (born 1st May 1894, Bristol; died 1946, Bristol) on 30th July 1921 at Moorfields St. Matthew Church, Bristol. They had one child.

James, Ellen (Nelly) and child.

The 1939 Register shows the family living at 32 Cobden Street, Bristol, where James's occupation is shown as being involved in Maintenance and Repair.

James was buried at Avonview Cemetery, Bristol.

- **Sarah Millicent Bullock** (born 9th November 1900, Bristol; died 1979, Leicester, aged 78).

Sarah was baptised at Holy Trinity Church, Bristol, on 6th March 1912. The family address at the time was recorded 28 Barton Hill Road, Bristol, and her father's occupation a Carman.

She married Cecil Thomas Cartlidge (born 24th July 1900, Derby; died 1968, Melton Mowbray, aged 67) on 4th September 1926 at St. Philip and Jacob Church, Bristol. They had no children.

The 1939 Register shows the couple living at The Bungalow, Melbourne Drive, Melton Mowbray, where Cecil's occupation was that of a Railway Signaller.

- **Matilda Frances Bullock** (born 30th July 1902; died 26th January 1979, Bristol, aged 76).

Matilda was baptised at Holy Trinity Church, Bristol, on 20th August 1902. The family address at the time was recorded 2 Unity Place, Lawrence Hill, Bristol, and her father's occupation a Carman.

Matilda married Frederick 'Jerry' Morgan in 1923.

See Chapter 4.

2.   **Emily Bullock** (born 25th October 1865).

Albert was baptised at St. Philip & Jacob Church, Bristol, on 12th November 1865. The family address was shown as being Barton Vale, Bristol, with her father's occupation recorded as being a Labourer.

She married Henry Benjamin Lucas (born 1861, Bath; died 1916, Newport, Monmouthshire, aged 55) at St. Luke's Church, Barton Hill, Bristol, on 13th February 1884.

The family moved from Bristol to Wolverhampton and finally to Newport, Monmouthshire.

They had ten children:

- **William Henry Lucas** (born 19th April 1884, Bristol; died 27th November 1946, Newport, Monmouthshire, aged 62).

William was baptised at St. Philip & Jacob Church, Bristol, on 11th May 1884. The family address at the time was vaguely recorded as 4 Barton Hill, Bristol, and his father's occupation a Labourer.

He married Gladys Hewitt (born 16th June 1891, Newport, Monmouthshire; died 1971, Newport, Monmouthshire, aged 80) on 10th January 1916 in Newport, Monmouthshire, and had three children.

The 1939 Register shows the family residing at 23 Morris Street, Newport, Monmouthshire, with William working as an Iron Worker.

- **Albert Lucas** (born 15th April 1886, Bristol).

Albert was baptised at St. Philip & Jacob Church, Bristol, on 9th May 1886. The family address at the time was recorded as Beaufort Road, Bristol, and his father's occupation a Labourer.

- **Emily Lucas** (born 24th May 1887, Bristol; died 30th September 1967, Bristol, aged 80).

Emily was baptised at St. Philip & Jacob Church, Bristol, on 10th June 1887. The family address at the time was records as Beaufort Road, Bristol, and her father's occupation a Labourer.

She married Sidney Thomas Norman (born 13th November 1891, Bristol; died 1967, Bristol, aged 75) on 25th May 1931 at St. Philip & Jacob Church, Bristol. Her home address was shown as 32 William Street, Bristol, whilst that of Sidney was 30 Barton Road, Bristol. He was a Labourer by trade. They had no children.

The 1939 register shows the couple living at 7 Osborne Terrace, Bristol, where Sidney's occupation shown as a Jointer in Gas Company.

- **Frederick James Lucas** (born 22nd September 1889, Bristol; died 1948, Newport, aged 58).

Frederick was baptised at St. Luke's Church, Barton Hill, Bristol, on 11th October 1889. The family address at the time was recorded as 27 Factory Street, Bristol, and his father's occupation a Dipper at Galvanizer Works.

He married Gladys Rogers (born 22nd June 1896, Birkenhead; died 1975, Newport, Monmouthshire, aged 78) in 1916, in Bedford, and had six children.

The 1939 Register records the family living at 9 Ashley Road, Newport, Monmouthshire, where Frederick is shown as being employed as a worker at Iron and Steel Works.

- **James Lucas** (born 1892, Wolverhampton; died 1950, Newport, aged 58).

James was baptised at St. James' Church, Wolverhampton, on 21st January 1892.

He married Elsie Gertrude Rees (born 1897, Cardiff; died 1944, Newport, Monmouthshire, aged 47) in 1918, in Newport, Monmouthshire. They had six children.

- **George Lucas** (born 9th August 1894, Hampton, Staffordshire).

George was baptised at St. James' Church, Wolverhampton, on 5th February 1896.

He married Amelia Maud Yoxall (born 20th February 1899, Bilston, Staffordshire; died 1964, Newport, Monmouthshire, aged 64) on 27th December 1916, in Newport, and had three children.

The 1939 Register reveals the family living at 9 Park Drive, Newport, Monmouthshire, with George's occupation shown as a Club Steward.

- **Nellie Jane Lucas** (born 2nd November 1896, Wolverhampton; died 1986, Newport, aged 89).

Nellie was baptised at St. James' Church, Wolverhampton, on 26th January 1898.

She married Ivor Edward Harris (born 15th August 1896, Newport, Monmouthshire; died 1962, Newport, Monmouthshire, aged 65) on 7th April 1917, also in Newport, Monmouthshire. They had one child.

The 1939 Register has revealed the family were living at 12 Rensel Street, Newport, Monmouthshire, where Ivor worked as a Lorry Driver.

- **Florence Lucas** (born 15th February 1899, Newport, Monmouthshire; died 1981, Newport, Monmouthshire, aged 81).

Florence was baptised at Maindee Parish Church, Newport, Monmouthshire, on 6th October 1899. The family address recorded was 20 Gaskell Street in Newport, with her father's occupation shown as being a Sheet Wire Worker

She married William Stevens (born 6th November 1894, Wolverhampton; died 1953, Newport, Monmouthshire, aged 58) in 1921, in Newport, Monmouthshire. They had one child.

The family remained at 20 Gaskell Street for the 1939 Register, where William's occupation was described as a Steel Sheet Checker.

- **Jane Lucas** (born 1901, Newport).

Jane was baptised at St. Mary's Church, Maindee, Newport, Monmouthshire, on 16th April 1901. The family address was recorded as 20 Gaskell Street in Newport, with her father's occupation an Ironworker.

- **Annie Lucas** (born 19th June 1904, Newport; died 2000, Newport, aged 95.

She married Charles William Sealey (born 26th March 1902, Bishops Lydeard, Somerset; died 22nd September 1958, Newport, Monmouthshire, aged 56) in Newport, Monmouthshire in 1928.

The 1939 Register saw the family residing at 19 Gaskell Street, Newport, Monmouthshire, where Charles was recorded as working as a Lorry Driver.

3.   **Alice Bullock** (born 25th November 1867; died 13th August 1929, Bristol, aged 61).

She married William John Morgan, son of John Morgan and Matilda Williams, on 13th October 1884 at Bristol Registry Office.

See Chapter 4.

4.   **George Bullock** (born 21st December 1870; died 9th March 1927, Bristol, aged 56).

George was baptised at St. Philip & Jacob Church, Bristol, on 12th February 1871, with the family address recorded as Wellington Terrace, Easton Road, Bristol, with his father's occupation being a Labourer.

He married Emma Coates (born 1872, Marshfield; died 26th February 1956, Bristol, aged 84) on 3rd August 1891 at Holy Trinity Church, Bristol. He was boarding at the Coates household according to the 1891 Census, living at 31 Winsford Street, St. Philips, Bristol, where Emma was living with her family. They had no children.

George and Emma were both buried at Greenbank Cemetery, Bristol, George on 16th March 1927, and Emma on 2nd March 1956.

5.   **James Bullock** (born 1873; died 31st August 1937, Bristol, aged 64).

He married Sarah Maria Rossiter (born 1878, Bristol; died 14th February 1946, Bristol, aged 68) on 4th December 1897 at Moorfields St. Matthew Church, Bristol.

Both James and Sarah were buried at Avonview Cemetery, Bristol, James on 4th September 1937, and Sarah on 19th February 1946.

They had four children.

- **Rosina Matilda Bullock** (born 19th April 1898, Bristol; died 1965, Bristol, aged 66).

Rosina was baptised at St. Philip & Jacob Church, Bristol, on 8th May 1898. The family address at the time was shown as 'Barton Hill, Bristol' and her father's occupation a Labourer.

She married Edward George Pickford (born 22nd June 1893, Bristol; died 1966, Weston-super-Mare, aged 72) on 26th December 1918 at St. Luke's Church, Bristol. They had four children, and lived at 44 Granville Street, Bristol at the time of the 1939 Register.

- **Albert Edward Bullock** (born 28th July 1902, Bristol; died 28th November 1989, Bristol, aged 87).

Albert was baptised at St. Philip & Jacob Church, Bristol, on 17th August 1902. The family address at the time was shown as 41 Granville Street, Barton Hill, Bristol and his father's occupation a Labourer.

He married Annie Louisa Miell (born 22nd June 1906, Bristol; died 1st March 1996, Bristol, aged 93) at St. Paul's Church, Bedminster, Bristol, on 29th June 1929. They had three children, and lived at 11 Cuffington Avenue, Bristol, as recorded on the 1939 Register.

- **Lilian Florence Bullock** (born 12th December 1906, Bristol; died 27th December 1980, Bristol, aged 74).

Lilian was baptised at St. Philip & Jacob Church, Bristol, on 9th January 1907. The family address at the time was shown as 41 Granville Street, Barton Hill, Bristol and her father's occupation a Labourer.

She married Arthur Tarzey Hodge (born 3rd November 1902, Bristol; died 7th June 1982, Bristol, aged 79) at St. Luke's Church, Barton Hill, Bristol, on 13th February 1926. They had three children, and the 1939 Register shows them living at 7 Matthews Road, Bristol.

- **Phyllis Arabis Bullock** (born 2nd June 1916, Bristol; died 17th March 1996, Bristol, aged 79).

She married William Albert Frederick McCormick (born 22nd July 1915, Ilminster, Somerset; died 27th April 1982, Bristol, aged 66) at St. James' Church, Bristol, on 17th April 1937.

They had three children, and the 1939 Register records the family living at 1 Ninth Avenue, Bristol.

6. **Thomas Bullock** (born 26th May 1876; died 7th November 1922, Bristol, aged 46).

Thomas was baptised at St. Philip & Jacob Church, Bristol, on 11th June 1876, with the family address recorded as Wellington Terrace, Bristol, his father William noted as being a Sugar Refiner.

He married Eliza Parker (born 18th June 1875, Bristol; died 25th October 1942, Bristol, aged 67) in 1912, in Bristol, Eliza had one child from a previous marriage, and they had one additional child together.

- **Lily Eliza Bullock** (born 16th December 1914, Bristol; died 14th November 2009, Bristol, aged 94).

She married Reginald James Weeks at St. Agnes Church, Bristol, on 21st December 1935. They had one child. The 1939 Register shows Lily and Reginald living at 18 Walcot Street, Bristol.

Eliza married Joseph Ford in 1925 in Bristol.

Thomas was buried at Greenbank Cemetery, Bristol on 15th November 1922, and Eliza was buried at the same location in 1942.

7. **Matilda Bullock** (born 30th January 1879; died 1960, Bristol, aged 80).

Matilda was baptised at St. Philip & Jacob Church, Bristol, on 16th February 1879, with the family address recorded as Wellington Terrace, Bristol, her father's occupation being a Labourer.

She married George Earl Miles (born 5th September 1875, Bristol; died 1939, Bristol, aged 63) on 7th April 1901 at St. Luke's Church, Bristol. They had no children. They lived at 14 Dunkery Road, Bristol, according to the 1939 Register.

8.   **Ellen Bullock** (born 12th April 1883; died 11th February 1972, aged 88).

She married Arthur Patrick Rowe (born 1878, Bristol; died 15th May 1938, Bristol, aged 60), a policeman by trade, on 31st May 1903 at St. Luke's Church, Bristol. He served in the Boer War and was wounded in action in November 1899.

Ellen and Arthur were both buried at Greenbank Cemetery, Bristol, Arthur on 19th May 1938, and Ellen on 16th February 1972.

They had eight children,

- **Ivy Ellen Rowe** (born 9th September 1904, Bristol; died 6th March 1979, 55 Brendon Road, Bedminster, Bristol, aged 74).

Ivy was baptised at St. Michael's Church, Bedminster, Bristol, on 5th October 1904. The family address at this time was 80 Upper Cotswold Road, Bristol, with her father's occupation recorded as a Police Constable.

She married Horace Frederick James Brown (born 3rd October 1903, Bristol; died 17th December 1974, Bristol, aged 71) on 23rd August 1930 at St. Michael's Church, Bedminster, Bristol. They had no children.

The 1939 Register shows the family living at 55 Brendon Road, Bedminster, Bristol, an address they remained at for their entire lives.

- **Winifred Grace Rowe** (born 27th August 1906, Bristol, died 18th October 1993, Bristol, aged 87).

Winifred was baptised at St. Michael's Church, Bedminster, Bristol, on 12th September 1906. The family address at this time was 20 Dunkery Road, Bristol, with her father's occupation recorded as a Policeman.

She married Sydney Harris (born 24th November 1905, Bristol; died 25th September 1940, Bristol, aged 34) on 11th April 1936 at St. Michael's Church, Bedminster, Bristol.

The 1939 Register has recorded the family living at 55 Highbury Road, Bristol. Sydney was sadly killed during a German air raid on Filton, Bristol, on 25th September 1940.

> HARRIS, SYDNEY, age 34. Son of Mrs. Harris, of 4 Sunrise Grove, Bloomfield Road, Brislington; husband of W. G. Harris, of 55 Highbury Road, Parson Street, Bedminster. Injured 25 September 1940, at Filton; died same day on way to Bristol Royal Infirmary.

Sydney Harris's WW2 Civilian Death record.

- **Elsie May Rowe** (born 24th December 1908, Bristol; died 11th April 1941, Bristol, aged 32).

Elsie was baptised at St. Michael's Church, Bedminster, Bristol, on 13th January 1909. The family address at this time was 37 Dunkery Road, Bristol, with her father's occupation recorded as a Policeman.

She married William Henry Mugridge (born 13th July 1909, Bristol; died 11th April 1941, Bristol, aged 31) at St. Michael's Church, Bedminster, Bristol, on 30th May 1936. They had no children.

Elsie and her husband were both killed at home (33 Leighton Road, Southville, Bristol) on 11th April 1941 as a result of a German bombing raid.

> MUGRIDGE, ELSIE MAY, age 32; of 33 Leighton Road, Southville. Daughter of Mrs. E. Rowe, of 37 Dunkerry Road, Bedminster; wife of William Henry Mugridge. 11 April 1941, at 33 Leighton Road.
>
> MUGRIDGE, WILLIAM HENRY, age 31; Fire Guard; of 33 Leighton Road, Southville. Son of Mr. J. Mugridge, of 16 Talbot Street, Ashton Gate; husband of Elsie May Mugridge. 11 April 1941, at 33 Leighton Road.

Elsie and William's WW2 Civilian Death record.

- **Doris Matilda Rowe** (born 2nd October 1910, Bristol, died 1992, Nottingham, aged 81).

Doris was baptised at St. Michael's Church, Bedminster, Bristol, on 23rd November 1910. The family address at this time was 37 Dunkery Road, Bristol, with her father's occupation recorded as a Policeman.

She married Frederick Ernest Rogers (born 5th August 1911, Bristol; died 1973, Eton, Buckinghamshire) at St. Michael's Church, Bedminster, Bristol, on 11th September 1937.

The 1939 Register saw Doris living at home with her mother and sisters at 37 Dunkery Road, Bristol.

- **Arthur William Rowe** (born 10th May 1912, Bristol; died 16th January 1999, Bristol, aged 86).

The 1939 Register shows Arthur living at home with his parents at 37 Dunkery Road, Bristol, were his occupation was recorded as being a a Depot Foreman at Coal Merchants.

He married Alice Caroline Durnell (born 10th October 1913, Totnes, Devon; died 4th March 1988, Bristol, aged 84) in Bristol, in 1941. They had four children.

- **Alfred George Rowe** (born 28th March 1914, Bristol; died 2002, Bristol, aged 87).

The 1939 Register also shows Alfred living at home with his parents at 37 Dunkery Road, Bristol, where his occupation was stated as being a Sheet Metal Worker.

He married Vera Maud Caddick (born 21st May 1915, Bristol; died 2nd November 2011, Bristol, aged 96) in Bristol, in 1947. They had one child.

- **Mildred Vera Rowe** (born 5th April 1916, Bristol; died 31st October 1997, Bristol, aged 81).

Like her brothers, the 1939 Register shows Mildred living at home at 37 Dunkery Road, Bristol, her occupation being recorded as a Factory Hand at Paper Factory.

She married Frederick George Levi Jones (born 18th October 1915, Bristol; died 2003, Bristol, aged 88) in Bristol, in 1940. They had three children.

- **Hilda Maud Rowe** (born 1918, Bristol; died 15th June 1982, Bristol, aged 63).

Hilda also features on the 1939 Census as living at home at 37 Dunkery Road, Bristol, her occupation revealed as also being a Factory Hand at Paper Factory.

She married Royston Joseph Ernest Cavill (born 23rd June 1917, Bristol; died 3rd August 1982, Bristol, aged 65) in Bristol, in 1941. They had one child. Hilda was cremated at South Bristol Crematorium on 21st June 1982, and Roy was cremated at the same location on 6th August 1982.

Another distant Bullock family member, Lilian May Bullock (1895-1975), married William (Billy) Henry Vaughan (1898-1976) on 5th August 1922 in Bristol. Billy played football for Bristol Rovers in the 1920-21 season, alongside Frederick 'Jerry' Morgan, making 6 appearances and scoring 1 goal.

Her sister, Gladys Mabel Bullock (1905-1969), was a keen Bristol Rovers supporter in the 1930s, regularly assisting in kit washing duties.

The Coles (or Cole) family.

During the early 1900s, the family name evolved into 'Coles', having been 'Cole' for numerous years. The reasoning for the change remains a family mystery.

Elizabeth Coles (born 10th May 1875, Bristol, died 20th August 1963, Bristol, aged 88) married James Morgan, one of the sons of John Morgan and Matilda Williams, on 24th May 1896 at St. Lawrence Church, Easton, Bristol.

Elizabeth was the eldest of five children born to Henry Cole (born 1851, Bristol; died 1884, Bristol, aged 33) and Mary Ann Bidder (born 1856, Bristol, died 10th August 1902, Bristol, aged 46). Henry and Mary Ann married on 17th February 1873 at St. Jude's Church, Bristol.

The 1881 Census shows the family living at 3 Lamb Street, St. Judes, Bristol, where Henry earned his living as a Hawker, plying his trade around the Lawrence Hill and Barton Hill areas of the city.

By 1891 most the family were still living in Lamb Street, in one of the many small courtyards which backed on to the main thoroughfare. In this case, the family was living at 3 Crockers Court, no doubt in cramped and unsanitary conditions. Henry was employed as a Dock Labourer, Mary Ann a Tailoress, whilst son Henry was a 'Boot Stamper'.

It is worth recalling here the absolute poverty in which people lived in these small Courts in the St. Jude's area of Bristol. A report from 1864 describes the conditions in detail:

"It must be premised that the inhabitants are essentially poor. We cannot think that crime finds a haunt in this quarter. It is rather a densely-populated neighbourhood of people who struggle to get an honest living - but such miserable living that it barely deserves the name. Some families have to exist on half-a-crown a week - while others get more. The average may be from six to seven shillings. It can hardly be urged, in the face of this, that these poor creatures are "a drunken lot". And yet this has been urged. It is necessary to touch upon this matter in order fully to grasp the question before us, viz., what has occasioned the epidemic sickness in this particular locality? The details we subjoin will, we think, fully answer this. It is "filth" that is the prime cause of all of it. Insufficient accommodation, want of ventilation, and bad drainage are conspicuous almost everywhere.

True - the Board of Health have been very busy and energetic, since the appearance of the fever, in cleansing and improving, but why was not all this done long ago? Nearly every court visited contained but one privy - and that until very recently has all outlet stopped up. The drought of the past season, acting upon the collected filth, would be in itself enough to cause disease. But there are other evils. Pigsties and stables are attached to many of the houses, and the manure in these has often been allowed to remain for months. In one place we visited there was absolutely no water closet at all, but a hole in the floor, communicating with a sort of underground passage, was made to answer the purpose. In that room lived five people; and, when we saw it, a woman was down in the fever, and two little children were "squatted" down in a state of perfect nudity. We dare not, in a question like this, stop to mince matters, or allow any false delicacy to prevent our laying bare such evils. The subject demands more careful attention, and our readers will be able to form for themselves some idea of it by perusing the accounts we have given of the places which we yesterday examined."

The article continues:

"Crocker's Court, the next in that street, was tolerably free from the pollutions which are rife in many other quarters, and a somewhat profuse distribution of chloride of lime imparted to the atmosphere of the place's wholesomeness, which was quite refreshing in such a neighbourhood."

In the mid 1880's, Mary Ann had a relationship with John 'Jack' Hennessy (born 1852, Waterford, Ireland), and they had two children together. Despite claims on the 1891 Census that they had married, no evidence has been found to confirm this. Their children were:

- **John William Hennessy** (born 6th May 1888, 9 Little Ann Street, Bristol; died 29th May 1964, Bristol, aged 76). He married twice, and had eight children.

- **Maurice Joseph Hennessy** (born 20th August 1890, 14 Little Ann Street, Bristol; died 1945, Bristol, aged 54). He married Elsie Eliza Jefferies in 1918 and had two children.

The 1891 Census shows Mary Ann's surname recorded as 'Hennessy' and living with John and their two children along with her own children Mary Ann, and Henry, at 14 Little Ann Street, Bristol. John's occupation was recorded as being a Hawker.

The 1901 Census shows Mary Ann living with John Hennessy and their two children at 24 Brick Street, Bristol, under her surname of 'Coles' and described as a 'Housekeeper'.

Mary Ann died on 10th August 1902 in Bristol, and is buried in the Morgan family grave at Avonview Cemetery Bristol, under her 'Coles' surname.

HENRY AND MARY ANN'S CHILDREN:

1. **Elizabeth Coles** (born 10th May 1875, Bristol; died 20th August 1963, Bristol).

Also see Chapter 7.

Elizabeth had a hard and poverty-stricken upbringing. The 1891 Census shows her living with her Uncle and Aunt Henry and Phoebe Fuller and family at 11 Orchard Square, Redfield, Bristol, where she worked as a cotton weaver, no doubt at the cotton factory at Barton Hill. It was only when she married James Morgan in 1896 that the quality of her life improved.

Elizabeth Morgan (nee Coles), 1935, just after the passing of her husband James Morgan. Picture taken at the Rising Sun.

After her husband James died in 1935, she took over the running of the 'Rising Sun' public house in Church Road, Redfield, Bristol, before moving to 38 Victoria Avenue, St. George, which suffered a direct hit during the Bristol Blitz. Thankfully Elizabeth and the other inhabitants of the house had found a safe haven in the local air raid shelter.

She married William Edwin Stokes (born 3rd October 1876, Bristol; died 28th August 1946, Bristol, aged 69) on 3rd May 1943 at St. Mary's Church, Fishponds, Bristol.

Elizabeth passed away on 20th August 1963 at 61 Queen's Road, St. George, Bristol, the home of her daughter Grace and husband Arthur Stanley Hodge.

2. **Mary Ann Coles** (born 18th July 1878, Bristol; died 28th August 1970, Bristol)

Elizabeth's sister Mary Ann had a very eventful life. She married 3 times:

- **Thomas Hodges:** Married on 21st June 1896, St. Matthews Moorfield, Redfield, Bristol.

Their marriage registration shows they both lived at 10 Lyppiatt Road, Bristol. It would appear that they separated between 1904 and 1907.

The 1939 Register shows him living with the Sharpe family at 55 Victoria Parade, Bristol, employed as a Market Gardener.

- **William Henry Packer:** Married in 1917, in Bristol.

He died on 9th July 1925, and was buried at Avonview Cemetery, Bristol, on 16th July 1925.

- **Edward James Haines**: Married in 1933, Bristol. He died on 27th January 1959 in Bristol.

He had previously been married to Lucy Ann Ferris (born 1874, Bristol, died 1931, Bristol), and they had seven children together. He was buried at Avonview Cemetery, Bristol, on 31st January 1959.

Mary Ann had nine children, all born in Bristol, many of whom were born out of wedlock, and took on various surnames during their early years:

- **Rose Emily (Flossie) Coles** (born 7th September 1899; died 30th March 1990, Bristol, aged 90).

Her father was not stated on her birth registration. However, the baptism registration from 27th September 1899 shows her being baptised as Rose Emily Packer, which would suggest the father would have been William Henry Packer.

The address of both parents is shown as being 11 Orchard Square, Redfield, Bristol.

She married William Edwin Lucas (born 12th July 1902, Bristol; died 1949, Bristol, aged 46), on 21st March 1921 at Holy Trinity Church, Kingswood, Bristol.

The marriage certificate gave Rose's name as Rose Emily Packer, living at 4 Blackhorse Road, Kingswood, Bristol, her father's occupation noted as being a Labourer.

William was living at 3 Wood Road, Kingswood, Bristol, an Engineer by trade.

They had five children.

William was buried at Avonview Cemetery, Bristol on 18th March 1949, and Rose was buried at the same location on 6th April 1990.

- **William Coles** (born 28th August 1901; died 23rd February 1947, Bristol, aged 45).

His father again not stated on birth registration. However, the 1911 Census shows him entered as 'William Packer Hodges' which could indicate that his father was again William Henry Packer.

He was also known as 'William Coles Packer', and can be found on the 1939 Register under the name of William C. Packer living with his mother Mary Ann Haines and his brother Ernest at 11 Orchard Square, Redfield, Bristol, working as a Potato Stores Labourer.

He never married, and was buried at Avonview Cemetery, Bristol on 28th February 1947 under the name of William Charles Packer, the 'Charles' possibly being a transcription error.

- **Lily Hodges** (born 21st March 1904; died 10th December 1985, Bristol, aged 81).

Father recorded as Thomas Hodges. She married Herbert Bennett (born 2nd August 1893, Bristol; died 30th December 1976, Bristol, aged 83) on 18th April 1925, at St. Matthew Moorfields Church, Bristol.

They had six children.

The 1939 Register shows the family living at 129 Lichfield Road, where Herbert was employed as a Chemicals Labourer (Heavy Work).

Herbert was buried at Avonview Cemetery, Bristol on 6th January 1977, and Lily was buried at the same location on 18th December 1981,

- **Mary Ann Packer** (born 1st January 1907; died 15th January 1958, Bristol, aged 51).

Father recorded as William Henry Packer.

She married Sidney John Birch (born 12th October 1907, Bristol; died 21st April 1976, Bristol, aged 68) on 23rd December 1933 at St. Matthew Moorfields Church, Bristol. They had no children.

The 1939 Register records them living at 77 Fishponds Road, Bristol, where Sidney's occupation was noted as being an Aeroplane Erector.

Mary Ann was buried at Greenbank Cemetery, Bristol on 21st January 1958, and Sidney at the same location on 27th April 1976.

- **George Henry Packer** (born 27th September 1909; died 1988, Bristol, aged 79).

Father shown as William Henry Packer. He never married.

The 1939 Register shows him as an inmate at the Stapleton Institution, 200 Manor Road, Bristol, with his occupation recorded as being a Carter.

He was cremated at Canford Cemetery, Bristol, on 19th April 1988.

- **Elizabeth Emily (Betty) Packer** (born 1912; died 23rd January 2010, Bristol, aged 98).

Her father was William Henry Packer.

She married Frederick Ernest Evans (born 22nd September 1911, Bristol; died 20th July 1990, Bristol, aged 78) on 26th October 1935 at St. Ambrose Church, Whitehall, Bristol. They had one child.

- **Ernest Charles Packer** (born 2nd October 1915; died 10th August 2002, Bristol aged 86).

His father was William Henry Packer.

The 1939 Register shows him at home, with his mother and brother William, at 11 Orchard Square, Redfield, Bristol, his occupation being a Woodworker (Aircraft).

He married Irene Kate White (born 13th May 1919, Bristol; died 6th November 1975, Hillfields Park, Bristol, aged 56), on 13th May 1940, in Bristol.

They had three children.

Irene was buried at Avonview Cemetery on 11th November 1975.

- **Bertie Packer** (born 1st January 1918; died 2005, Colchester, Essex, aged 87).

His father was William Henry Packer,

He married Irene (date unknown), and died in 2005, in Colchester, Essex.

- **Gilbert Edward Packer** (born 6th September 1921; died 29th March 2009, Bristol, aged 87).

His father was William Henry Packer.

He married Pamela Nicholls (died 2015, Bristol) in 1947 in Bristol, and they had four children.

He was cremated at South Bristol Crematorium on April 7th 2009. Pamela was cremated at the same location on 24th April 2015.

The 1911 Census is revealing in that it shows William Packer living with Mary Ann and her children living at 17 Orchard Square, Redfield, Bristol. William's trade is described as a 'Carter for Employed Acid Hawker' and his marital status shown as 'single'.

Mary Ann has her surname shown as 'Hodges' but her marital status is shown as 'married' but 'separated from husband'. The children's surnames are shown as being 'Packer Hodges' rather than those by which their births were registered.

By the 1921 Census, the family were still living at 11 Orchard Square, now all with the surname 'Packer'. William continued his trade as a carter, Mary Ann with daughters Rose and Lillian working as cotton weavers, William being shown as a general labourer, and daughter Mary Ann as a charwoman.

The 1939 Register shows Mary Ann with new husband Edward James Haines residing at the same address; Edward described as being a Steel Erector, with Mary Ann undertaking unpaid domestic duties. Sons William and Ernest Packer were still living at home, employed as a Potato Stores Labourer and an Aircraft Woodworker respectively.

Mary Ann died on 28th August 1970 and she is interred in the Morgan Family grave at Avonview Cemetery in Bristol, under her final married name of Haines.

3. **Rosina (Rose) Coles** (born 19th August 1880, Bristol).

Little can be found about Rosina, often known as Rose or Rosie. She was baptised at St. Jude's Church, Bristol, on 22nd September 1880, with the home address appearing to be Redcross Street, Bristol and her father's occupation being a Hawker.

She appears on the 1881 Census, living at 3 Lamb Street, Bristol, but does not appear on the 1891 Census with her mother and brother. No further trace of her has been found.

4. **Henry (Harry) Coles** (born 3rd April 1882, Bristol; died 18th May 1951, Bristol, aged 69).

Henry (known as Harry) was baptised at St. Jude's Church, Bristol, on 12th May 1882, at the same date as his twin sister Eliza (see below). Their home address was recorded as 3 Lamb Street, Bristol, and their father's occupation shown as being a Rag Picker.

He never married, and was noted on the 1939 Register as living with the Bewley family at 8 Robert Street, Bristol, where his occupation was noted as being a Builder's Labourer.

He was buried at Avonview Cemetery, Bristol.

5. **Eliza Coles** (born 3rd April 1882, Bristol; died 1883, Bristol, aged less than 1); twin to Henry.

Eliza was baptised at St. Jude's Church, Bristol, on 12th May 1882, at the same date as her twin brother Henry.

She was buried at Holy Trinity Church, Bristol, on 11th February 1883.

The Dawes Family.

The link to the Morgan family can be found via John McGoldrick (Frederick) Dawes, who married Florence Beatrice Morgan on 27th May 1900 at St. Matthew Moorfields, Bristol.

His father was Charles James Dawes (born 1851, died 22nd May 1922, Bristol, aged 79) and his mother Jane Glover Cheese (born 11th May 1853, Wraxall, North Somerset; died 30th December 1935, Bristol, aged 82). They married on 13th April 1871, in Bristol.

The 1881 Census shows the family living at 23 Winsford Street, Bristol, where Charles was recorded as being a Baker, and Jane a Boot Binder.

By 1891, the family had moved to 46 Pennywell Road, Bristol, where Charles was now a Dairyman and Jane a shopkeeper.

1901 saw Charles return to his work as a Baker, and the family had relocated to 34 Pennywell Road, Bristol, an address where they stayed when the 1911 Census took place. By then, Charles was working alongside his son Frank as a Labourer with a Shipping Agent.

The 1921 Census records Charles and Jane living at 44 Goodhind Street, Bristol, where Charles is noted as being an Out of Work Baker, and children Frank. Myrtle and Elizabeth still living with them.

Charles died in Bristol on 13th January 1931, aged 79, and was buried at Greenbank Cemetery, Bristol, on 17th January 1931. Jane died in Bristol in on 30th December 1935, aged 82, and was also buried at Greenbank Cemetery on 4th January 1936.

CHARLES AND JANE'S CHILDREN:

1. **William Charles Dawes** (born 27th July 1872, Bristol; died 14th September 1944, Bristol, aged 72), was a Baker by trade.

He was baptised at Holy Trinity Church, St. Philips, Bristol, on 8th September 1872, with the family home recorded as being Clifton Wood, Bristol, and his father's occupation being a Baker.

He married Lilly Elizabeth Jayne (born 18th May 1872, Bristol; died 9th April 1951, Bristol, aged 78) on 24th December 1892 at St. Matthias Church, Bristol. At the time of their marriage both William and Lilly were living at Merchant Street, Bristol.

They had ten children:

- **Oliver Charles Dawes** (born 7th May 1894, Bristol; died 15th January 1951, Bristol, aged 56).
- **Mabel Lilian Dawes** (born 22nd September 1895, Bristol; died 1982, Bristol, aged 86).
- **Gilbert Francis Dawes** (born 2nd February 1900, Bristol; died 9th March 1981, Bristol, aged 81).
- **Albert Clarence Dawes** (born 1902, Bristol; died 20th August 1963, Bristol, aged 61).

- **Violet Frances Dawes** (born 10th January 1904, Bristol; died 1983, Taunton, aged 78).
- **Ethel Beatrice Dawes** (born 6th March 1906, Bristol; died 1985, Poole, aged 78).
- **Daisy Ethel Dawes** (born 1908, Bristol; died 1st May 1908, Bristol, aged less than 1 year).
- **Percival Arthur Dawes** (born 7th September 1908; died 5th October 1972, Bristol, aged 64).
- **Hilda Gladys Dawes** (born 21st November 1910, Bristol; died 13th October 1992, Bristol, aged 81).
- **Leslie Frank Dawes** (born 16th June 1913, Bristol; died 20th September 1968, Bristol), aged 55).

2. **Arthur Godwin Dawes** (born 1874, Bristol; died 31st March 1937, Bristol, aged 63).

Arthur worked on the Midland Railway as a carriage cleaner.

He was baptised at Holy Trinity Church, St. Philips, Bristol, on 11th October 1874, with his family address shown as Lansdown Terrace, Redland, Bristol, and his father's occupation being a Baker.

He married Lilly Southall (born 1875, Bristol; died 9th June 1941, Bristol, aged 66) on 28th January 1899 at St. Luke's Church, Bristol. At the time of their marriage, Arthur was living at 3 St. Luke's Street, Bristol, and Lilly at 9 Granville Terrace, Bristol.

They had three children:

- **Charlotte Beatrice Ellen Dawes** (born 30th October 1899, Bristol; died 26th January 1979, Bristol, aged 79).
- **Arthur Leslie Dawes** (born 29th January 1905, Bristol; died 1905, Bristol, aged less than 1).
- **Grace Annie Maud Dawes** (born 27th December 1906, Bristol; died 16th May 1955, Bristol, aged 48).

3. **Albert Edward (Edwin) Dawes** (born 1877, Bristol; died 11th March 1880, Bristol, aged 3).

He was baptised at Holy Trinity Church, St. Philips, Bristol, on 13th July 1879, with the family home recorded as being Pennywell Road, Bristol, and his father's occupation being a Baker.

At the time of his death, caused by Atrophy, the family home was recorded as being 5 Wellington Terrace, Easton Road, Bristol. He was buried at Greenbank Cemetery, Bristol.

4. **Ralph James Dawes** (born 15th May 1879, Bristol; died 21st March 1957, Bristol, aged 77).

He was baptised at Holy Trinity Church, St. Philips, Bristol, on 13th July 1879, with the family home recorded as being Pennywell Road, Bristol, and his father's occupation being a Baker.

He worked as a Coal Haulier and then a Carter on the Railways.

He married Matilda Marsh (born 18th December 1880, Bristol; died 11th June 1959, Bristol, aged 78). Ralph lost one of his legs in 1915 when he fell off his cart and was run over by its wheels.

They had eight children:

- **Gladys Winifred Dawes** (born 22nd May 1901, Bristol; died 8th June 1986, aged 85).
- **Lilian May Dawes** (born 1903, Bristol, died 9th November 1984, aged 81).
- **William Charles Dawes** (born 23rd November 1905, Bristol, died 15th February 1998, Dorset, aged 92).
- **Edna Beatrice Dawes** (born 13th August 1908, Bristol; died 19th December 2009, Braunton, Devon, aged 101).
- **Alice Maud Dawes** (born 4th December 1909, Bristol; died 19th March 2001, South Gloucestershire, aged 91).
- **Frederick John Dawes** (born 1st August 1912, Bristol; died 22nd July 1995, Sodbury, aged 82).
- **Ellen Dawes** (born 13th August 1914, Bristol; died 19th March 1992, Bristol, aged 77).
- **Frank Dawes** (born 1916, Bristol; died 2nd August 1919, 33 Cabot Street, Bedminster, Bristol, aged 3).

5. **John McGoldrick Dawes** (born 1883, Bristol; died 20th October 1926, Bristol, aged 43).

See Chapter 11.

6. **Winifred Dawes** (born 3rd June 1884, Bristol, died 20th March 1976, Bristol, aged 91).

She was baptised at Holy Trinity Church, St. Philips, Bristol, on 16th July 1884, with the family home recorded as being 23 Winsford Street, Bristol, and her father's occupation being a Milkman.

She married Ernest George Hemmings (born 9th June 1884, Bristol; died 2nd February 1948, Bristol, aged 63) at Holy Trinity Church, Bristol, on 27th August 1905. Ernest was a Carter by trade, and also served in the Royal Berkshire Regiment during WW1. At the time of their marriage, Winifred was living at 34 Pennywell Road, Bristol, and Ernest at 26 Winsford Street, Bristol.

They had nine children:

- **Ernest George Hemmings** (born 4th July 1907, Bristol; died 26th June 1981, Fishponds, Bristol, aged 73).

- **Harold Hemmings** (born 6th March 1909, Bristol; died 28th November 1957, Bristol, aged 48).
- **William Henry Hemmings** (born 18th August 1911, Bristol; died 23rd October 2001, Bristol, aged 90).
- **Leonard George Hemmings** (born 27th December 1914, Bristol; died 20th November 1992, Bridport, aged 77).
- **Winifred Glover Hemmings** (born 11th May 1917, Bristol; died 2nd July 1994, Bristol, aged 77).
- **Henry John Hemmings** (born 27th August 1919, Bristol; died 25th January 1921, Bristol, aged 1).
- **Ronald Arthur Hemmings** (born 6th September 1922, Bristol; died 16th September 2004, Stroud, aged 82).
- **Joan Violet Hemmings** (born 30th March 1926, Bristol; died 7th February 2013, Bristol, aged 86).
- **Kenneth Edward Hemmings** (born 30th March 1926, Bristol; died 22nd September 2005, Bristol, aged 79).

After Ernest's death, she married Frederick George Pile (born 19th January 1896, Bristol; died 1967, Sodbury, aged 70) in 1955 in Bristol.

7.   **Frank Frederick Dawes** (born 1887, Bristol; died 4th February 1946, Southmead Hospital, Bristol, aged 59).

He served in the Tank Corps in France during WW1 but was disciplined on a couple of occasions for disobeying orders and using obscene language. He never married. His last known address was 45 Bedford Street, Stapleton Road, Bristol.

8.   **Claudia Florence Dawes** (born 29th July 1888, Bristol; died 14th September 1980, Bristol, aged 92).

She was baptised at Holy Trinity Church, St. Philips, Bristol, on 19th September 1888, with the family home recorded as being 40 Pennywell Road, Bristol, and her father's occupation being a Dairyman.

She married Albert Jesse Morgan (born 1887, Bristol; died 20th April 1937, Bristol, aged 50) on 9th August 1909 at Holy Trinity Church, Bristol. Albert, not related to 'our' Morgan family, was employed as a Brewer's Labourer, and had served in the Army in World War 1, being discharged in 1917 due to 'displacement of cartilage of knee, not caused by active service'.

At the time of their marriage, Claudia was living at 34 Pennywell Road, Bristol, and Arthur at 17 Pennywell Road, Bristol, subsequently moving to 32 Thrissell Street, Bristol.

They had two children:

- **Lilian Marion Morgan** (born 24th June 1914, Bristol; died 1996, Bristol, aged 81).
- **Olive Gwendoline Morgan** (born 30th April 1918, Bristol).

A concerning report about Albert was reported on 20th August 1937 in the local press:

'UNCONSCIOUS MAN IN BRISTOL BUILDING'

"Albert Morgan (48*) of Thrissell Street, Stapleton Road, Bristol, was taken to the Royal Inirmary last night suffering from a cerebral haemorrhage.

He was discovered unconscious on the premises of the Bristol United Brewery, Lewin's Mead, shortly after nine o'clock last night, and it appeared he had been unconscious for about four hours.

Morgan ceased work at the brewery at about five o'clock, and it was not until about nine o'clock that his brother, calling at his house, found that he had not yet reached home.

He at once returned to the brewery, and found Morgan lying on the floor near his hat and coat.

The City and Marine Ambulance took him to the Royal Infirmary, and early this morning his condition was serious."

The following day, it was confirmed that Albert had passed away:

'FATAL ILLNESS'

"Albert Morgan (48*) of Thrissell Street, Stapleton Road, Bristol, who was found lying ill on the premises of Bristol United Brewery on Monday, died in the Bristol Royal Infirmary yesterday."

The actual age of death was confirmed as 50 on death records.

After Albert's death, she married Sidney Alfred Farrow (born 2nd April 1882, Bristol, died 1962, Bristol, aged 79) in 1943, again in Bristol.

9. **Edward Charles Dawes** (born 1889, Bristol; died 1889, Bristol, aged only a few weeks).

10. **Harold Lionel Dawes** (born 28th June 1890, Bristol; died 23rd June 1984, Cossham Hospital, Bristol, aged 93).

He married Elsie Eveline Harze (born 8th July 1891, Islington, London; died 18th March 1959, Bristol, aged 67) at Holy Trinity Church, Bristol, on 29th April 1917.

Harold was another Baker by trade before becoming a General Stores shopkeeper in Goodhind Street.

At the time of their marriage both Harold and Elsie were living at 44 Goodhind Street, Bristol.

They had one child:

- **Edwin John Dawes** (born 17th July 1927, Bristol; died 24th September 2002, Bristol, aged 75).

He married Winifred Cron (born 14th February 1926, Bristol; died 19th September 1994, Oldbury Court, Bristol, aged 68) in 1944, in Bristol. They had two children.

11.   **Myrtle Maria Dawes** (born 20th November 1893, Bristol; died 1980, Bristol, aged 86).

She married Henry Mining (born 2nd June 1893; died 2nd January 1962, Bristol, aged 68) at Holy Trinity Church, Bristol, on 2nd December 1922. Henry's occupation was a Furniture Upholsterer.

At the time of their marriage, Myrtle was living at 44 Goodhind Street, Bristol, and Henry at 32 Thrissell Street, Bristol.

They had two children:

- **Dennis Henry Mining** (born 31st March, 1924, Bristol; died 15th February 1999, Bristol, aged 74).

He married Grace Gwendoline Fletcher in 1943, in Bristol.

- **Edgar Alfred Mining** (born 1928, Bristol; died 28th April 2015, Keynsham, aged 87).

In true family tradition, Edgar was the landlord of a couple of public houses; The 'New Inn', Keynsham, and the 'Compton' at Compton Dando.

He married Sylvia M. Jones in 1950, in Bathavon.

One of their children, Keith, was tragically killed in a car accident in 1969, aged only 11.

12.   **Elizabeth Beatrice Dawes** (born 26th February 1899, Bristol; died 9th November 1980, Bristol, aged 81)

She married John (Jack) Frederick Herbert Condick (born 23rd February 1901, Bristol; died 1981, Bristol, aged 79) on 26th December 1924 at Holy Trinity Church, Bristol. John, a Lorry Driver by trade, served in the R.A.F. after WW1 and then the R.A.F. reserve.

At the time of their marriage, Elizabeth was living at 44 Goodhind Street, Bristol, and John at 64 Goodhind Street, Bristol.

They had one child:

- **Charles Edwin John Condick** (born 1933, Bristol, died 12th May 2010, Bristol, aged 77).

He married Winifred E. R. Poole (born 8th March 1933, Bristol; died 11th November 2015, Bristol, aged 82) in 1958, in Bristol. They had three children.

The Foley Family.

The link to the Morgan family is via Daniel Foley (born 1st October 1888, Bristol; died 27th March 1961, Bristol, aged 72) married Clara Morgan, youngest daughter of John Morgan and Matilda Williams on 10th April 1908 at St. James Church, Bristol. Both Daniel and Clara lived at 7 Priory Place, Bristol, according to their marriage registration, with Daniel's occupation being a Collier.

Daniel's grandparents were Michael Foley (born 1832, Cork, Ireland) and Alice Prendergast (born 1833, Clonmel, Ireland). They married at St. Mary-on-the-Quay Roman Catholic Church, Bristol, on 20th June 1852, and they had seven children.

The 1871 Census shows the family living at 2 James Court, Bristol, where Michael's occupation is recorded as being a Stoker, wife Alice a Dressmaker, and children Mary Ann a Fishmonger, Margaret a Domestic Servant, John a Shoe Maker, and the remainder of the children at school.

By 1881 the family had relocated to 4 Cherry Alley, Bristol. Michael was now a General Labourer, Alice a housewife, and children Edward and Samuel both Boot Makers, and Bridget a Brush Maker.

1891 saw Michael and Alice residing at 4 Sim's Alley, Bristol, where Michael was now employed as a Stoker at Gas Works.

The 1901 Census indicated that Michael and Alice had moved to 13 Little James Street, Bristol, with Michael still working at the Gas Works.

Finally, the 1911 Census records Michael (by now a widower and pensioner) boarding at the hoe of the Hayden family at 4 Lower Cottage Place, Eugene Street, St. James, Bristol.

Alice died on 1st December 1907, in Bristol, aged 74, and Michael died on 1st December 1911, aged 79, also in Bristol.

MICHAEL AND ALICE'S CHILDREN:

1. **Mary Ann Foley** (born 1853, Bristol; died 1919, Bristol, aged 65).

She married John Pickett (born 1846, Cork, Ireland; died 1915, Bristol, aged 69) in 1906 in Cardiff. She died in 1919 in Bristol.

The 1881 Census reveals the family living at 3 Cherry Alley, Bristol, next door to Mary Ann's parents, where John is recorded as being General Labourer.

The next Census in 1891 shows the family living at 12 Hammonds Buildings, Bristol, John having found work as a Coster Monger.

1901 saw the family residing at 5 Jarman's Court, Bristol, John now working as a Dock Labourer.

The 1911 Census reveals that Mary Ann was living with three of her children at 5 Cherry Alley, Bristol, her occupation being that of a Fish Hawker.

They had twelve children, six of whom sadly passed away at a young age.

2.   **Margaret Foley** (born 3rd January 1856, Bristol).

Margaret was baptised at St. Nicholas of Tolentino Church, Lawford's Gate, Bristol, on 6th January 1856.

3.   **John Foley** (born 10th September 1857, Bristol; died 29th June 1900, Bristol, aged 42).

John was baptised at St. Nicholas of Tolentino Church, Lawford's Gate, Bristol, on 13th September 1857.

He joined the Royal Navy; however it seemed that he was not cut out for Navy life and in 1876 he appeared on the official list of deserters, having left his ship at Portsmouth on 14th June of that year. He was described as a Shoemaker from Bristol, 5'5" tall, light brown hair, grey eyes, and a sallow complexion. Despite this, in 1881 he could be found amongst the crew of HMS Invincible;

By 1891 he had returned to civilian life and married. His address at that time was at 14 Dove Lane, Bristol, where he returned to his original trade as a shoemaker. His marriage took place in 1884 to Hester (or Esther) Jane Hawkes (born 28th August 1861, Bristol; died 1940, Bristol, aged 78), and they had seven children:

- **Esther Sarah Foley** (born 23rd October 1886, Bristol; died 23rd February 1948, Bristol, aged 61).

Esther was baptised at St. Mary-on-the-Quay Church, Bristol, on 23rd November 1886. The family address was recorded as being 3 Gabriel's Court, Broad Quay, Bristol.

She married James Murphy (born 1880, Bristol; died 8th December 1926, Bristol, aged 46) on 7th October 1906 at St. Philip & Jacob Church, Bristol. Esther was living at 6 David Street, Bristol, whilst James' address was shown as being Leadhouse Lane, Bristol. His occupation was recorded as being a Sawyer.

They had twelve children.

Both Esther and James were buried at Greenbank Cemetery, Bristol.

- **Daniel Foley** (born 1st October 1888, Bristol; died 1961, Bristol, aged 72).

Daniel, the link with the Morgan family through his marriage to Clara, was baptised at St. Nicholas of Tolentino Church, Lawford's Gate, Bristol, on 1st January 1889.

He appeared in the 1891 Census above, living at 14 Dove Lane, and by 1901 he was living at 3 Church Lane, Old Market Street, Bristol, where he worked as an Errand Boy.

It was recorded in the local press on 17th March 1900 that; "Daniel Foley, 13, and Albert Lloyd, 13, were summoned for advertising the sale of newspapers by crying, so as to be a nuisance and annoyance to the residents of Cooperation Road." The boys were let off with a severe caution.

As noted in an earlier chapter, Daniel's wife Clara committed suicide on 24th February 1937 whilst the family were living in Twinnell Road, Lawrence Hill. Daniel subsequently married Rosina Sampson (nee Cook, born 10th May 1892, Bristol). They had no children together.

The 1939 Register shows Daniel and Rosina living at 32 Daventry Road, Bristol, along with Rosina's daughter Violet and Daniel's son John.

Daniel died in 1961 in Bristol, aged 72, and was buried at St. Barnabas Church, Knowle, Bristol. His last known address was 107 Kenmare Road, Bristol. Rosina passed away on 14th June 1977, aged 85, also in Bristol.

See also Chapter 13.

- **James Alfred Foley** (born 2nd September 1890, Bristol; died 30th October 1962, Ham Green Hospital, Bristol, aged 72).

James was, by all accounts, a colourful character.

He was baptised at St. Nicholas of Tolentino Church, Lawford's Gate, Bristol, on 17th August 1892.

He was sentenced to one year's imprisonment in 1910 for stealing, as a newspaper article dated 29th June 1910 reports:

"William Baxter (17), fitter, and James Alfred Foley (19), labourer, pleaded guilty to feloniously stealing two iron tram plates and a quantity of scrap iron, the property of Charles Bridgeman, on April 29th 1910, at Stoke Gifford.

Mr. Jordan prosecuted.

The prisoners had each previous convictions, and a police officer mentioned that there was a warrant out against the young men for theft at Weston-super-Mare for goods found upon them at their arrest.

The chairman, taking into consideration the charge from Weston-super-Mare, ordered each prisoner 12 months detention under the Borstal system."

Prison records at the time show that they spent a short time at Stapleton Institute before being transferred to Wormwood Scrubs. The 1911 Census shows him as an inmate at Rochester Borstal Institute in Kent.

It would appear that after his release he joined the Mercantile Marine, as his World War 1 medal card confirms:

James Alfred Foley's Medal Card.

He married Amelia Phelps (born 18th March 1890, Bristol; died 4th April 1957, Bristol, aged 67) on 13th October 1917, at Bristol Registry Office.

James' occupation was listed as a Fireman (Merchant Service) and his home address shown as 12 Wellington Street, Lawrence Hill, Bristol. Amelia, a widow, was registered under her married surname of Moss. Her address was shown as 12 Wellington Hill, Lawrence Hill, Bristol. They had three children:

James was buried at Avonview Cemetery, Bristol.

- **Martha Catherine Foley** (born 19th October 1894, Bristol; died 17th February 1978, Bristol, aged 83).

She was baptised at St. Philip & Jacob Church, Bristol, on 18th November 1894, her home address vaguely recorded as being St. Pauls, Bristol, and her father's occupation a Boot Maker.

She married Ernest James Rowden (born 3rd November 1893, Bristol; died 24th November 1971, Bristol, aged 78) on 5th August 1922 at Holy Trinity Church, Bristol. On the marriage registration document Martha's middle name was recorded as 'Kathleen'; she was living at 4 Fear's Buildings, Bristol, with Ernest living at 12 Wellington Street, Bristol, his occupation noted as being a Warehouseman.

They had one child.

Ernest and Martha were both buried at Greenbank Cemetery, Bristol.

- **Adelaide Foley** (born 2nd December 1898, Bristol; died 6th February 1956, Bristol, aged 57).

She was baptised at St. Mark's Church, Easton, Bristol, on 10th January 1899, with her home address shown as being 5 Bellevue Road, Bristol, and her father's occupation a Boot Finisher.

She married Arthur Gilbert Parker (born 18th September 1897, Bristol; died 1975, Bristol, aged 77) in 1928, in Bristol. They had four children.

- **Edward Foley** (born 2nd December 1898, Bristol; died 1902, Bristol, aged 3); twin of Adelaide.

He was baptised at St. Mark's Church, Easton, Bristol, on 10th January 1899, with his home address shown as being 5 Bellevue Road, Bristol, and his father's occupation a Boot Finisher.

4.   **Edward Foley** (born 1860, Bristol, died 1910, Bristol, aged 51).

Known as Fred, he married Alice Frizlo (born 1868, Bristol, died 27th May 1898, Bristol, aged 30) in 1888 in Bristol. They had no children.

The 1891 Census shows Edward and his wife Alice living at 7 Leonard Court, Broadmead, Bristol, with Edward employed as Boot Maker.

By 1901, Edward was back living with his parents following the death of his wife Alice in 1898.

Alice was buried at Ridgeway Park Cemetery, Bristol.

5.   **Alice Foley** (born 24th August 1861, Bristol, died 1890, Bristol, aged 28).

Alice was baptised at St. Nicholas of Tolentino Church, Lawford's Gate, Bristol, on 8th September 1861.

Alice married George William Malpas (born 1857, Bristol, died 1933, Bristol, aged 76) in 1882 in Bristol. They had three children.

6.   **Daniel Foley** (born 17th December 1863, Bristol; died 1883, Bristol, aged 19).

Daniel was baptised at St. Nicholas of Tolentino Church, Lawford's Gate, Bristol, on 25th December 1863.

He appears on the 1881 Census living with his family at 4 Cherry Alley, Bristol, where his occupation is listed as a Boot Maker.

7.   **Bridget Foley** (born 14th July 1866, Bristol; died 1929, Bristol, aged 62).

Bridget was baptised at St. Mary-on-the-Quay Roman Catholic Church, Bristol, on 29th July 1866. She married Thomas William Hawkes (born 1866, Bristol; died 1912, Bristol, aged 46) in 1885, in Bristol.

They had eight children, two of whom had died by 1911.

The 1891 Census records the family living at 34 Water Street, Bristol, where Thomas is employed as a Dock Labourer and Bridget a Brush Maker.

1901 saw the family now residing at 4 King William Court, St. Philips, Bristol, with their five children. Both their occupations remain unchanged.

The 1911 Census shows Bridget as head of the family (although still married), living at 15 Great James Street, Bristol, with two of her sons, William and Thomas.

By 1921 she was living at 47 Dale Street, Bristol, with her occupation noted as being a Brush Maker. Living with her was son Thomas (a Labourer), daughter Alice (a Modellit* Maker), daughter Kathleen and grandson William.

*Modellit was a plasticine-like modelling material, popular at the time.

The Langford family.

The Langfords are related to the Morgans through Lillian (Lily) Rosina Langford (born 16th October 1885, Bristol; died 17th July 1952, Bristol, aged 66) who married Thomas (Tom) Morgan, son of John Morgan and Matilda Wiliams, on 1st December 1904 at Emmanuel Church in Bristol.

Lillian's parents were James Langford (born 1854, Kilburn, London) and Elizabeth Bull (born 1857, Bristol). They married on 2nd July 1882 at St. Bartholomew's Church, Montpelier, Bristol and had four children, all born in Bristol.

The 1891 Census indicated the family were living at 19 Kingsland Road, St. Philips, Bristol. James' employment was noted as being a 'Smith's Striker'. By 1901 the family had moved to 20 Great Western Street, Barton Hill, Bristol, otherwise known as the 'Weaver's Arms' – a public house which Lillian's husband Tom would eventually take over.

The 1911 Census shows James and Elizabeth living at 18 Weston Street, Barton Hill, Bristol, where James was noted as being a 'Licensed Victualler out of business'. All their children had left home by this time.

James died at Bristol Royal Infirmary on 5th February 1918 aged 64, whilst wife Elizabeth died later the same year, aged 60. Her burial register states that her last known address was 78 Barton Hill Road, Bristol.

After Thomas Morgan died on 19th January 1944, Lillian married Ernest Meredith (born 16th July 1891, Lancaster) in 1947, but sadly she passed away a few years later on 17th July 1952, aged 66, at 'The Clarence', 60 Chelsea Road, Easton, Bristol. She was buried at Avonview Cemetery, Bristol.

Ernest had already been married and had one child from that relationship.

JAMES' AND ELIZABETH'S CHILDREN:

1. **Henry James Langford** (born 28th July 1883, Bristol; died 28th February 1899, Bristol, aged 16).

He was baptised on 17th August 1883 at St. James' Church, Bristol, his parents' address recorded as 10 Willway Street, Bristol. His father's occupation was noted as being a Labourer.

He was buried at Greenbank Cemetery, Bristol.

2. **Lillian Rosina Langford** (born 16th October 1885, Bristol; died 7th July 1952, Bristol, aged 66).

See Chapter 10.

3.   **Arthur Edward Langford** (born 10th October 1887, Bristol; died 1950, Bristol, aged 63).

He was baptised on 20th October 1891 at Emmanuel Church, St. Philips, Bristol. His parents' address was shown as being 19 Kingsland Place, Bristol, his father's occupation being a Labourer.

It seems that his middle name became 'Hodgson' at some time, replacing Edward for reasons yet unknown.

He joined the Royal Navy in 1906 and served as a Stoker for many years on various vessels, serving up to 1911, and then joining the Royal Naval Reserve in 1915, leaving in 1919.

He married Louisa Selina Betty (born 1888, Bristol; died 1923, Bristol, aged 35) on 22nd November 1910, at Holy Trinity Church, St. Philips, Bristol. Arthur's address was shown as 44 Webb Street, Bristol, with his father James accurately noted as a Licensed Victualler. Arthur himself was recorded as being an R.N. Stoker. Louisa was living at 2 Beaufort Street at the time of her marriage.

The 1911 Census shows the couple living at 37 Leadhouse Lane, Easton, Bristol, with Arthur's occupation being a Beer Retailer. They had three children together.

By the 1921 Census, Arthur was landlord of the Three Horseshoes public house at 70 Old Market, Bristol, which he had taken over in 1915. He lived there with wife Louisa and their three children, along with two of Louisa's sisters.

After Louisa died in 1923, he married Florence Price on 2nd July 1924 at St. Matthew Moorfields Church, Bristol, his address noted as being 70 Old Market Street (The Three Horseshoes), his occupation being a Licensed Victualler. Florence was living at 9 Milton Park, Bristol, a widow.

Louisa was buried at Avonview Cemetery, Bristol.

4.   **Ethel Elizabeth Langford** (born 28th September 1891, Bristol; died 25th November 1963, Bristol, aged 72).

Ethel was baptised on the same day as her elder brother Arthur at Emmanuel Church, St. Philips, Bristol.

The family tradition of running public houses continued when Ethel married William Walter Webb (born 13th December 1889, died 19th November 1966, Bristol, aged 76) at St. Silas' Church, Bristol, on 17th January 1911; he was landlord of the 'Fox' in Peter Street, Bristol, where Ethel assisted in the business.

A photograph of the 'Fox' can be found in ***Appendix 3.***

Ethel's address at the time of their marriage was shown as being 36 St..Silas Street, Bristol, whilst William was living at the Victoria Hotel, Bristol. Both fathers were noted as being Licensed Victuallers.

The 1921 Census shows the family still at the 'Fox' in Peter Street, with their 3 sons and one adopted son.

According to a 1938 directory of Bristol, Walter ran the Weaver's Arms at Maze Street, Barton Hill, which was previously run by Thomas Morgan, William's brother-in-law.

The 1939 Register shows the family residing at The King George VI public house, Station Road, Filton, where William was the landlord, assisted by their son Arthur. A photograph of the pub can also be found in *Appendix 3.*

Other son Reginald was an Engineer at the nearby Bristol Aeroplane Company, and daughter Joyce a 'lady secretary'.

Ethel died on 25th November 1963, aged 71, in Bristol, and William died on 19th November 1966, at home at the pub, which he had run since 1939, aged 76.

The Mansfield Family.

William Mansfield (born 1885, Bristol; died 1915, France & Flanders, aged 30), married Alice Morgan on 28th January 1911 at St. Luke's Church, Barton Hill, Bristol.

He was one of nine children of William Mansfield (born 1852, Marshfield, Gloucestershire; died 24th February 1932, Bristol, aged 82) and Mary Matilda Smith (born 1851, Sherston, Wiltshire; died 5th August 1912, Bristol, aged 60). They married on 6th February 1877 at St. Swithin's Church, Walcot, Somerset, where William's occupation was noted as being a Waggoner.

The 1881 Census saw the Mansfield family living at 43 Croydon Street, Barton Hill, Bristol. William was shown as being a Drayman.

The 1891 Census indicated that family were living at Cannon Street, St. George, Bristol, where William Sr. had his occupation noted as being a Cart Haulier.

The 1901 Census shows the family living at 1 Chapter Street, St. George, Bristol, where William Sr. was recorded as being a Gas Fitter Labourer; Henry a Brewery Labourer, with Ethel and William both Cotton Spinners.

By 1911, the family were now living at 3 Chapter Street, and William was still employed as a Gas Works Labourer.

William's first wife Mary died on 5th August 1912, in Bristol, aged 60, and was buried at Avonview Cemetery, Bristol, on 11th August 1912.

The 1921 Census shows William with new spouse Mary Jane Bennett (born 10th May 1867, Bristol, died 9th December 1945, Bristol, aged 78) who he married in 1916, in Bristol and his stepchildren at 3 Clarence Street, Newtown, Bristol, where William's occupation was shown as a Navvy at the Bristol Gas Company.

Mary had been married before, to George Perryman, and they had 3 children together.

William died on 24th February 1934, in Bristol, aged 82, and was buried at Avonview Cemetery, Bristol, on 1st March 1934. Mary died on 9th December 1945 and was also buried at Avonview Cemetery on 13th December 1945.

WILLIAM AND MARY SMITH'S CHILDREN:

1. **Walter Mansfield** (born 19th July 1877, Sherston, Wiltshire; died 27th November 1956, Bristol, aged 79).

He married Sarah Phelps (born 9th December 1876, Bristol; died 6th January 1930, Bristol, aged 53) in 1896, in Bristol. She was buried at Greenbank Cemetery, Bristol. They had ten children.

1901 Census showed the family living at 10 Horton Street, St. George, Bristol, where Walter's occupation was shown as being a Coke Wheeler at Gasworks. By 1911, the family had relocated to 13 Lower Proctor Street, Moorfields, Bristol, and Walter's occupation recorded as being a Gas Stoker.

The 1921 Census shows the family living at 8 Charlton Street, Bristol, with Walter still working at the Bristol Gas Works at Canon's Marsh, Bristol.

By the time of the 1939 Register, Walter had remarried to Rosina James (born 24th March 1877, Bristol; died 28th January 1946, Bristol, aged 68). They married in 1931 and were living at 9 White Street, Pennywell Road, Bristol. Walter was shown as being retired.

Walter and Rosina were both buried at Greenbank Cemetery, Bristol.

2. **Henry Charles Mansfield** (born 10th May 1879, Marshfield, Gloucestershire).

He married Mary Jane Martin 'Jennie' King (born 26th November 1880, Bristol; died 16th December 1962, Bristol, aged 82) on 22nd February 1902 at St. Matthew Moorfields, Bristol. His address at the time was shown as being 2 Chapter Street, Bristol, his occupation being listed as a Labourer, whilst Mary was living at 14 Clare Street, Bristol. They had six children.

The 1911 Census indicated that the family were living at 17 Beam Street, Barton Hill, Bristol, where Henry was shown as working as a Packer on the Great Western Railway. By 1921 the family was residing at 6 Barton Street, Easton, Bristol, with Henry still working for the GWR at Kingsland Road as an 'Underman'.

By the time of the 1939 Register, the family were living at 6 Bush Street, Barton Hill, Bristol, where Henry was recorded as working as a Permanent Way Labourer.

Mary was buried at Avonview Cemetery, Bristol, on 20th December 1962.

3. **Arthur Mansfield** (born 1881, Bristol; died 21st July 1898, Bristol, aged 17)

Arthur sadly died at a young age, and was buried at Avonview Cemetery, Bristol on 31st July 1898.

4. **Ethel Matilda Mansfield** (born 3rd August 1882, Bristol; died 27th December 1959, Bristol, aged 77).

She married Francis Edward Warren (born 29th August 1877, Bristol; died 4th March 1949, Bristol, aged 71) on 2nd April 1904 at Moorfields St. Matthew Church, Bristol. They had six children.

The 1911 Census shows the family living at 1 Charlton Street, Barton Hill, Bristol, where Francis's occupation was recorded as being a Railway Carriage Cleaner.

By 1921, the family were living at 15 Hampton Street, Bristol, where Francis was shown as being employed as a Steam Wagon Driver for United Alkia Co., Feeder Road, Bristol.

The 1939 Register shows the family still residing at 15 Hampton Street, where Francis was by now a retired Motor Driver.

Both Ethel and Francis were buried at Avonview Cemetery, Bristol, Francis on 9th March 1949, and Ethel on 30th December 1959.

5.   **William Mansfield** (born 1885, Bristol; died 19th December 1915, France & Flanders, aged 30).

Details of his life can be found under the Alice Morgan section.

See Chapter 4.

6.   **Alfred James Mansfield** (born 1888, Bristol; died 3rd May 1909, Bristol, aged 21).

Alfred sadly died at a young age, and was buried at Avonview Cemetery, Bristol on 9th May 1909.

7.   **Ada Mansfield** (born 1890, Bristol; died 1913, Pontypridd, aged 23).

She married Charles Henry Hathway (born 8th September 1879, Bristol; died 30th October 1951, Bristol, aged 72) on 4th August 1912 at St. Matthew Moorfields, Bristol. The marriage registration shows Ada living at 22 Chapter Street, Bristol, and Charles residing at 13 Proctor Street, a Collier by trade.

They had one child, William Charles Hathway (born 13th February 1913, Pontypridd).

8.   **Bertie Mansfield** (born 13th July 1892, Bristol; died 3rd January 1957, Bristol, aged 64).

Bertie could be found on the 1911 Census living at home with his family, working with his brother Reuben at Lysaghts in Bristol as a Tinsmith. In August 1914 he signed up to join the Royal Gloucestershire Regiment before being transferred to the Royal Hampshire Regiment and then the Army Reserve.

He was discharged from the Army in 1918 and his records have revealed an interesting reason; "This man is quite healthy except for a hernia, and is being discharged for reasons other than medical".

He married Edith Stace (born 20th August 1895, Faversham, Kent; died 23rd February 1992, Bristol, aged 96) in Blean, Kent, in 1918. They had four children.

By 1921 the family could be found living at Kenilworth House, Kenilworth Terrace, Bristol. Bertie could be found working as a Sheet Metal Worker again with his brother Reuben at Wilmott & Co., St. Philips, Bristol.

By 1939 the family were living at 4 Ripley Road, Bristol, with Bertie still working as a Sheet Metal Worker.

9.   **Reuben Mansfield** (born 8th April 1894, Bristol; died 23rd January 1953, Bristol, aged 58).

Reuben married Lily Florence Peacock (born 25th September 1894, Bristol; died 26th August 1983, Bristol, aged 88) on 22nd April 1916, at St. Lawrence Church, Easton, Bristol. They had eight children.

At the time of their marriage, Reuben was living at 99 Lawrence Hill, Bristol, his occupation being registered as a soldier, currently serving in WW1. Lily was living at the same address, with no occupation being displayed on the marriage registration.

The 1921 Census reveals the family now residing at 30 Dean Street, St. George, Bristol, with Reuben employed as a Sheet Metal Worker at Wilmott & Co, St. Philips, Bristol.

The 1939 Register shows the family living at 84 Sandholme Road, Bristol, with Reuben still working as a Sheet Metal Worker.

The Stephens Family

The Stephens family are linked to the Morgans through Clara Morgan, who married Albert James Stephens on 10th July 1904.

Albert was one of eight children born to William and Sarah Ann Stephens (nee Dale) who married in Bristol on the 4th June 1876. William was born in Bristol in 1856, and Sarah was born in Bristol in 1859.

The 1861 Census shows young William (aged 5) living with his family at 7 Zion (Sion) Road, Bristol. William's father (also called William) was shown as being an Earthenware Potter, and his mother Sarah (nee Roberts) had no occupation recorded.

By 1871, William's father had passed away, and his mother Sarah became head of the family, still living at 7 Zion Road, Bristol. William was recorded as being a Painter.

The 1881 Census shows that William and Sarah Ann Dale were now married and were still living at the family home at 7 Zion Road. William's occupation was now that of a General Labourer.

By the time of the 1891 Census, the family were again at 7 Zion Road, but William Stephens Sr. was not shown on the document. Albert appears on the Census for the first time, noted as being a Scholar.

1901 saw the return of William to the Census records, his employment (and that of Albert) shown as being a General Labourer. The Zion Street address was maintained.

1911 saw a career change for William; he was now a Licensee, running the Globe at Catherine Street, Barrow Road, Bristol. He took over the pub in 1906 and ran it until his death on 24th March 1921, the pub then being taken over by his widow Sarah and son Thomas. William was buried at Greenbank Cemetery, Bristol.

Albert had married Alice Morgan by this time and was living at 79 Belle View Road, Easton, Bristol, running a General Stores.

The 1921 Census saw Sarah Ann and Thomas running the Globe public house, whilst Albert and Alice were also by now running their own pub, the Lord Raglan at Stapleton Road.

Albert's mother Sarah died on 15th October 1924, and was also buried at Greenbank Cemtery, Bristol.

WILLIAM AND SARAH ANN'S CHILDREN (all born in Bristol):

1. **Sarah Emily Louisa Stephens** (born 7th February 1877; died 30th November 1922, Bristol, aged 45).

Sarah was baptised at St. Philip & Jacob Church, Bristol, on 25th February 1877. The family address was recorded as Zion Road, Stapleton Road, Bristol, with her father's occupation shown as being a Labourer.

She married Frederick Hurley (born 12th February 1874, Bristol; died 27th December 1920, Bristol, aged 46) on 6th June 1897 at Holy Trinity Church in Bristol.

Both Sarah and Frederick were living at 7 Zion Road, Bristol at the time of their marriage, with Frederick's occupation noted as being a Greengrocer.

They had four children.

Sarah and Frederick were buried at Greenbank Cemetery, Bristol.

2.   **Mary Ann Elizabeth Stephens** (born 18th March 1880; died 13th April 1920, Bristol, aged 40).

Mary was baptised at St. Philip & Jacob Church, Bristol, on 16th May 1880. The family address was recorded as 7 Zion Road, Bristol, with her father's occupation shown as being a Labourer.

She married William Arthur Burnard (born 1878, Bristol; died 13th June 1915, Bristol, aged 37) on 25th December 1899 at Holy Trinity Church, Bristol. Both Sarah and William (a Greengrocer) were living at 7 Zion Road, Bristol, at the time of their marriage. The 1901 Census has Mary Ann referred to as 'Polly', and on the 1911 Census, their surname appears as 'Bernard', on both occasions living at 17 Catherine Street, Bristol.

They had no children.

William was buried at Greenbank Cemetery, Bristol.

After William died, she married Fred Brunt (born 1877, Bristol, died 4th April 1920, Bristol, aged 44) on 30th July 1917, again at Holy Trinity Church, Bristol. Mary was living at 15 Zion Road, Bristol, and Fred (a Butcher by trade) was living at 8 Catherine Street, Bristol, at the time of their marriage.

Fred was buried at Arno's Vale Cemetery, Bristol, and Mary was buried at Greenbank Cemetery, Bristol.

3.   **Albert James Stephens** (born 27th November 1883, died 30th December 1960, Bristol, aged 77).

See Chapter 12.

4.   **Thomas Stephens** (born 9th March 1888; died 14th October 1958, Bristol, aged 70).

Thomas was baptised at St. Philip & Jacob Church, Bristol, on 1st April 1888. The family address was recorded as 7 Zion Road, Stapleton Road, Bristol, with his father's occupation shown as being a Labourer.

He married Lilian Harriet Manley (born 21st November 1888, Bristol; died 4th March 1955, Bristol, aged 66) on 18th June 1929, at St. Luke's Church, Barton Hill, Bristol. His address at the time of marriage was shown as 44 Ducie Road, Bristol, and his occupation a Licensed Victualler. Lilian was living at 196 Avon Vale Road, Bristol. They had no children.

Thomas took over the running of the Globe public house at 4 Barrow Road, Bristol, from his mother until 1953.

Thomas and Lilian are both buried at Greenbank Cemetery, Bristol.

5.   **John Henry Stephens** (born 6th April 1890; died 25th October 1972, Bristol, aged 82).

John (known as Jack) was baptised at St. Philip & Jacob Church, Bristol, on 27th April 1890. The family address was recorded as 7 Zion Road, Stapleton Road, Bristol, with his father's occupation shown as being a Labourer.

His surname was erroneously recorded on his Baptism Register as 'Stevens'.

He married Kate Watkins (born 20th July 1889, Bristol; died 21st March 1970, Frenchay Hospital, Bristol, aged 80) on 10th April 1911, at Holy Trinity Church, Bristol. His address was shown on the registration as 15 Zion Road, Bristol, and his occupation described as a 'Dealer'. Kate's address was 14 Canning Street, Bristol.

They had five children.

The 1921 Census shows John as a Baker's Roundsman, living with Kate and their two children at 15 Zion Road, Bristol.

The 1939 Register shows the family living at 10 Edward Place, Bristol, Thomas's occupation shown as being a Licencee and Garage Proprieter, with his wife Kate a Bar Assistant.

He ran the Royal Oak public house in Pennywell Road, Bristol, for over 38 years.

John and Kate were both buried at Greenbank Cemetery, Bristol.

6.   **Frederick Dale Stephens** (born 9th October 1892; died 29th July 1971, Bristol, aged 78).

Frederick was baptised at St. Philip & Jacob Church, Bristol, on 30th October 1892. The family address was recorded as Stapleton Road, Bristol, with his father's occupation shown as being a Labourer.

He joined the Royal Navy and served throughout WW1 and the early part of WW2. He married Blanche Lydia Hopkins (born 23rd March 1892, Bristol; died 15th April 1920, Bristol, aged 28) on 14th March 1917, in Bristol. They had one child.

Blanche was buried at Greenbank Cemetery, Bristol.

Frederick subsequently married Ethel Beatrice Price (born 15th November 1890, Bristol; died 19th July 1965, Manor Park Hospital, Bristol, aged 74), in 1923, in Bristol.

Frederick took over the running of the Albert Hotel, West Street, Bristol in 1938, and also ran the King's Head, Cathay, Redcliffe, and the Black Horse, Bedminster.

His obituary which appeared in the *'Bristol Evening Post'* on 30th July 1971 gave an excellent description of his life:

'MR. F. D. STEPHENS.'

"Mr. Frederick Dale Stephens, a member of the Bristol licence trade, has died in hospital after a long illness.

Mr. Stephens (79), of Littlecross House, Ashton, was a life member of the Licensed Victuallers' Association and served on the association's committee.

He was also a member of the Bedminster branch of the Royal Antediluvian Order of Buffaloes.

Mr. Stephens was landlord of the Black Horse, Bedminster, before his retirement five years ago. Before that he had been landlord of the Albert Hotel, Bedminster, and the King's Head, Cathay, Redcliffe.

The funeral will take place next Thursday."

Ethel was cremated at Arno's Vale Cemetery, Bristol.

Frederick was cremated on 3rd August 1971, recorded in the parish of St. Francis, Ashton Gate, Bristol.

7.   **Lillian Stephens** (born 12th March 1898; died 17th July 1964, Bristol, aged 66).

Lillian was baptised at St. Philip & Jacob Church, Bristol, on 3rd April 1898. The family address was recorded as Zion Road, Clarence Road, Bristol, with her father's occupation shown as being a Labourer.

She married Albert William Price (born 12th August 1892, Bristol; died 18th May 1979, Bristol, aged 86) on 23rd December 1918, at Holy Trinity Church, Bristol. Her address at the time was 4 Barrow Road, Bristol (The Globe Public House), with her father a Licensed Victualler. Albert's address was recorded as 8 Catherine Street, with his occupation shown as a Shipwright.

They had one child.

The 1921 Census reveals the couple living at 71 St. Nicholas Road, Bristol, where Albert was shown as being an 'out of work' Shipwright. They stayed at this address for the 1939 Register, where Albert was still listed as being a Heavy Worker Shipwright.

Lillian and Albert were both buried at Greenbank Cemetery, Bristol.

8.   **Frank Stephens** (born 8th April 1901; died 1971, Bristol, aged 89).

Frank was baptised at St. Philip & Jacob Church, Bristol, on 28th April 1901. The family address was recorded as 7 Zion Road, Stapleton Road, Bristol, with his father's occupation shown as being a Labourer.

He married Ethel Louisa Farwell (born 10th October 1898, Bristol; died 8th November 1965, Frenchay Hospital, Bristol, aged 67) in 1920, in Bristol.

They had three children.

The 1921 Census shows the family living at 10 Beaufort Road, Bristol, where Frank's employment was recorded as being a Labourer.

By 1939 the family had moved to 78 Padstow Road, Bristol, where Frank's occupation was simply recorded as being 'Mainten', no doubt being an abbreviation of Maintenance.

The Tranter Family.

The Tranters were a very well-known family in the Barton Hill area, and it is not surprising that one of their members married into the Morgan family. The whole family lived at various addresses in Tichborne Street, Barton Hill for many years, and were close neighbours of the Morgan family.

The Tranter family, 1909.

Sarah Tranter, who married John (Jack) Morgan on 25th November 1894 at St. Luke's Church, Barton Hill, was one of five children of Reuben Henry Tranter (born 1848, Bristol;

died 1906, Bristol, aged 58) and Amy Iles (born 14th December 1852, Bristol; died 4th July 1918, Bristol, aged 65), all born in Bristol.

Reuben and Amy married at St Philip & Jacob Church in Bristol on 12th March 1871. Reuben's occupation at the time was recorded as being a Mason, with his home address noted as being Union Road, Bristol. Amy had no occupation recorded, with her home address shown as being Oxford Road, Bristol.

The 1891 Census shows the Tranter family living at 11 Tichborne Street, Barton Hill, a well-known street for members of the Morgan family. Reuben's employment was noted as being a Mason, with wife Amy and daughter Sarah being Cotton Spinners.

Reuben does not appear on the 1901 Census, which shows Amy at home at 5 Tichborne Street, Barton Hill, a few doors down from the 1891 address. She was employed as a laundress, whilst children Amy, John and Sarah (with her husband John Morgan and children John, George and Williams) were also present at this address. It would seem that Reuben had either left or been removed from the family home by this time, as reports from the time report a 'Reuben Tranter' from Bristol wandering the country in search of work.

By 1911, Amy was a widow, Reuben having died in 1906. She was now living at 10 Tichborne Street, along with children Reuben and John. Also in the house was daughter Amy, husband Alfred John Cheesley (who she married in 1904) and their 3 children Alfred, William and Sarah.

Amy died on 4th July 1918, aged 65, and is buried at Avonview Cemetery, Bristol.

As alluded to above, Reuben appears to have lived an 'interesting' life, with many of his exploits and misdemeanours reported in the local press:

2nd February 1861: "On Monday a poor little boy, named Reuben Tranter, whose friends reside in the Dings, met with a very sad accident, whilst engaged in tending some machinery. The boy, who was only twelve years of age, working in the employ of Mr. Brown, lucifer match manufacturer, West Street, and while engaged at the machine, his foot in some way became caught by the drum; by which it became very much lacerated. The little fellow's cries at once attracted attention; and he was taken to the Bristol Royal Infirmary, where his wounds were at once dressed, and he was received as an inpatient."

15th September 1874: Somerset Prison Records state that Reuben Henry Tranter was committed to 2 months' hard labour for "assaulting and resisting John Laver, a Police Constable whilst in the execution of his duty at Weston-super-Mare on the 12th September 1874." He entered Shepton Mallet prison on 15th September 1874 and was released on 14th November 1874.

26th November 1878: Reuben Tranter, labourer, was charged with unlawfully wounding Amy Tranter, his wife, at St. George's, on Friday last. Complainant, who had an infant in her arms, said she had only been confined about six weeks. The prisoner had been drinking hard all last week. At three o'clock on Tuesday morning he beat her, and turned her out of bed and beat her head against the fire-place. On the night in question he came home very drunk, and went to bed without taking off his clothes. She afterwards went to bed with the baby, and was woken up in the night by the prisoner assaulting her. He knelt on her chest, and threatened to murder her. He was also injuring the baby. She tried to get him away, but he struck her over the eye with something, and for a few minutes she was insensible.

On recovery she found that she had a deep wound over the temple, and it bled very much. The baby's clothes were nearly covered with blood. One of the officers in court informed the bench that the chemist who dressed the wound said that if it had gone any further it would certainly have been very dangerous, if not fatal.

In cross-examination by the prisoner, the wife admitted that she took one of their children away from him when he was at a public house. She also admitted that she bit his arm before he wounded her, but that was in her efforts to prevent him from kneeling on her and the baby. The prisoner wished the magistrate to see the bite on his arm, but Mr. Harford told him that that was unnecessary as the wife admitted that she did it when he was making a brutal assault upon her.

The prisoner: "She bit my arm badly".

The Clerk: "I don't wonder at her biting you, if you were kneeling upon her and the baby in the manner she here described".

The wife, in reply to the magistrate, said the chemist who dressed the wound said it was inflicted with a sharp cutting instrument. The prisoner, who complained that he woke up and found not enough clothes on him, said he did not cut his wife's head with any weapon. He struck her and she fell against the bedpost. He was remanded till Thursday."

29th November 1878: Reuben Tranter, a mason, was charged with assaulting his wife. The woman said her husband and herself had been quarrelling all the week, and on Wednesday night she woke up and found him kneeling on her chest. He was the worse for liquor, and struck her violently on the forehead. She was rendered senseless by the blow, and her baby was now lying dead. The husband had been several times previously convicted. Inspector Bird said the wife was a quiet, hard-working woman, but the man was a drunken fellow. Mrs. Tranter asked the magistrates to deal mercifully with her husband, and the bench, in consideration of the appeal, gave him four instead of six month's imprisonment with hard labour."

Prison records of the time show that he was committed in prison from 29th November 1878 until 27th March 1879.

13th May 1884: Reuben Tranter was fined 20s and costs, or in default a month's hard labour, for being drunk and disorderly, and assaulting P.C. Uzzell, at St. Georges."

28th July 1886: "Yesterday afternoon a man named Reuben Tranter, aged 36, living at 9 Tichborne Street, St. George's, was knocked down and run over by a passing cart while crossing the street near his residence. Tranter sustained a fractured thigh and an injury to his arm. He was detained at the Infirmary."

9th November 1901: "At the Gloucester Police Court on Friday, Reuben Tranter, a tramp, from Bristol, was charged with attempting to commit suicide by placing his head on the railway lines at Barton Gates on Thursday night.

The D.C.C., in asking for a remand, said prisoner was found lying on the rails at the Barton Gates immediately after a goods train had passed. A remand was granted till Wednesday. Prisoner, an old man, cried bitterly in the dock."

On the same day:

"At Gloucester City Petty Sessions day, before D. Batten (in the chair), Messrs. J. M. Collett and E. Lea, Reuben Tranter, a miserable looking fellow, who was described as a tramp belonging to Bristol, was charged with attempting to commit suicide on Nov. 7.

D.C.C. Philpott said that between eleven and twelve o'clock on Thursday night prisoner was found with his head across the railway metals at the Barton Street crossing, a goods train having just passed on the outer line.

Being unable to give an account of himself, accused was taken into custody, and he (the Deputy Chief Constable) asked for a remand until Wednesday. Remanded accordingly."

13th November 1901: "At the Gloucester Police Court on Wednesday, before Messrs. T. Powell (in the chair) and J. Ward, Reuben Tranter, tramp, was placed in the dock charged with attempting to commit suicide by placing his head on the railway metals on November 7th.

Mr. Philpott said in this case he was of the opinion that the prisoner did not intend to commit suicide at all, but simply acted as he had done a ruse to get in for the night. He (Mr. Philpott) had got his history from Bristol, where he had been before the Court upon fifteen occasions. He hoped their Worships would send him back to Bristol.

Prisoner said he had been travelling in search of work, and not being able to get any, and having no food, he got into a weak state. He was pleased in one way that he had been saved from self-destruction, and if he were discharged he would promise to leave the town at once, but he should go a different way to Bristol, because if he went back there they would be on to him about this. Prisoner was discharged."

18th June 1904: "Alleged assault in Silver Street, Reading. P.C. Skelton reports that on 10.35 on Thursday evening he found a man lying on the footway in London Road. Dr. Freeman was passing at the time and ordered his removal to the Hospital, where he was found to be suffering from a fractured rib. The man gave his name as Reuben Tranter, aged 61, of Tichborne Street, Bristol, and was tramping the country in search of work.

He stated that he was assaulted in Silver Street by some person unknown, and that the blow he received caused the fracture. Tranter was afterwards removed to the workhouse infirmary."

REUBEN AND AMY'S CHILDREN (all born in Bristol):

1.   **Sarah Tranter** (born 20th January 1872; died 1st February 1951, Bristol, aged 79).

Sarah was baptised on 21st July 1872 at St. Philip & Jacob Church, Bristol. The family address at the time was vaguely recorded as Lawrence Hill, Bristol, and her father's occupation stated as being a Labourer.

See Chapter 8.

2.   **George Henry Tranter** (born 3rd September 1873; died 4th December 1930, Bristol, aged 57).

George was baptised on 28th September 1873 at St. Philip & Jacob Church, Bristol. The family address at the time was vaguely recorded as Lawrence Hill, Bristol, and his father's occupation stated as being a Labourer.

He married Eliza Annie White (born 1875, Bristol), on 25th November 1894 at Christ Church, Barton Hill, Bristol. At the time of their marriage, both George and Eliza were living at 9 Morley Street, Bristol, George being a Labourer and Eliza a Tailoress.

They had fifteen children.

The 1901 Census shows the family living at 8 Tichborne Street, Barton Hill, Bristol, where George's occupation is recorded as being a Labourer in Gas Works.

The 1911 Census reveals the family had relocated to 2 Corbett Street, Barton Hill, Bristol. George had continued his employment as a worker at the Gas Works.

By the time of the 1921 Census, the family were still at 2 Corbett Street, Barton Hill, Bristol, with George working for the Bristol Gas Company.

George was buried at Avonview Cemetery on 10th December 1930.

3.   **Mary Ann Tranter** (born 13th October 1878; died 28th November 1878, aged 6 weeks).

Mary was baptised on 3rd November 1878 at St. Philip & Jacob Church, Bristol. The family address at the time was vaguely recorded as Lawrence Hill, Bristol, and her father's occupation stated as being a Labourer.

4.   **Reuben Edward Tranter** (born 3rd April 1883; died 27th August 1943, Bristol, aged 60).

Reuben was baptised on 28th January 1888 at St. Luke's Church, Bristol. The family address at the time was recorded as 9 Tichborne Street, Bristol, and his father's occupation stated as being a Mason.

He was mentioned in the local press for 'Gambling in the Streets' on 22nd May 1900 when it was reported that he (with others) was charged with playing 'Banker' at Victoria Square, Barton Hill, Bristol. He was fined 5s without costs.

He married Florence Emily Aldridge (born 23rd October 1896, Stroud; died 21st February 1974, Bristol, aged 77) on 23rd October 1920, in Stroud, Gloucestershire. They had one child.

He had obviously not learned his lesson from his earlier charge when it was reported on 29th April 1938 that "Reuben Edward Tranter (55) of Granville Street, Barton Hill, and Alfred Thomas Cole (56) of Factory Street, Barton Hill, pleaded guilty at Bristol Police Court yesterday to a charge of loitering at Barton Hill for the purposes of betting. Each was fined £4 and ordered to pay £1 costs."

Reuben was buried at Avonview Cemetery on 1st September 1943. Florence was buried alongside her husband on 26th February 1974.

The grave of Reuben Edward and Florence Elizabeth Tranter.

5.   **Amy Tranter** (born 31st August 1884, died 23rd May 1958, Bristol, aged 73).

Amy was baptised on 28th January 1888 at St. Luke's Church, Bristol. The family address at the time was recorded as 9 Tichborne Street, Bristol, and her father's occupation stated as being a Mason.

She married Alfred John Cheesley (born 4th December 1883, Bristol; died 23rd April 1943, Bristol, aged 59) on 16th April 1904 at St. Luke's Church, Barton Hill, Bristol. Amy's address on the marriage registration was shown as 10 Tichborne Street, Barton Hill, Bristol, and her occupation a Cotton Weaver. Alfred was living at 16 Ford Street, Barton Hill, Bristol, and was employed as a Labourer.

They had thirteen children.

The 1911 Census reveals that Amy and Alfred were living at 10 Tichborne Street, Barton Hill, Bristol, with their three children at the time. Sadly, two of their children had died in infancy. Alfred's occupation was a Worker at Galvanising Works.

By 1921, the family were still at 10 Tichborne Street, Barton Hill, Bristol, and Alfred remained working as a Galvaniser. Five of their children were living with them at this time.

The 1939 Register saw no change in address or Alfred's employment, but six of their children remained in the family home.

Alfred was buried at Avonview Cemetery on 29th April 1943, and his wife Amy buried at the same location on 29th May 1958.

6. **John (Jack) Tranter** (born 2nd January 1888, died 1970, Ham Green Hospital, Bristol, aged 81).

John was baptised on 28th January 1888 at St. Luke's Church, Bristol. The family address at the time was recorded as 9 Tichborne Street, Bristol, and his father's occupation stated as being a Mason.

He married Florence Rosina Dauncey (born 20th October 1890, Bristol; died 28th March 1974, Bristol, aged 83) on 5th June 1911 at St. Luke's Church, Barton Hill, Bristol. John's address at the time was 10 Tichborne Street, Barton Hill, Bristol, and Florence lived close by at 9 Tichborne Street. John's occupation was a Labourer, and Florence was a Machinist.

They had six children.

The 1921 Census shows John as an out of work Galvaniser Pickler at Lysaghts, a well-known local employer, and the family still at 10 Tichborne Street, Barton Hill, Bristol.

By 1939 the family had moved next door, to 8 Tichborne Street, Barton Hill, Bristol, where John was still working as a Galvaniser Pickler.

The Wagland Family

The Waglands were another family from the Barton Hill area of Bristol. Laura Wagland married George Morgan (born 1891) on 12th August 1918, after previously marrying Robert William Hitchings on 11th February 1913. Robert was sadly killed on HMS Goliath during WW1.

Laura was one of the children of William Wagland, 4th child of Edward and Esther.

William's father Edward was born in 1833 in Bristol, and he married Esther Winterson on 6th November 1859 at Holy Trinity Church, Bristol. Both Edward and Esther were living at Brick Street at the time. They went on to have six children, all born in Bristol.

The 1861 Census records Edward (erroneously entered as Edwin) and Esther (Hester) living at Harding Court, St. Philips, Bristol, were Edward's occupation noted as being a Labourer.

The next Census from 1871 shows the family at Hammersmith Place, Bristol, where Edward's occupation was again recorded as being a Labourer.

The 1881 Census indicated that the family were living at 3 Canterbury Street, Bristol, where Edward was working as a Gas Stoker. Children Elizabeth and Esther were working in the Cotton Factory, whilst William was a Printer's Compositor.

By 1911 Edward was living at 49 Barton Street, Barton Hill, being described as a Widower and Pensioner.

He died on 9th July 1917, aged 79 in Bristol, and was buried at Avonview Cemetery, Bristol on 15th July 1917.

EDWARD AND ESTHER'S CHILDREN:

1. **Mary Ann Wagland** (born 1860, Bristol; died 1910, Prescot, Lancashire, aged 50).

Mary was baptised on 4th August 1861 at St. Luke's Church, Bristol. The family address at the time was recorded as Kingsland Road, Bristol, and her father's occupation stated as being a Labourer.

She married Charles Cuthbert (born 1857, Stanwick, Northamptonshire; died 13th November 1934, Vancouver, Canada, aged 77) in Ashton-under-Lyme in 1877.

They had three children:

- **Albert Cuthbert** (born 29th November 1879, Mossley, Manchester; died 1890, Ashton-under-Lyme).

He was baptised on 21st December at Primitive Methodist Chapel, Canal Street, Stalybridge, Cheshire. The family's home address was recorded as 14 Bank Side, Mossley, Manchester, and his father's occupation shown as a Cotton Operative.

- **Emma Cuthbert** (born 25th February 1884, Mossley, Manchester).

She was baptised on 27th March 1884 at Stamford Road Wesleyan Methodist Chapel, Monsall, Lancashire. The family's home address was recorded as Mossley, Manchester.

- **Rose Myer Cuthbert** (born 1891, Ashton-under-Lyme; died 1893, Ashton-under-Lyme, aged 2).

She was buried at Mossley Cemetery, Manchester.

The 1881 Census shows that Charles was boarding at the Evans family home in Tintwhistle, Cheshire, his occupation being a Cotton Operator. Meanwhile, Mary was boarding with the Mayall family in Ashton-under-Lyme with their son Albert.

By 1891 Charles and Mary were living together with their two children in Ashton-under-Lyme, Charles still working in a cotton factory.

The 1901 Census reveals that Charles had re-married in 1899 to Hannah Loftus in Oldham, Lancashire, and was living with his mother and new wife at Middleton, Lancashire. He was still working in a Cotton Mill; mystery surrounds the whereabouts of Mary and surviving child Emma at this time.

2.   **Elizabeth Selina Wagland** (born 8th August 1863, Bristol; died 17th May 1942, Brisbane, Australia, aged 78).

Elizabeth was baptised on 13th September 1863 at St. Luke's Church, Bristol. The family address at the time was recorded as Hammersmith Place, Bristol, and her father's occupation stated as being a Labourer.

She emigrated to Australia in 1889, and married William Arthur Tompkins (born 9th October 1848, Delaware, USA; died 20th May 1919, Townsville, Australia, aged 78). Elizabeth and William had five children together.

- **William Edward Tompkins** (born 27th July 1890, Townsville, Queensland, Australia; died 23rd July 1917, Wulvergem, West-Vlaanderen, Belgium, aged 26).

The grave of William Edward Tompkins, West-Vlaanderen, Belgium.

- **Arthur Henry Tompkins** (born 1892, Queensland, Australia; died 14th May 1955, Queensland, Australia, aged 62).

- **Elizabeth Amelia (Milly) Tompkins** (born 19th November 1893, Townsville, Queensland, Australia; died 1975, Eventide Charters Towers, Queensland, Australia, aged 81).

- **Esther Ann (Etty) Tompkins** (born 9th November 1896, Townsville, Queensland, Australia; died 5th January 1970, Townsville, Queensland, Australia, aged 73).

- **David John Tompkins** (born 5th January 1899, Townsville, Queensland, Australia; died 27th July 1967, Townsville, Queensland, Australia, aged 68). William had previously been married to Kate Lysaght and had three children with her.

3. **Hester (Esther) Wagland** (born 5th September 1865; died 1932, Weston-super-Mare, aged 66).

Hester was baptised on 24th September 1865 at St. Philip & Jacob Church, Bristol. The family address at the time was recorded as Kingsland Road, Bristol, and her father's occupation stated as being a Labourer.

She married Alfred Ernest Wade (born 5th February 1858, London; died 1943, Weston-super-Mare, aged 84) at Christ Church, Weston-super-Mare on 5th August 1895. Esther's address was recorded as Glenavon, Montpelier, Bristol, and Alfred was living at 2 Shellabears Cottages, Weston-super-Mare, and was working as a Blacksmith.

They had eight children:

- **Alfred Ernest (Fred) Wade** (born 27th July 1896, Weston-super-Mare; died 1972, Weston-super-Mare, aged 75).

- **Florence Agnes (Flossie) Wade** (born 22nd October 1897, Weston-super-Mare; died 1996, Weston-super-Mare, aged 98).

- **Henry Bertie Wade** (born 3rd July 1899, Weston-super-Mare; died 1993, Weston-super-Mare, aged 93).

- **Edith Maud Wade** (born 1901, Weston-super-Mare; died 1969, Wincanton, Somerset, aged 68).

- **Rosina Wade** (born 23rd March 1903, Weston-super-Mare; died 2003, North Somerset, aged 99).

- **Beatrice Wade** (born 5th June 1904, Weston-super-Mare; died 2006, North Somerset, aged 101).

- **Maurice Wade** (born 17th June 1905, Weston-super-Mare; died 1982, Weston-super-Mare, aged 76).

- **Lily Wade** (born 11th June 1910, Weston-super-Mare; died 1965, Wells, Somerset, aged 54).

Alfred had previously been married to Mary Jane Ralph, who died in 1894. They had two children together.

The 1901 Census shows Hester and Alfred living at with their five children at 18 Locking Road, Weston-super-Mare, where Alfred was employed as a General Smith.

By 1911, Alfred, Hester, and their eight children had moved to 1 Furland Terrace, Milton, Weston-super-Mare, continuing his work as a General Smith.

The 1921 Census reveals that the family had moved again, this time to 1 South Terrace, Milton, Weston-super-Mare, Alfred still working as a Blacksmith.

4. **William Thomas Potter Wagland** (born 30th July 1867, Bristol; died 30th January 1909, Bristol, aged 41).

William was baptised on 1st September 1867 at St. Philip & Jacob Church, Bristol. The family address at the time was recorded as Kingsland Road, Bristol, and his father's occupation stated as being a Labourer.

He married Ellen Rosina Davis (born 1869, Bristol; died 15th February 1957, aged 88) on 24th December 1892, at the Wesleyan Methodist Church in Bristol. They had four children, details of which are shown at the end of this Wagland Family section.

The 1901 Census shows the family living at 13 Beaufort Road, Bristol, where William's occupation is shown as a Gas Stoker.

William died on 30th January 1909, and was buried at Avonview Cemetery, Bristol, on 7th February 1909.

By 1911, the family were now living at 44 Corbett Street, Barton Hill, Bristol, William's widow Ellen now head of the household. Laura was working in the Cotton Factory, whilst son William was an Errand Boy.

William was buried at Avonview Cemetery, Bristol, on 7th February 1909, and Ellen buried at the same location on 20th February 1957.

WILLIAM AND ELLEN WAGLAND'S CHILDREN:

1. **Laura Wagland** (born 17th November 1893, Bristol; died 1st January 1981, Bristol, aged 87).

See Chapter 4.

2. **William George Wagland** (born 3rd May 1897; died 3rd August 1974, Bristol, aged 77).

He married Florence Mary Pollard (born 25th August 1899, Bristol) in 1922, in Bristol.

They had three children.

- **Doreen Florence Wagland** (born 1923, Bristol).

She married Alfred William (Bill) Hook (born 1919, Bristol; died 2009, Bristol, aged 90) at St. Philip & Jacob Church, Bristol, in 1943.

They had no children.

- **Irene Claris Wagland** (born 7th June 1925, Bristol; died 1st March 2017, Bristol, aged 91).

She married James Edward Light (born 27th September 1923, Bristol; died 1992, Bristol) in 1945, in Bristol.

They had three children.

- **William J. Wagland** (born 1936, Bristol).

Florence died on 7th November 1972 and was buried at Avonview Cemetery on 10th November 1972.

William was buried at Avonview Cemetery, Bristol on 7th August 1974.

3. **Edward Henry Wagland** (born 12th January 1898, Bristol; died 12th May 1971, Bristol, aged 73).

He joined the Royal Navy in September 1914, and served on various vessels during WW1.

He married Emily Sarah White (born 7th September 1896, Bristol; died 18th January 1934, Bristol, aged 37) at St. Silas Church, Bedminster, on 25th October 1924, and his address shown as 17 Short Street, St. Philips, Bristol, with his occupation recorded as being a Builder's Labourer.

Emily was buried at Avonview Cemetery, Bristol on 25th January 1934.

Edward subsequently married Emma Selina Ada Walker (born 24th May 1902, Bristol; died 1980, Bristol, aged 77) on 20th April 1935 at St. Simon's Church, Bristol. His occupation on the registration document was shown as a Scaffolder, and his address noted as being 52 Beaumont Street, Bristol.

The 1939 Census shows the family living at 94 Charfield Road, Bristol, where Edward's occupation was noted as being a Builder's Constructor's Ganger.

He died on 12th May 1971, in Bristol, aged 72.

Emma died in 1980 aged 77, in Bristol, and her funeral took place on 29th December 1980 at Arno's Vale Cemetery, Bristol.

Edward and Emily had four children together:

- **Edward George Wagland** (born 3rd December 1926, Bristol; died 10th January 1945, near Galveston, Indiana, U.S.A.).

He joined the Royal Navy and was working as an aircraft test pilot for the Fleet Air Arm at the time, based at the Naval Air Station, Bunker Hill, U.S.A.

He was 18 years old when he was killed in an aircraft accident and was buried at Kokomo (Crown Point) Cemetery, Indiana, U.S.A.

The death certificate advises that Edward, of 94 Charfield Road, Southmead, Bristol, died of 'multiple fractures and extensive mutilating lacerations'.

It would appear that the aircraft he was flying collided with another, resulting in his death.

He is commemorated on the Westbury-on-Trym War Memorial, Bristol.

Edward's War Grave at Kokomo Cemetery.

> **KOKOMO (CROWN POINT) CEMETERY**
> Index No. U.S.A. 56
>
> WAGLAND, Ldg. Airman Edward George, FX605591. R.N. H.M.S. Saker. 10th January, 1945. Age 18. Son of Edward and Emma Wagland, of Southmead, Gloucestershire, England. Sec. 26. Lot 26.

Edward Wagland's War Grave details.

- **Ronald Henry Wagland** (born 1928, Bristol; died 23rd January 1930, Bristol, aged 1 year 8 months).

He was buried at Avonview Cemetery, Bristol, on 29th January 1930.

- **Jean Wagland** born 1929, Bristol; died 14th January 1930, Bristol, aged 9 months).

She was buried at Avonview Cemetery, Bristol, on 21st January 1930.

- **Audrey Wagland** (born 1931, Bristol).

She married Guy Lewis Wensley (born 15th September 1931, Bristol; died 18th October 2001, Hampshire).

They had one child.

- **Harry Wagland** (born 1909, Bristol; died 17th November 1913, Bristol, aged 4).

He was buried at Avonview Cemetery, Bristol, on 23rd November 1913.

5.   **Edward Wagland** (born 12th July 1869, Bristol; died 1872, Bristol, aged 3).

Edward was baptised on 8th August 1869 at St. Philip & Jacob Church, Bristol.

The family address at the time was recorded as Kingsland Road, Bristol, and his father's occupation stated as being a Labourer.

6.   **Edward William Wagland** (born 25th May 1885, Bristol; died 1887, Bristol, aged 19 months).

Edward was baptised on 18th October 1885 at St. Philip & Jacob Church, Bristol. The family address at the time was recorded as 4 Canterbury Road, Barton Hill, Bristol, and his father's occupation stated as being a Labourer.

The Williams family.

There were two unrelated Williams families with direct links to the Morgan family:

1. **Matilda Williams**, who married John Morgan, and;
2. **Jane Williams**, who married Harry Morgan.

Both are described below.

Matilda Williams.

The earliest family we can trace with any certainty on 'our' Morgan line is the Williams family from the Oldland/Bitton area, between Bristol and Bath. Matilda Williams married John Morgan on 2nd March 1834 in Bitton, from whom all the Morgans featured in this book are descended. *See Chapter 2.*

Matilda was the fifth child of John Williams (born 1808, Oldland, near Bristol; died 1868, Bristol aged 60) and Eliza Cox (born 1811, Oldland, near Bristol; died 1889, Bristol, aged 78). They married on 2nd March 1834, in Bitton.

Matilda's siblings, all born in Bitton, near Bristol, are recorded as:

1. **Emma Williams** (born 1834; died 5th April 1891, Bristol, aged 56).

Baptised on the 14th December 1834 at Holy Trinity Church, Bitton, Gloucesterhire, She married William Haynes (born 1831, Bitton, Bristol; died 12th November 1901, Bristol, aged 70) on 5th May 1855 at Holy Trinity Church, Kingswood, Bristol, and had nine children. William, recorded as being a Collier on the marriage registration, was living at Potter's Wood, Bristol, along with Emma.

Emma and William were buried at Avonview Cemetery, Bristol.

2. **Harriet Williams** (born 1836; died 1844, Bristol, aged 8).

She was baptised on 19th February 1836 at Holy Trinity Church, Bitton, Gloucestershire, and buried at the same location in 1844.

3. **William Williams** (born 1838; died 3rd September 1904, Bristol, aged 66).

He was baptised on 11th August 1839 at Holy Trinity Church, Bitton, Gloucestershire. He married Sarah Gingell (born 1840, Bristol; died 15th July 1926, Bristol, aged 86) on 9th November 1861 at Holy Trinity Church, Stapleton, Bristol, and had nine children.

William and Sarah were buried at Avonview Cemetery, Bristol.

4. **Samuel Williams** (born 1842; died 2nd June 1852 Bristol, aged 10).

He was baptised on 15th May 1842, at Holy Trinity Church, Bitton, Gloucestershire.

He was sadly killed in a Kingswood coal mine accident after being run over by a wagon, and was buried at Holy Trinity Church, Kingswood, Bristol.

5.   **Thomas Williams** (born 1847; died 18th April 1930, Bristol, aged 83).

He was baptised on 5th August 1849 at Holy Trinity Church, Kingswood, Bristol.

He married Emma Sweet (born 1850, Bristol; died 10th November 1921, Clutton, North Somerset, aged 71) on 7th August 1870 at Holy Trinity Church, Stapleton, Bristol. Both Thomas and Emma were recorded as living at Stapleton, with Thomas's occupation being a Miner.

They had eleven children.

Emma was buried at St. James' Church, Cameley, North Somerset, whilst Thomas was buried at Greenbank Cemetery, Bristol.

6.   **George Williams** (born 1850; died 29th July 1924, aged 74, Bristol).

He was baptised on 1st September 1850 at Holy Trinity Church, Kingswood, Bristol.

He married Elizabeth Humphries (born 1852, Saltford; died 2nd November 1913, Bristol, aged 61) in 1872 and had six children.

The 1911 Census shows that Elizabeth was the licencee of the 'Bell Inn' at 79 Old Bread Street, St. Philips, Bristol. She and husband George ran the pub until their deaths, when their son Francis Williams took over until the early 1930s.

George was buried at Avonview Cemetery, Bristol.

7.   **Isaac Williams** (born 1854; died 26th February 1936, Bristol, aged 81).

Isaac was baptised at Holy Trinity Church, Kingswood, Bristol, on 4th October 1857, the address of his parents being recorded as Kingswood Hill.

He married Elizabeth Packer (born 1860, Bristol) in Bristol in 1880. The 1881 Census saw Isaac and Elizabeth living at 29 Derby Street, Bristol, along with Elizabeth's son William, who they later adopted. Isaac's occupation was recorded as being a Coal Miner.

By 1891 the family had moved to 6 Albert Place, Bristol, with Isaac maintaining his job in a colliery, and by 1901 they had moved to 15 Orchard Square, Avonvale Road, Bristol. Isaac was by now a Groom in local stables. The 1911 Census shows the family now at 25 Netham Road, St. George, Bristol, with Isaac's occupation described as a 'Labourer when at work'.

By 1921, Isaac was living with daughter Violet and adopted son George Packer at 10 Orchard Square, Bristol, close to their address in 1901. Isaac was sadly a widower at this time, Elizabeth having died since the previous Census.

They had seven children together.

Isaac was buried at Avonview Cemetery, Bristol.

8.   **Harriet Elizabeth Williams** (born 1857; died 28th January 1922, Bristol, aged 65).

She was baptised at Holy Trinity Church, Kingswood, Bristol, on 4th October 1857.

She married Walter Woodland in 1878. Sadly Walter died that same year, and he was buried at St. George Parish Church. At the time of his death, he was living with Harriet in Derby Street, Bristol.

Harriet then married John Cureton (born 1844, Plymouth; died 15th December 1925, Bristol, aged 81) on 5th July 1903 at St. Philip & Jacob Church, Bristol. John had been married before, to Sarah Jane Lanham, and they had five children together. The address of both Harriet and John was recorded as 4 Tower Hill, Bristol, and John's occupation shown as being a Collier.

No children resulted from either of Harriet's marriages.

Both Harriet and John were buried at Avonview Cemetery, Bristol.

Jane Williams.

Another unrelated Williams family (not from the Oldland/Bitton area) has links to the Morgan family through Jane Williams (born 1873, Bristol), who married Harry Morgan, son of John Morgan and Matilda Williams on 26th May 1889 at St Luke's Church, Barton Hill.

Jane was one of the children of Robert Williams (born 1833, Bristol), and Elizabeth Iles (born 1834, Bristol), who married on 12th June 1853 at St. Simon's Church, Bristol.

Before marriage, Robert lived at:

1851 Census: 5 Colstons Place, St, Pauls, Bristol. Robert was noted as being a Turner's Apprentice. He was living with his brother James and half-sister Mary Youlten.

1861 Census: 16 Norfolk Street, St. Pauls, Bristol, where his occupation was shown as a Turner. He with his widowed mother Mary Williams, a dressmaker.

The 1871, 1881 and 1891 Censuses show the family living at 15 Leigh (or Lee) Street, Bristol, where father Robert is shown as being employed as a labourer.

The Censuses of 1901 and 1911 saw Robert and Elizabeth living at 16 Wellington Street, Bristol.

Elizabeth died on 29th March 1914, in Bristol, aged 80. Robert died on 18th January 1919, and was buried at Greenbank Cemetery, Bristol.

Robert and Jane had eight children:

1. **Elizabeth Mary Williams** (born 4th June 1856, Bristol).

Elizabeth was baptised at St. Philip & Jacob Church, Bristol, on 29th June 1856. The family address at the time was recorded as Lawrence Hill, Bristol, and her father's occupation shown as being a Labourer.

2. **John Williams** (born 30th April 1859, Bristol; died 20th November 1939, Bristol, aged 80).

John was baptised at St. Philip & Jacob Church, Bristol, on 22nd May 1859. The family were noted as living at Lawrence Hill, Bristol, with his father recorded as being a Labourer.

He married Mary Jane Wilkins (born 1861, Taunton, Somerset; died 21st December 1912, Bristol, aged 51) on 10th October 1880 at St. Philip & Jacob Church, Bristol. John was living at Tower Hill, Bristol and employed as a Labourer at the time, and Mary was residing within the St. Philip's parish in Bristol.

The 1881 Census shows John and Mary living at 2 Berkeley Street, Bristol. John was employed as a Railway Porter, and Mary a Tailoress.

1891 saw the family relocate to 30 Isherman Street, Birmingham, no doubt due to John's work with the railways as a Railway Goods Guard.

By 1901 the family had returned to Bristol, and were living at 50 Croydon Street, Bristol, with John still employed as a Goods Guard on the Railway.

The 1911 Census shows the family still at 50 Croydon Street, Bristol, but John was by now working as a Labourer at a Chocolate Factory.

The 1939 Register saw John in his final year living with his daughter Alice and family at 9 St. Gabriel's Road, Bristol.

They had ten children, two of whom had sadly died by 1911.

John and Mary were both buried at Greenbank Cemetery, Bristol.

3. **Eliza Williams** (born 1st October 1862, Bristol).

Eliza was baptised at St. Philip & Jacob Church, Bristol, on 28th October 1862. The baptism records show the family living at Easton Road, Bristol, with her father's occupation being a Labourer.

She married James Smith (born 1863, Bristol; died 1918, Bristol) at St. Philip & Jacob Church, Bristol, on 10th October 1881. Both Eliza and James were recorded as living at Old Mead Street, Bristol, at the time of their marriage, James' occupation being a Labourer.

The 1891 Census shows the family living at 43 Harding Street, Bristol, with five children and James' father. James' occupation was that of a Brewer's Labourer. They remained at that address for the 1901 Census, James still being employed as a Labourer, and with four more children.

One of their children, Edwin Smith (born 1889, Bristol), was killed by a cart outside of the Waverley Hotel, Bristol, in 1892.

4. **George Williams** (born 15th February 1865, Bristol; died 20th August 1946, Bristol, aged 81).

He married Martha Jane Upton (born 13th September 1868, Bristol; died 4th April 1915, Bristol, aged 46) at St. Luke's Church, Bristol, on 14th September 1890. He was living at 15 Factory Street, Bristol, at the time of his marriage, and employed as a Carter. Martha was living at 32 Church Street, Bristol.

It is interesting that on the 1891 Census, George and Martha were living at 12 Charlton Park, Bristol, in the same house as his sister Jane and husband Harry Morgan.

By 1901, George and Martha were living at 19 Gladstone Street, St. Philips, Bristol, George working as a Carter at Cocoa Works, and by 1911 the couple had moved to 28 Milsom Street, Stapleton Road, Bristol, George continuing his work as a Carter.

They had no children.

After Martha died in 1915, George married Mary White (born 23rd March 1874) in 1917, in Bristol.

The Census of 1921 reveals that George (still working as a Housekeeper at J.S. Fry & Sons Ltd (Cocoa Manufacturers) in Bristol) and Mary and two of her sons (Thomas and George) living at 33 Winsford Street, Bristol.

The 1939 register shows George and Mary still living at 33 Winsford Street, Bristol along with Mary's son Thomas.

George and Martha were buried at Greenbank Cemetery, Bristol.

5. **Robert Williams** (born 16th December 1868, Bristol).

Robert was baptised at St. Philip & Jacob Church, Bristol, on 10th January 1869. The family address was noted as being Lee (Leigh) Street, Easton Road, Bristol, with his father's occupation shown as being a Labourer.

6. **Jane Williams** (born 5th May 1873, Bristol, died 19th March 1914, Bristol, aged 40).

Twin of Samuel.

She was baptised at St. Philip & Jacob Church, Bristol, on 1st June 1873. The family address was noted as being Easton Road, Bristol, with her father's occupation shown as being a Labourer.

See Chapter 6.

7. **Samuel Williams** (born 5th May 1873, Bristol, died 12th November 1875, Bristol, aged 2).

Twin of Jane.

Samuel was baptised at St. Philip & Jacob Church, Bristol, on 1st June 1873. He died at home at Leigh Street, Bristol, and was buried at Greenbank Cemetery, Bristol, on 21st November 1873.

8. **Florence Henrietta Williams** (born 1877, Bristol, died 1878, Bristol, aged 15 months).

Florence was baptised at St. Philip & Jacob Church, Bristol, on 2nd September 1877. The baptism records show the family living at Easton Road, Bristol, with her father's occupation being a Labourer.

She died at home in Leigh Street, Bristol, on 25th December 1878, and was buried at Greenbank Cemetery, Bristol, on 29th December 1878.

APPENDIX 1.

FREDERICK 'JERRY' MORGAN – APPEARANCES FOR BRISTOL CITY AND BRISTOL ROVERS FOOTBALL CLUBS.

DATE	VENUE	OPPONENTS	SCORE	SHIRT NUMBER	GOALS
\multicolumn{6}{c}{FOR BRISTOL CITY F.C. - LEAGUE DIVISION TWO}					
4/5/1912	H	Bristol Rovers (Titanic Disaster Fund)	W 3-1	4	0
7/12/1912	A	Leeds City	D 1-1	4	0
14/12/1912	H	Grimsby	D 2-2	4	0
\multicolumn{6}{c}{FOR BRISTOL ROVERS F.C. SOUTHERN LEAGUE (1919/20); LEAGUE DIVISION THREE (S) (1920/21 – 1924/25)}					
1/5/1920	A	Gillingham	D 2-2	10	0
30/10/1920	A	Norwich	D 1-1	10	0
27/11/1920	H	Southampton	L 1-2	10	1
4/12/1920	A	Reading	L 1-2	10	0
11/12/1920	H	Reading	W 3-2	10	1
18/12/1920	H	Worksop (F.A. Cup)	W 9-0	10	3
25/12/1920	H	Swansea	L 1-2	10	0
27/12/1920	A	Swansea	D 2-2	10	0
1/1/1921	A	Luton	W 2-1	8	0
15/1/1921	A	Swindon	L 2-1	4	0

22/1/1921	H	Swindon	W 3-1	8	0
29/1/1921	A	Gillingham	L 0-1	8	0
5/2/1921	H	Gillingham	W 2-0	8	0
12/2/1921	A	Portsmouth	L 0-1	10	0
26/2/1921	A	Watford	L 1-2	10	0
5/3/1921	H	Watford	W 2-0	10	0
2/4/1921	A	Southend	L 0-1	7	0
9/4/1921	H	Merthyr	D 1-1	8	0
16/4/1921	A	Merthyr	D 2-2	10	1
23/4/1921	H	Plymouth A.	W 2-0	8	0
30/4/1921	A	Plymouth A.	L 1-2	8	0
2/5/1921	H	Exeter	W 5-0	8	0
7/5/1921	A	Exeter	L 0-1	9	0
27/8/1921	H	Plymouth A.	L 1-3	10	0
29/8/1921	A	Southend	L 0-3	8	0
31/8/1921	A	Portsmouth	L 0-1	8	0
3/9/1921	A	Plymouth A.	L 0-1	8	0
7/9/1921	H	Portsmouth	D 1-1	8	0
10/9/1921	H	Charlton	W 4-2	8	1
14/9/1921	H	Brentford	D 0-0	8	0
15/10/1921	A	Q.P.R.	W 2-1	8	0
22/10/1921	H	Merthyr	W 2-0	8	0
29/10/1921	A	Merthyr	W 2-0	8	1
5/11/1921	A	Norwich	W 1-0	8	0
12/11/1921	H	Norwich	W 4-2	8	2

19/11/1921	H	Reading	W 2-0	8	0
3/12/1921	H	Exeter (F.A. Cup)	D 0-0	8	0
7/12/1921	A	Exeter (F.A. Cup)	W 2-0	8	0
10/12/1921	A	Southampton	L 0-1	8	0
17/12/1921	A	Swansea (F.A. Cup)	L 0-2	8	0
24/12/1921	A	Brentford	L 2-4	8	0
26/12/1921	H	Brighton	L 1-2	8	0
14/1/1922	H	Aberdare A.	W 5-1	8	2
21/1/1922	H	Newport	L 3-4	8	0
28/1/1922	A	Newport	W 1-0	8	1
4/2/1922	H	Luton	W 2-0	8	0
11/2/1922	A	Luton	W 2-1	8	0
18/2/1922	H	Swindon	D 1-1	8	0
25/2/1922	A	Swindon	W 1-0	8	0
11/3/1922	A	Gillingham	L 2-3	8	0
25/3/1922	H	Millwall	D 0-0	8	0
1/4/1922	A	Exeter	D 2-2	8	1
14/4/1922	H	Southampton	D 0-0	8	0
15/4/1922	A	Swansea	L 1-8	8	0
17/4/1922	A	Watford	L 0-1	8	0
18/4/1922	H	Watford	D 1-1	8	0
22/4/1922	H	Swansea	D 0-0	8	0
1/5/1922	H	Bristol City (Glos. Cup)	L 0-2	8	0
6/5/1922	H	Southend	W 1-0	8	0
26/8/1922	A	Portsmouth	D 0-0	10	0
28/8/1922	H	Newport	W 3-1	10	1
2/9/1922	H	Portsmouth	L 0-2	10	0
7/9/1922	A	Newport	L 1-4	10	0

16/9/1922	H	Reading	D 1-1	10	0
23/9/1922	A	Bristol City	W 1-0	10	0
30/9/1922	H	Bristol City	L 1-2	10	0
4/10/1922	H	Southend	W 2-0	10	0
14/10/1922	A	Southend	D 0-0	10	0
21/10/1922	A	Millwall	L 0-1	10	0
28/10/1922	H	Millwall	D 0-0	10	0
2/12/1922	A	Reading (F.A. Cup)	W 1-0	10	0
16/12/1922	A	Stalybridge (F. A. Cup)	D 0-0	10	0
20/12/1922	H	Stalybridge (F. A. Cup)	L 1-2	10	0
23/12/1922	A	Brentford	W 1-0	8	0
25/12/1922	H	Exeter	D 3-3	8	0
26/12/1922	A	Exeter	D 0-0	8	0
6/1/1923	A	Norwich	D 0-0	8	0
20/1/1923	H	Northampton	D 0-0	8	0
27/1/1923	A	Northampton	L 0-1	10	0
3/2/1923	A	Luton	L 0-1	8	0
10/2/1923	H	Luton	D 1-1	8	1
17/2/1923	A	Q.P.R.	L 1-3	8	0
3/3/1923	A	Gillingham	W 1-0	8	0
10/3/1923	H	Gillingham	W 1-0	8	0
17/3/1923	H	Brighton	D 0-0	8	0
24/3/1923	A	Brighton	L 1-2	8	0
26/3/1923	H	Q.P.R.	L 1-3	8	0
31/3/1923	H	Swindon	W 2-0	8	0
2/4/1923	H	Merthyr	W 3-0	8	0
3/4/1923	A	Merthyr	D 1-1	8	1
7/4/1923	A	Swindon	L 0-1	8	0
14/4/1923	H	Aberdare	W 1-0	8	0
21/4/1923	A	Aberdare	D 0-0	10	0

23/4/1923	H	Norwich	W 3-2	10	3
28/4/1923	H	Swansea	D 0-0	10	0
30/4/1923	H	Brentford	D 1-1	10	0
7/5/1923	A	Bristol City (Glos. Cup)	L 0-1	10	0
1/3/1924	A	Charlton	W 3-1	10	0
8/3/1924	H	Charlton	W 2-0	10	0
15/3/1924	H	Norwich	W 3-1	10	2
22/3/1924	A	Norwich	L 1-3	10	0
29/3/1924	H	Swindon	L 0-1	10	0
19/4/1924	A	Watford	L 0-4	10	0
15/11/1924	A	Norwich	D 1-1	6	0
22/11/1924	H	Brentford	W 2-0	9	0
6/12/1924	H	Luton	D 1-1	10	0
29/11/1924	A	Yeovil & Petters	W 4-2	10	2
20/12/1924	H	Bournemouth	W 1-0	10	1
7/2/1925	H	Southend	L 1-3	10	0
11/2/1925	A	Gillingham	D 0-0	8	0
14/2/1925	A	Newport	L 1-4	8	0
21/2/1925	H	Plymouth A.	D 1-1	8	0
28/2/1925	A	Bristol City	L 0-2	8	0
7/3/1925	H	Swindon	L 0-1	8	0
14/3/1925	A	Aberdare A.	L 1-2	8	0
18/3/1925	H	Q.P.R.	W 3-0	10	2
21/3/1925	H	Norwich	W 3-0	10	2
28/3/1925	A	Brentford	D 1-1	10	0
30/3/1925	A	Merthyr	L 0-1	10	0
4/4/1925	H	Millwall	D 1-1	10	0
10/4/1925	H	Exeter	L 0-1	10	0
11/4/1925	A	Luton	D 1-1	10	0
13/4/1925	A	Exeter	D 1-1	10	0

14/4/1925	H	Reading	W 1-0	10	0
18/4/1925	H	Gillingham	D 0-0	10	0
29/4/1925	H	Bristol City (Glos. Cup)	W 2-0	10	1
2/5/1925	A	Reading	L 1-4	10	1

APPENDIX 2.
WILLIAM JAMES 'JIMMY' MORGAN – APPEARANCES FOR BRISTOL ROVERS FOOTBALL CLUB.

DATE	VENUE	OPPONENTS	SCORE	SHIRT NUMBER	GOALS
LEAGUE DIVISION THREE (S)					
19/4/1946	H	Torquay (Div. 3S Cup)	W 3-1	-	0
20/4/1946	H	Brighton (Div. 3S Cup)	W 6-1	-	2
22/4/1946	A	Brighton (Div. 3S Cup)	W 3-1	-	0
27/4/1946	H	Walsall (Div. 3S Cup)	L 1-3	-	0
23/11/1946	H	Northampton	L 0-3	10	0
30/11/1946	A	Merthyr (F.A. Cup)	L 1-3	10	0
1/2/1947	A	Bristol City	L 0-4	10	0
8/2/1947	A	Southend	W 3-2	10	0
15/2/1947	H	Q.P.R.	W 3-1	10	0
22/2/1947	H	Swindon	W 3-0	10	1
1/3/1947	A	Bournemouth	W 3-1	10	1
8/3/1947	H	Cardiff	W 1-0	10	0
15/3/1947	A	Norwich	D 3-3	10	0
22/3/1947	H	Notts County	W 4-1	10	0
29/3/1947	A	Northampton	W 2-1	10	1
4/4/1947	A	Leyton Orient	L 0-3	10	0

5/4/1947	H	Aldershot	D 0-0	10	0
7/4/1947	H	Leyton Orient	W 6-1	10	2
26/4/1947	A	Port Vale	L 1-2	10	0
10/5/1947	H	Ipswich Town	D 1-1	10	0
26/5/1947	H	Bristol City (Glos. Cup)	D 2-2	10	0
7/6/1947	A	Bristol City (Glos. Cup)	L 0-2	10	0
23/8/1947	A	Port Vale	D 1-1	10	0
25/8/1947	H	Swindon	W 3-1	10	0
30/8/1947	H	Q.P.R.	L 0-1	10	0
3/9/1947	A	Swindon	D 1-1	10	0
6/9/1947	A	Watford	L 2-3	10	0
8/9/1947	H	Crystal Palace	D 1-1	10	0
25/10/1947	A	Leyton Orient	W 4-2	10	0
1/11/1947	H	Exeter	D 2-2	10	1
8/11/1947	A	Newport	D 2-2	10	1
15/11/1947	H	Walsall	L 2-3	10	0
22/11/1947	A	Notts County	L 2-4	10	0
29/11/1947	H	Leytonstone (F.A. Cup)	W 3-2	10	1
6/12/1947	A	Bournemouth	L 0-3	10	0
13/12/1947	H	New Brighton (F.A. Cup)	W 4-0	10	2
20/12/1947	H	Port Vale	W 2-1	10	0
26/12/1947	H	Torquay	L 0-2	10	0
27/12/1947	A	Torquay	W 2-1	10	0

3/1/1948	A	Q.P.R.	L 2-5	10	1
10/1/1948	H	Swansea (F.A. Cup)	W 3-0	10	1
17/1/1948	H	Watford	W 3-0	10	0
24/1/1948	A	Fulham (F.A. Cup)	L 2-5	10	0
31/1/1948	A	Brighton	L 1-3	10	0
7/2/1948	H	Norwich	L 2-3	10	1
14/2/1948	A	Bristol City	L 2-5	10	1
21/2/1948	A	Northampton	W 3-1	10	1
28/2/1948	H	Reading	L 2-3	10	0
6/3/1948	A	Walsall	L 0-2	10	0
20/3/1948	A	Exeter	L 0-4	10	0
26/3/1948	A	Aldershot	L 0-2	10	0
27/3/1948	H	Newport	L 2-3	11	0
1/5/1948	A	Ipswich	W 4-0	10	1
8/5/1948	A	Bristol City (Glos. Cup)	W 2-1	10	1
28/8/1948	A	Notts County	L 1-4	10	0
30/8/1948	H	Bournemouth	W 4-0	10	2
4/9/1948	H	Walsall	W 3-0	10	0
8/9/1948	A	Crystal Palace	L 0-1	10	0
11/9/1948	A	Torquay	W 2-0	10	0
13/9/1948	H	Crystal Palace	W 1-0	10	0
18/9/1948	H	Bristol City	W 3-1	10	0
20/9/1948	H	Millwall	W 2-0	10	0
25/9/1948	H	Newport	W 3-1	10	1
2/10/1948	A	Swansea	L 0-5	10	0
9/10/1948	A	Swindon	D 1-1	10	0
16/10/1948	H	Leyton Orient	L 2-3	10	0
23/10/1948	A	Southend	W 1-0	10	0
30/10/1948	H	Northampton	W 1-0	10	1

Date	H/A	Opponent	Result		
6/11/1948	A	Aldershot	W 5-1	10	0
13/11/1948	H	Brighton	D 0-0	10	0
20/11/1948	A	Port Vale	L 0-2	10	0
27/11/1948	A	Walsall (F.A.Cup)	L 1-2	10	0
4/12/1948	A	Norwich	L 0-3	10	0
18/12/1948	A	Ipswich	W 1-0	10	1
25/12/1948	H	Watford	W 3-1	10	0
27/12/1948	A	Watford	D 0-0	10	0
1/1/1949	H	Notts County	W 3-2	10	1
15/1/1949	A	Walsall	W 1-0	10	0
22/1/1949	H	Torquay	W 1-0	10	0
5/2/1949	A	Bristol City	D 1-1	10	0
12/2/1949	H	Exeter	W 3-1	10	0
19/2/1949	A	Newport	L 1-2	10	1
26/2/1949	H	Swansea	D 1-1	10	0
5/3/1949	H	Swindon	D 1-1	10	0
26/3/1949	A	Northampton	W 1-0	10	0
2/4/1949	H	Aldershot	L 0-2	10	0
9/4/1949	A	Brighton	L 1-2	10	0
15/4/1949	H	Reading	W 4-1	10	0
16/4/1949	H	Port Vale	W 4-1	10	0
18/4/1949	A	Reading	L 0-1	11	0
23/4/1949	A	Millwall	D 1-1	11	0
7/5/1949	A	Exeter	L 1-2	10	0
14/5/1949	H	Bristol City (Glos. Cup)	W 2-0	11	1
20/8/1949	A	Port Vale	L 0-1	10	0
22/8/1949	H	Ipswich	W 2-0	10	0
27/8/1949	H	Notts County	L 0-3	10	0
30/8/1949	A	Ipswich	L 1-3	10	0
3/9/1949	A	Southend	L `1-3	10	0
10/12/1949	H	Port Vale	W 2-1	10	0
24/12/1949	A	Notts County	L 0-2	10	0

26/12/1949	A	Leyton Orient	L 0-1	10	0
27/12/1949	H	Leyton Orient	W 3-0	10	0
31/12/1949	H	Southend	D 1-1	10	0
14/1/1950	A	Bristol City	W 2-1	10	0
21/1/1950	A	Bournemouth	W 2-0	10	1
16/12/1950	A	Swindon	W 2-1	10	1
25/12/1950	A	Port Vale	D 0-0	10	0
26/12/1950	H	Port Vale	W 2-0	10	0
15/2/1951	A	Walsall	W 2-1	10	1
7/4/1951	A	Leyton Orient	L 0-1	10	0
22/9/1951	A	Plymouth	W 2-1	10	0
20/10/1951	H	Newport	D 1-1	10	0
27/10/1951	A	Southend	L 1-2	10	0
3/11/1951	H	Bournemouth	L 1-2	10	0
26/12/1951	A	Port Vale	D 1-1	10	1
29/12/1951	A	Aldershot	W 3-1	10	0
3/1/1952	A	Watford	W 3-0	11	1
26/1/1952	H	Plymouth	L 1-2	11	0

APPENDIX 3.
PUBLIC HOUSES OWNED BY MEMBERS OF THE MORGAN FAMILY.

This section shows the Public Houses in and around the Bristol area whose landlords and landladies were related to, or part of, the Morgan family.

Ownership of pubs in the Bristol area was commonplace within the Morgan family, many of them being handed down or passed on to other family members.

Sadly, many of them no longer exist, certainly the ones located in the Barton Hill and Easton areas of Bristol, all swept away for urban redevelopment. It seems that virtually every street in these areas had at least one Public House or Off Licence during the early part of the 20th Century, and they seemed to be at the centre of community activity at the time.

Unfortunately, photographs of the smaller pubs have proven difficult to locate.

However, those which are still in use are well worth a visit, and it is fascinating to visit these establishments today to follow in the footsteps of family ancestors.

THE ALBERT HOTEL, 1 WEST STREET, BEDMINSTER, BRISTOL.

The Albert Hotel.

The first mention of a public house on this site can be found in 1832, and an establishment known as the 'Spotted Horse' can be traced back to 1842. The address of the establishment was originally at 'Shim Lane', renamed 'Sheene Lane' and then 'Sheene Road'.

The pub was rebuilt on the same site around 1889, and was renamed the Albert Hotel, possibly due to names of streets and cottages known as Albert Lane and Albert Villas being in the close vicinity.

Between 1938 and 1941 the landlord was Frederick Dale Stephens (1892-1971), brother-in-law of Alice Morgan (1883-1940).

The pub was renamed the 'Albert Inn' in 1984.

The establishment closed (hopefully temporarily) in March 2023 and was latterly known as the Albert Lounge.

THE ALBION, 60 EASTON ROAD, BRISTOL.

The Albion.

The earliest known mention of 'The Albion' comes from 1870, when Charles Read was that landlord of the time.

Landlady of the pub between 1913 and 1953 was Ada Amelia Rodbourn (nee Peacock), mother-in-law of Harry Morgan (1890-1968). She was the mother of Rosina May Rodbourn (1895-1929) who married Harry in 1915.

It was reported that the annual rent for the establishment was £30. This was increased to £35 in March 1938, the landlords at the time were The Bristol Brewery Georges & Co. Ltd.

The pub dates to the mid-19th century, and its original address was 7 Wellington Place.

The pub and houses along Leigh Street (on the right) were among many of the properties demolished in the early 1970s so that the Lawrence Hill roundabout could be built.

THE APPLE TREE, ROSE STREET, TEMPLE, BRISTOL.

Sadly, no photographs of the pub could be located.

The establishment can be traced back to 1860, where the landlord was one Richard Thomas.

Between 1905 and 1907 the landlord was Thomas (Tom) Morgan (1878-1944). However, it appears the pub was not making enough money, so Thomas subsequently relocated to the more lucrative Weaver's Arms at Barton Hill.

The establishment was located in Rose Street, not far from Temple Meads railway station, and it appears that the pub was active until the early 1930s.

No sign of the pub or even the street remains, the site being flattened for expansion of the railway station and goods yards.

THE BELL INN, 79 OLD BREAD STREET, ST. PHILIPS, BRISTOL.

Again, no photographs of this pub can be located.

It should not be confused with another pub, simply called 'The Bell' in Bread Street.

It can be traced back to 1883, where the landlord was recorded as being Alice England.

The pub was run from 1906 until the mid-1920s by George Williams and his wife Elizabeth, and then taken over from 1925 until the early 1930s by their son Francis.

George Williams was the brother of Matilda Williams (1844-1912), who married John Morgan in 1864.

THE BLACK HORSE, NELSON PARADE, BEDMINSTER, BRISTOL.

The Black Horse.

The pub can be traced back to 1858, where the landlord at the time was Thomas Lute.

Nelson Parade, the address of the establishment, is located at the Bedminster Bridge end of East Street.

Between 1952 and 1956, the landlord was Frederick Dale Stephens (1892-1971), brother-in-law of Alice Morgan (1883-1940).

The pub was latterly renamed 'The Ropewalk' and is still active today.

THE CARPENTER'S ARMS, ST. JAMES CHURCHYARD, BRISTOL.

The Carpenter's Arms.

The earliest mention of the pub can be traced back to 1854, where Simon Dumble was the landlord. He was a Carpenter by trade, and could be the reason for the name of the establishment.

The Morgan family-related landlord was George Aldridge (1900-1986) between 1928 and 1941, husband of Ivy Morgan (1906-1992).

Due to its location in Central Bristol, the pub had numerous close calls during the blitz in 1940 and 1941, and George decided to move his family to the outskirts of Bristol.

The establishment was demolished in the early 1950s alongside other buildings in the area to make way for Lewis's department store.

THE CLARENCE, 60 CHELSEA ROAD, EASTON, BRISTOL.

The Clarence.

The earliest mention found of the Clarence (also known as the Clarence Inn), was in the 1901 Census, where the landlord was recorded as being Mary Clohesy.

Landlord of the Clarence between 1931 and 1944 was Thomas (Tom) Morgan (1878-1944), who had previous run other pubs in Bristol. His wife Lillian took over the pub after Thomas died. Lillian sadly died in 1952.

The building still exists but is no longer a public house.

THE COMPTON INN, COMPTON DANDO, NEAR BRISTOL.

The Compton Inn.

This village pub, located in the village of Compton Dando, a few miles east of Pensford, was once under the landlordship of Edgar Alfred Mining, linked to the Morgan family through his uncle, John McGoldrick Dawes, who married Florence Beatrice Morgan in 1900.

He took over the pub in the mid-1980s after running the New Inn at Keynsham for many years.

The establishment was known as The Gamekeeper for around 14 years before reverting to the Compton Inn in 1986.

It is an Historic England Grade II listed building, originally constructed in the early 19th Century.

The inn is still fully operational and remains a popular venue to this day.

THE FOX, PETER STREET, BRISTOL.

The Fox.

The pub, located in Peter Street, close to St. Peter's Church in Central Bristol, can be traced all the way back to 1752, where the first landlady appeared to be one Mrs. Taylor.

William Walter Webb (1889-1966) was landlord of the establishment from 1911 until 1921, taking over from his mother Ellen.

His wife Ethel Langford (1891-1963) also worked in the pub. Ethel was the sister of Lilian Langford, wife of Thomas Morgan (1878-1944), who was the landlord of other public houses in Bristol.

Peter Street (including the pub) was extensively damaged during the Blitz of WW2 and no longer exists, being built over by Castle Park in the city centre. Only the shell of St. Peter's Church remains of what was once a thriving and busy area.

THE GOLDEN LION, FISHPONDS, BRISTOL.

The Golden Lion.

The Golden Lion, located on the corner of Fishponds Road and Alexandra Park, can be traced back to 1875, where the first landlord was recorded as being William Hobbs.

The landlord between 1914 and 1918 was Harry Morgan (1869-1929).

The pub is still in regular use today and remains a very popular hostelry in the Fishponds area.

THE GLOBE, CATHERINE STREET, BARROW ROAD, BRISTOL.

The Globe (image courtesy of Barton Hill History Group).

The earliest date which can be found regarding the pub is 1871, where the landlord was recorded as being Anthony Lombardini.

This pub was in the hands of the Stephens family for many years.

Family landlords were William Stephens, between 1906 and 1921, his widow Sarah Ann Stephens between 1921 and 1925, and their son Thomas Stephens, between 1925 and 1953. Thomas Stephens was the brother-in-law of Alice Morgan (1883-1940).

The building has long been demolished and no trace of it exists today.

THE KING GEORGE VI, STATION ROAD, FILTON, BRISTOL.

The King George VI.

William Walter Webb (1889-1996) and his wife Ethel (1891-1983) took over the pub in 1938, having previously run the 'Fox' in Peter Street in Central Bristol. It would appear that he was the first landlord of the pub, as no earlier details have been located.

He ran this establishment until his death in 1966. Ethel (nee Langford) was the sister-in-law of Thomas (Tom) Morgan (1878-1944) who ran a few pubs in Bristol until his death in 1944. Their son Arthur Webb (1888-1950) also assisted in the running of the pub, which closed in 2012.

The building is still standing and now a Decorators' Centre.

THE KING'S HEAD, CATHAY, REDCLIFFE, BRISTOL.

The King's Head.

The King's Head, Cathay appears to have opened in 1839, with the landlord recorded as being George Cole. It was located on the corner of Cathay and Somerset Place.

Family-related landlords between 1925 and 1944 were William Stephens (1856-1921) followed by his son Frederick Dale Stephens (1892-1977), brother-in-law of Alice Morgan (1883-1940).

The establishment was demolished in 1959 when the area was redeveloped.

THE LORD RAGLAN, STAPLETON ROAD, BRISTOL.

The Lord Raglan.

Earliest records of the pub can be traced back to 1871 when the landlord was Joseph Viney.

Albert James Stephens (1883-1960), husband of Alice Morgan (1883-1940) was the landlord between 1914 and 1953.

In 1953, the pub was taken over by Ernest Frederick Dawes (1900-1994), son of John McGoldrick Dawes (1883-1926) and Florence Beatrice Morgan (1880-1956).

The earliest record of a public house at this location goes back to 1871 when the landlord was Joseph Viney, who also worked as a plumber.

The following photograph featuring a charabanc outing is interesting. According to information on the back of the original photograph, it was Charabanc No. 6 belonging to the

'Queen Of The Road' Charabanc Company owned by G. A. Gough, 571 Fishponds Road, Bristol. The vehicle was bought in April 1922 and subsequently re-bodied as a lorry for Smart Transport, Bristol by January 1931.

The Lord Raglan, Stapleton Road. Landlord Albert Stephens can be seen in the front row, extreme right.

The pub was located in an section of Stapleton Road called Raglan Place, between Alma Street and Gloucester Place, and was demolished many years ago to make way for urban development.

THE NEW INN, BATH HILL, KEYNSHAM, NEAR BRISTOL.

The New Inn, Keynsham.

This establishment can be traced back to 1860, with the first landlord noted as being William Ruddle.

The family-related landlord of the pub from the late 1960s to the early 1980s was Edgar Alfred Mining, linked to the Morgan family through his uncle, John McGoldrick Dawes, who married Florence Beatrice Morgan in 1900.

The establishment is still very much in business, and remains one of the more popular pubs in the area.

THE POST OFFICE TAVERN, HIGH STREET, STAPLE HILL, BRISTOL.

The Post Office Tavern.

The Post Office Tavern, located on the corner of High Street and Acacia Road in Staple Hill, Bristol, is where Thomas (Tom) Morgan (1878-1944) was landlord between 1927 and 1931. This was one of many public houses in the area where Tom was landlord.

It can be traced back to 1871, where the first landlord was noted as being Thomas James.

The building still stands today, and is known as 'The Old Mail House'.

THE RISING SUN, CHURCH ROAD, REDFIELD, BRISTOL.

The Rising Sun.

The first mention of the 'Rising Sun' comes from 1841 where the landlord was recorded as being Charles Hill.

The pub was subsequently run by numerous family members:

- James Morgan (1872-1935), landlord between 1912-1935;
- Elizabeth Morgan (1875-1963, widow of James Morgan), landlady between 1935-1939;
- Arthur Stanley Hodge (1914-1984, husband of Grace Morgan), landlord between 1939-1950;
- Albert Webber (1907-2000, husband of Violet Morgan (1908-1968), landlord between 1950-1953.

The pub was the headquarters and spiritual home of the Morgan family football team for many years, following the inauguration of the team in 1919 by James Morgan, landlord at the time.

Legend has it the pub was haunted, and reports of supernatural activity were rife amongst family members.

It closed in 1967, and latterly became a storage facility for the nearby Taylor's Builders Merchants, before being demolished in 1983.

THE ROYAL OAK, PENNYWELL ROAD, EASTON, BRISTOL.

The Royal Oak.

Located on the corner of Pennywell Road and Edward Place, the pub can be traced back to 1860, where the landlord at the time was J. Chappell.

The landlord related to the Morgan Family was John Stephens (1890-1972), brother-in-law of Alice Morgan (1883-1940), who ran the pub between 1924 and 1956.

The pub was demolished in the early 1970s to make way for the building of St. Nicholas Primary School.

THE SKINNER'S ARMS, PENNYWELL ROAD, EASTON, BRISTOL.

Sadly, no photographs of the pub could be located.

The establishment can be traced back to 1853, where the landlord was recorded as being John Sanger.

Between 1921 and 1925 the landlady was Louisa McTavish (1892-1970, nee Morgan), who married Robert John McTavish (1891-1958) in 1913.

The building, in common with many other public houses in Pennywell Road, no longer exists.

THE TALBOT, EASTON ROAD, BRISTOL.

The Talbot.

A coach waits outside the Talbot for a day out, late 1940s. Morgan family members in the photograph are Winifred Lottie Moore (nee Morgan), eighth from the left, and her daughter Jean in the front in the dark blazer.

The Talbot, Easton Road, formerly known as the Brickmaker's Arms, as a small alley near the pub led to the local Brickworks. It dates from 1840, when Sarah Pullin was recorded as being the landlady. It became the Talbot around 1874.

Landlord between 1904 and 1914 was Harry Morgan (1870-1929). The pub was demolished in the late 1960s as part of the development of the local area.

THE THREE HORSESHOES, 70 OLD MARKET STREET, BRISTOL

The Three Horseshoes.

Landlord of this pub was Arthur Edward (or Hodgson) Langford, brother of Lillian Langford who married Thomas Morgan in 1904. He ran this establishment from around 1914 to 1928.

The building was believed to have been built around 1670, and had its own Brewhouse, making its own ale. The first landlord appearing in records was one William Streeter, who was landlord from 1752 until 1764.

Due to its location close to the Empire Theatre, it became popular with artistes who appeared at the theatre in the early part of the 20th century. It is thought that Cary Grant worked at the pub for a short time, operating the lights for some of the performers who entertained the local clientele such as Flanagan & Allen and Gracie Fields.

The pub is still in existence and is known as the 'Long Bar'.

THE WEAVER'S ARMS, MAZE STREET, BARTON HILL.

The Weaver's Arms.

The Weaver's Arms, Barton Hill. Some directories have the pub listed as being in Great Western Street, but the majority have the address as Maze Street.

It can be traced back to 1851, where the first recorded landlord was James Skinner.

The landlord was Thomas (Tom) Morgan (1878-1944) between 1909 and 1921. Prior to this, the pub was run by James Langford, Thomas's father-in-law.

According to a late 1930s directory of Bristol, the landlord of the pub was William Walter Webb, husband of Tom's wife Lily's sister Ethel, who ran the establishment between 1925 and 1937.

This was a very popular and thriving pub in the local area for many years.

The building was demolished as part of the development of the Barton Hill area.

THE WELLINGTON ARMS, WELLINGTON PARK, CLIFTON, BRISTOL.

The Wellington Arms.

The Wellington Arms was located at Wellington Park, just off Whiteladies Road in the Clifton area of Bristol. It can be traced back to 1861 where the landlady was recorded as being Ann Waters.

The landlord between 1938 and 1939 was Gilbert Thomas Morgan (1912-1975), who took over from Alfred Martin.

The pub closed in 1958 when Courages bought out George's Brewery.

The building still exists but is now private accommodation.

APPENDIX 4.
PERSONAL MEMORIES OF IVY MORGAN.

I have so many fond and loving memories of Ivy, my Nan. She was a very religious person and her values have influenced many of us in the family. She had such a hard life growing up, as can be ascertained from her memories, with many struggles and setbacks, but her character saw her through those sad times.

Perhaps my earliest memories are of her and her husband George at their house in Park Place, Upper Eastville, Bristol. We used to get the bus from our house in Hillfields Park and then walk to her house from the nearby bus stop on Fishponds Road where she would greet us with cup of tea (made with sterilised milk) and a biscuit if we were lucky. A rare treat would be a Mars Bar, cut into slices, which she would pass around to everyone.

I can distinctly recall her singing and reciting rhymes to us when we were very young; one verse remains in my memory even today:

"Paddy on the railway, picking up stones.
Along came a choo-choo train and broke Paddy's bones.
'Hey' said Paddy, 'that's not fair'.
'Oh' said the choo-choo train; 'I don't care.'

I have no idea where this rhyme came from, or if it was one she made up.

Another phrase she used regularly was when we stayed with her for dinner; she used to say to us children:

"What are we having for dinner today? Sawdust and Hay!"

The house was a typical 1930s semi-detached residence with a carefully-tended garden. My grandfather kept a greenhouse in which he grew his tomatoes, and the smell of going in to his greenhouse remains with me to this day. He was always very proud of his flowers, and the colourful displays in the front garden added to the visual appeal of the house. His rhubarb plants, which were grown close to his greenhouse were plentiful.

All family conversations were held in the living room, and we would always eat in the kitchen; the front room was only used for special occasions and it was only then that we ventured into that room as children. Upstairs was also 'off limits' unless you needed the bathroom or were lucky enough to stay overnight.

There was a grandmother clock in the hall, which chimed on the hour and had a loud 'tick' caused by the pendulum swinging in the cabinet, giving an air of calmness to the house. She also had an old musical box which played *'Oh Mein Papa'* which she used to love to play to us.

A regular trip was a visit to the local cemeteries; we used to take sandwiches and a drink with us, and I remember that as a small child I used to collect the different-coloured stones which adorned the graves. Nan was also a regular attendee at the Spiritualist Church in Grosvenor Road in the St. Pauls area of the city; we used to get on the bus from Eastville and I was regularly despatched around the church, plate in hand, to take the collection from amongst the congregation.

I also remember going on the bus on a few occasions with her to visit Chepstow for a day; it was great fun to travel over the newly-completed Severn Bridge, and also to take the trip on a 'Red-and-White' bus which provided the service, rather than the usual green 'Bristol' buses.

We always referred to grandfather George as 'Trant' for some reason; no-one in the family seems to know why. He loved his Fox's Glacier Mints and there was always a pocketful of them in his jacket when required. He was a builder by trade and was known as 'The Gentleman Builder' amongst his colleagues, following his insistence on wearing a collar and tie at work.

Ivy and George on holiday, probably during the 1960s.

George was a lovely man. He loved all of his grandchildren, and he used to take us to Eastville Park to play on the swings or go fishing for tiddlers in the lake. Sometimes he'd let us have a go on the paddle-boats which you could hire for a short time.

He liked to stop to watch the bowling or watch football on a Wednesday. Often he would take us back to Park Place along an access lane to the back of the house. We always called it the 'Lucky Lane' as we would always find a penny on the ground, which we later found out that he had dropped when out of our sight!

His other great love was gardening and tending his beloved chrysanthemums. In fact his skill was recognised in a *'Bristol Evening Post'* newspaper report from 31st October 1960, when it reported that:

"Two names, Morley Densley and Stanley Morgan, between them dominated the list at Bristol Chrysanthemum Society's late flowering show at St Aidan's Parish Hall, Nags Head Hill, on Saturday.

But for Mr. G. Aldridge of Park Place, Eastville, the day was one to remember. Although this is only the first year he has grown and exhibited chrysanthemums, his efforts won him the Hawkins Cup for the most points in the open classes for novices, plus a special money voucher."

On a Saturday at Park Place we would often hear a muffled noise from the other side of Eastville Park; I was told this was the famous 'Eastville Roar' which went up when Bristol Rovers scored a goal.

My grandfather took one of my cousins and myself to my first Bristol Rovers match in September 1966; I was six years old and can well remember wearing a scarf and bobble hat which were knitted for me and carrying a rattle to make some noise with! Rovers beat Swindon 3-0, which was the start of my affection for the team. I've been going to Bristol Rovers matches regularly since then. He used to joke that the team had signed two new Chinese players; 'Wee Wun Once' and 'Hao Long Since'!

Nan always made wonderful meals. Her stews were tasty and thoroughly enjoyable, but it was only some time after her passing that I found out what went in the pot; had I known about the ingredients then I'm sure I wouldn't have been so enthusiastic.

Every Christmas we all used to go to Auntie Grace's house (Grace being Ivy's youngest sister) in St. George, Bristol. My father couldn't drive at the time, so Grace's husband Stan used to pick us up in his Ford Cortina. We all had Christmas lunch and then depart to the lounge area where we would exchange presents and the adults would have a few drinks and play Newmarket. For some reason I remember winning regularly, although I do suspect that I was allowed to win the few pennies we played for.

Other family members would come and go during the day, many bringing presents for us children. I can vividly remember being given model fire engines and model aeroplanes by numerous family members, all smartly-dressed in grey or brown suits. I had no idea who they were, but as they always brought presents for me, they were certainly well appreciated.

A Christmas family gathering at Auntie Grace's house, c. 1966.

Sometimes we used to visit these family members who all lived locally, but of course I was too young to understand who all these old people were; it was only when I was much older that I started to take an interest in her extended family.

Nan used to love to talk about her family, and growing up in Redfield and St. George. She would also regularly talk about the war and the bombing raids on Bristol. We used to watch episodes of Dad's Army together but she would turn it off before the end so as not to hear the air-raid siren sound which still haunted her.

She was very much 'old school' in her outlook on life, never shirking away from hard work and although outspoken on occasions, never wished harm on anyone, following her Christian beliefs instilled in her from her schooldays. Any minor cuts and bruises we suffered as children were always dealt with by Nan's handkerchief, moistened by saliva and rubbed vigorously over the wound! She was also a formidable ally should any of us be picked on at the local park; she was certainly not afraid to confront anyone who dared to upset her beloved grandchildren!

Other regular trips were to Bath, on the old Midland Railway line which went through Fishponds and Staple Hill to Bath Green Park. I recall running around the canopy supporting the pillars at Fishponds station, waiting for the train to arrive. And the smell of the station was wonderful!

We once travelled to Bournemouth for a week's holiday along the old Somerset & Dorset Railway route, our luggage being taken by Uncle Stan in his car, while we all filled one compartment in one of the carriages. We stayed in a nice 'Bed & Breakfast' establishment at Southbourne, called *'Ad Astra'*, a short walk from the beach. An abiding memory of mine is travelling on the yellow trolleybuses which operated in the area at the time. I can also remember the cliff railway which took us up and down, to and from the beach.

Ivy and George moved house later in the 1960s, to a smaller terraced house at Hill Street, St. George, just off Whiteway Road, and well within walking distance from our family home. They stayed there for a few years before moving again to a ground floor flat at Hawkesbury Road, Fishponds, directly opposite their daughter Joy and family.

It was a regular occurrence for us all to take 'day trips' in their car, Tetbury always being a favourite destination. The first car I can remember was a yellow-green Ford Popular (VWN 567), and this was followed by a grey Ford Anglia 105E. Nan always used to wander around the numerous antique shops in the Cotswold town, and we always used to take sandwiches and a drink with us; it was a rare treat when we would eat in a local café or restaurant. They also owned a 4-door Morris (or Austin) 1000 in duck-egg blue, but this was sold when my younger brother fell out of it on Rodway Common, Mangotsfield.

George in particular was very interested in my career in radio, and when I obtained my amateur radio licence we bought him a small radio receiver which covered the amateur bands so that he could listen in to me. Many's the time I'd mention his name when contacting other radio amateurs in the area and he loved it when other stations passed their best wishes to him.

The final car they owned was a white Morris 1300 estate, one of the early automatic versions. Sadly my grandfather George started to lose confidence in his driving, and after one particularly stressful drive he decided to give up driving altogether.

Another move ensued a few years later, this time to managed flats at Beaufort Court, Blackhorse, Bristol, where they stayed for a short time.

There was to be one final move, this time to another managed flat at St. Clements Court, Soundwell. She lived on the first floor of the building, and to many of her great-grandchildren she was known as 'Nanny in the lift'. She never really settled at that flat, and it wasn't a happy place for her.

She always used to love visitors, and I always made a point of visiting her every time I visited my parents in Bristol. I was of course made most welcome and enjoyed endless cups of tea in china crockery. She was always interested in the careers of all her grandchildren, and whilst she didn't quite understand the role of my own somewhat technical work, she would always ask me about it. When I moved away from Bristol in the early 1980s, I used to get regular letters and cards from her, and the occasional 'food parcel' of essentials such as soup, tinned vegetables and packets of biscuits.

I used to take the occasional female companion with me on my visits, and she often confused their names – a little embarrassing perhaps but she was instantly forgiven.

She used to love talking about the 'olden days' and growing up in the Redfield and St. James' areas. She was very fond of the city, and used to write to the local newspapers with fond memories, such as one below which appeared in the *'Bristol Evening Post'* in the mid-1970s:

"I have lived in Bristol Centre from 1929, and I say to Mrs. Dorothy Brown, yes, you are quite right. Bristol city was like an egg. The yolk was the little shops, squares and alleys.

There was Sims Alley, Dalton Square, Cumberland Street, Barrs Street, Mibbs Court, Moon Street, and the Alms Houses.

Our address then was St. James right up to St. James Square. Has the name St. James disappeared?

The shop fronts in those days were narrow and went far back. Here and there were lanes and cottages where people lived. They were poor but happy.

In summer people would sit outside in the little squares laughing and talking, perhaps knitting and darning socks.

The biggest blunder was the Bristol Bus Station and the demolition of St. James National Day School for children in the parish of St. James. My children attended there.

Now there is a plaque in the Bus Station on left as a tombstone.

Yes, leave Canon's Marsh alone."

Sadly Ivy's health deteriorated towards the end of her life which meant it became more difficult for her to remember her wonderful stories; it was sad to see her in such a condition. She was never quite the same after losing her husband George.

I have nothing but fond memories of such a lovely lady.

God Bless Nan.